GLOBAL AND MULTINATIONAL ADVERTISING

Edited by

Basil G. Englis
Rutgers University

LAWRENCE ERLBAUM ASSOCIATES, PUBLISHERS
1994   Hillsdale, New Jersey   Hove, UK

Lawrence Erlbaum Associates, Inc., Publishers
365 Broadway
Hillsdale, New Jersey 07642

Library of Congress Cataloging-in-Publication Data

Global and multinational advertising / edited by Basil G. Englis.
    p. cm. — (Advertising and consumer psychology)
  Includes bibliographical references and index.
  ISBN 0-8058-1137-0. — ISBN 0-8058-1395-0 (pbk.)
    1. Advertising—Cross-cultural studies. 2. Marketing—Cross
-cultural studies. 3. Consumer behavior—Cross-cultural studies.
  I. Englis, Basil G.
  HF5821.G55 1994
  659.1—dc20   94-22421
                                           CIP

Books published by Lawrence Erlbaum Associates are printed on acid-free paper, and their
bindings are chosen for strength and durability.

Printed in the United States of America
10 9 8 7 6 5 4 3 2 1

Contents

PART III.   CROSS-CULTURAL ISSUES

PART IV.   METHODS AND PARADIGMS

Preface

By 1990 U.S. advertisers were spending more than $130 billion dollars annually in non-U.S. markets, and the share of global advertising expenditures accounted for by U.S. companies had reached nearly 50% of total global expenditures (Levin & Lafayette 1990). With the recent opening of Eastern European and Chinese markets, these figures are likely to grow at even faster rates as the turn of the century approaches. Advertising is part of the increased globalization of mass media — rapidly evolving into a truly global media village. The effects of global media on individuals, nations, and cultures demand critical and empirical attention by practitioners and academicians alike. For practitioners the question of when and for what products a global versus a multinational strategy, tailored to individual cultural groups, may prove more effective has obvious ramifications for creative and media buying decisions. For academics, critical concerns include how to conceptualize culture and the question of how culture-bound are current theories and the empirical corpus of data upon which these theories rest.

The theme for the Ninth Annual Advertising and Consumer Psychology Conference concerned cultural variation and its impact on advertising practice and on audience response. The papers presented at the conference covered a broad range of theoretical perspectives and methodologies. Topics ranged from analyses of differences in advertising strategy as a function of culture of origin and target culture to how consumers' responses to advertising are influenced by their culture. One focal point of the conference, and of this volume, was the need for consumer researchers to consider the extent to which their theories and empirical findings are culture-bound. A concern voiced in this book is how empirical paradigms can be used in widely divergent cultural groups and how cultural factors can be separated from other effects on research findings. As was evident by the submissions received for the conference, many researchers are employing subcultural groups as models for studying cultural differences.

This collection of chapters is not meant to provide strong conclusions, but instead to raise questions and, hopefully, to point out some directions for future research. In that sense we viewed this undertaking as an exploration of a new field, whose development will need to keep pace with the rapid changes occurring in international economic, political, and cultural realities. These changes should provide a range of interesting and challenging opportunities for practitioners and academics.

This volume is divided into four sections. The first deals with the broad issues of values and culture and how these are conceptualized and interrelated. The second section examines subcultural groups as models for the study of cultural influences on advertising audiences and for studying the assumptions made by advertisers when they target different cultural groups. The third section deals with cross-cultural issues. These chapters all focus on advertising in the international media community. Finally, section four explores different methodological approaches relevant to consumer research with diverse cultural groups.

PART I: VALUES AND CULTURE

In the first chapter of Part I, Ellie Lester argues that international advertising research needs to be placed theoretically within the broader context of international communication research. She provides a critique of current international advertising research as often being ill-informed regarding the status of theory in international communication. Theoretically informed research should prove both more interesting and more viable to advertising researchers and practitioners alike. The major paradigms of international communication are reviewed in an effort to provide an alternative to both the older "dominant paradigm" and the new "cultural imperialism thesis."

In the next chapter John McCarty takes up the issue of cultural values. He argues that although there has been a great deal of interest in recent years in the relationship of consumer values to consumption, most of this work has dealt with personal values. McCarty argues that *cultural values* are of primary importance in international marketing efforts. He shows how cultural value orientations (e.g., individualism vs. collectivism) can profoundly affect the way products are used in a culture. McCarty stresses that knowledge and understanding of cultural values are essential to successful international marketing efforts.

If one wants to understand and communicate with a culture, investigation of the values of people in that culture provides a promising starting point. In their chapter, Kahle, Beatty, and Mager present analyses of the diffusion of several core values in the various European countries that comprise the European Economic Community. In their coverage of the structural changes that occurred in Europe in 1992 (and subsequently), these authors consider how broad political and legal changes are likely to impact on consumers—their behavior, attitudes, values. The authors also consider how the structural changes in Europe may provide an impetus for increased cultural homogeneity or may, conversely, result in an heightening of cultural differentiation. They also discuss how the restructuring of the European political and national landscape is likely to affect international communication.

PART II: SUB-CULTURAL ISSUES

Barbara Stern considers women as a distinct cultural group—the culture of "other"—to clarify how women use language and how language uses women. Her purpose is to render women's language visible in order to help advertisers design persuasive appeals and more effectively position (or reposition) products to the women's market. The chapter begins by discussing some cultural differences between men and women that give rise to three qualities characteristic of women's language: propriety, hesitancy, and verbal excess. It next describes the influence of sex-specific language on advertising dialogue and male/female role portrayals. Stern concludes by discussing two contributions that awareness of women's language can make to the creation of better advertising.

Gender positioning, whereby gender is made an explicit marketing positioning variable, has been examined by focusing on the gender of the product being promoted, the sex of the individuals portrayed in advertisements, and/or the sex of the buyer. In her chapter, Milner argues that although a great deal of research has been devoted to understanding the dynamics underlying gender positioning, the majority of studies done thus far have concentrated on U.S. markets. Her chapter reviews the limited amount of research done on gender positioning in other countries. In her review, she calls attention to the need to study the meaning of gender in diverse cultural contexts.

Roberta Astroff considers how cultural, ethnic, racial, and national groups are treated by marketers and advertisers as distinct market segments. Her analysis focuses specifically on the construction of a "Latino market" and the "sale" of that market to advertisers as viable and profitable. In her analysis, Astroff uncovers processes of identity formation, defining the "other," the interpretation of nondominant cultures, and the role played by cultural brokers. One important issue raised by this work concerns the primacy of category (or label) versus "true" (empirically demonstrable) group differences. In addition, Astroff identifies the advertising trade press as a site in which industry discourse (in this case about cultural identity) is played out and made public:

PART III: CROSS-CULTURAL ISSUES

Fairfid Caudle provides a qualitative analysis of advertising strategies employed when products are advertised outside of their country or culture of origin. A taxonomy is presented of verbal and nonverbal communication strategies designed to cross barriers of language and nationality. The verbal strategies illustrated include retention of the original language, parallel multi-language product naming, linguistic variation in isolated phrases, and linguistic "mosaics," in which sentences combine words from different languages. Several of the nonverbal communication strategies discussed involve reliance on visual content such as national symbols, visual metaphors, and works of art. Caudle concludes by drawing our attention to the need for greater emphasis on visual aspects of marketing communications.

Bradley, Hitchon, and Thorson present an empirical study designed to operationalize the concepts of brands as "leading ladies" (central to an advertisement) or "bit players" (when brands play a more peripheral role). They employ content analysis to determine which of these two very different approaches dominate in British as compared with American television advertising. They also analyze structural characteristics such as time when a product first appears and how much visual and audio time is devoted to it, number of product attributes included and time spent with them, clarity about what product and brand is being advertised, relationship of the product to the characters, emotional relationship of the commercial environment to the product, camera and editing techniques used to represent the product, and type of appeal.

The purpose of the next chapter, by Prabhaker and Sauer, is two-fold. First, a macro-analytic framework is developed within which international advertising and marketing research can be framed. The authors elaborate their framework by discussing some of the difficulties in conducting consumer research in China. Second, the current state of advertising in the People's Republic of China is reviewed and some conclusions drawn. The People's Republic of China, with its vast consumer market potential, has always been of interest to advertisers and marketers. But now, with the economy opening up to Western ideas and Western products, general interest has given way to action. A number of western corporations are attempting to make their presence felt in this market via advertising.

Taylor, Miracle, and Chang take up the question of advertising standardization. They present a content analysis of over 1000 Japanese, 1000 U.S., and 850 Korean television commercials representing a broad range of product and service categories. Hypotheses about expected differences in the mean values of several objectively measured variables are derived from the research literature and also from additional knowledge of cultural variation among the three countries. Results of statistical hypothesis tests are presented and the implications for marketers and advertisers desiring to standardize international advertising are discussed.

The chapter by Gould and Minowa explores Levitt's hypothesis concerning standardized advertising by analyzing Japanese and American automobile advertising. The results of their content analysis reveal more differences than similarities in advertising appeals and in the symbolic components of the ads. These authors delineate the idea of cultural interpretation, where cultural symbols may become transplanted from one culture to another. In the process these symbols acquire new meaning, and yet retain a link in the minds of consumers to the culture of origin. Although the results are provisional, they support the idea that standardizing advertising in these two countries is unlikely to be effective.

PART IV: METHODS AND PARADIGMS

Corey and Williams present a methodology for analyzing language use by market segments defined by gender and ethnicity. Their general premise is that speech patterns and language use can serve as mirrors of mental processes and underlying attitudes, values, and beliefs. Corey and Williams employ an interpretive method based on the theory of the index, and then a text-theoretic approach to provide quantitative analysis of focus group discussions. Emphasis is placed on providing an interpretive account of how different market segments of car buyers manage language to create meaning and present social reality. Their approach can shed light on the "hows" and "whys" of the consumption experience, and thus provide useful information to advertisers.

The chapter by Bozzolo and Brock offers a structured paradigm for studying the processing of brand information. The paradigm is derived from current illusory correlation theory in social psychology. The method allows microspecification of the cognitive processing of strong and weak brands as well as their product categories. The authors present data from both student and nonstudent (adult female consumers) populations. They also consider the usefulness of the paradigm in a multicultural context, and suggest that reexamination of multicultural marketing in terms of the illusory correlation paradigm has practical implications for advertisers.

REFERENCE

Levin, G., & Lafayette, J. (1990), "Ad spending hikes may lag inflation," *Advertising Age,* 17(December 17), pp. 3, 34.

ACKNOWLEDGMENTS

The chapters that appear in this volume are based on papers presented at the Ninth Annual Advertising and Consumer Psychology Conference held at the offices of the McCann-Erickson advertising agency in New York City in May of 1990. The conference was made possible by the joint sponsorship of the Society for Consumer Psychology, the Marketing Science Institute, and, of course, the host agency, McCann-Erickson.

I would like to thank Katherine Jocz, Director of Research Management of MSI, Susan Irwin, Director of Public Relations at McCann-Erickson, and John Dooner, President of McCann-Erickson, for providing the resources and support needed to organize the conference and to make the event a success. D. Frederick Baker, Senior Vice President and Director of Market Research at McCann-Erickson, co-chaired the meeting and provided valuable support throughout the planning process. Fred helped to set the agenda for the conference and to select the papers that were presented at the meeting.

In preparing the chapters for their publication in this volume, I would like to acknowledge the considerable help provided by the staff at Lawrence Erlbaum Associates. In particular, Judith Amsel was always encouraging and patient as the process of preparing the volume progressed. Once the volume was placed in production, Kathleen Dolan and Linda Eisenberg provided invaluable in shepherding the book to the presses.

Last, but not least, I would like to thank John Cacioppo and Mike Solomon for getting me involved with this undertaking in the first place and for their continued support throughout the project.

Basil G. Englis

I VALUES AND CULTURE

1 International Advertising Research and International Communication Theory

Elli Lester
University of Georgia

IS THERE ANY INTERNATIONAL ADVERTISING THEORY?

The purpose of this chapter is to critique current international advertising research for being uninformed about the status of theory in international communication and to suggest that international advertising research must be placed theoretically within the broader context of international communication research. Theoretically informed research should prove both more interesting and more viable to advertising researchers and practitioners. However, it may also prove more challenging because the theoretical perspective may lead to critical questions that suggest significant dilemmas that the industry itself may not care to pursue.

Critical approaches have been suggested by a number of industry and academic researchers as work that is important and useful, though not immediately practicable. My contention is that critical work (i.e., work that does not necessarily seek to solve an immediate problem and thus, is not product oriented) will in fact prove useful to both academics and practitioners because such work is more analytical, revealing problems of process at the social and cultural levels and at the levels of individual consumers, campaigns, or advertisements. International advertising in particular, linked as it is to political and economic policy decisions, must be analyzed at a theoretically informed level.

INTERNATIONAL ADVERTISING RESEARCH IN THE "CHAMELEON DECADE"

Outside of academia the importance of international communication (advertising as well as other forms such as journalism, film, and telecommunication) has been clearly linked with policy concerns, as policy analyst Mark Fowler suggested:

> International Communications . . . has become an important expression of the posture of the United States toward the rest of the world, a significant aspect of our foreign policy, and a vital tool in the economic interdependence which is becoming a fact of life for all international policy. . . . (Schiller, 1976, p. 43)

Even within academia, advertising is recognized as part of the increasing globalization of the communications industries. As international communication researcher Hachten (1987) pointed out in his analysis of ideology and media trends:

> Recent "mega-mergers" among advertising and marketing services companies point up how internationalized Madison Avenue, the symbolic home of advertising, has become. . . . Increased communication . . . leads to increased organization and consequently some concentration of control. . . . Regional and continental media organizations are playing increasingly crucial roles in international news communication. (p. 83)

Hachten's thesis is that free and independent journalism is a key to democratic political practices. But his very brief reference to the increasing concentration of advertising practice is suggestive because it links the growth in international advertising to political–economic and cultural concerns.

Advertising is also acknowledged in the UNESCO MacBride Report on international communication as an important major force in international communication. The MacBride Report was commissioned by UNESCO in an effort to both describe and make recommendations about the current state of mass communication globally, with special reference to transnational communication. The importance of mass media is acknowledged as being especially significant in recently independent nations; as such the report comes down heavily on the side of recommending a "more balanced flow of information, both worldwide and within individual societies" (UNESCO, 1984, p. 12). The report shows that much media content is commodified (i.e., packaged and available for sale) and furthermore that advertising supports most mass media whatever its other content. The report continues by enumerating a number of research questions:

[Research] should ascertain the direct and indirect, intentional and unintentional effects of advertising and could lay the groundwork for new policy decisions, if and as required. . . . How can commercial considerations be harmonized with broad social and cultural goals? How can any negative effects be lessened? (UNESCO, 1984, p. 123)

In terms of recommendations, the one area in which the MacBride Report includes advertising specifically is in the area titled "strengthening cultural identity." The specific recommendation is: Introduction of guidelines with respect to advertising content and the values and attitudes it fosters, in accordance with national standards and practices. Such guidelines should be consistent with national development policies and efforts to preserve national identity" (UNESCO, 1984, p. 205). The MacBride Report is of concern to advertising researchers for two reasons. First it was authored by a multinational panel and carries a certain amount of prestige among national planners and decision makers. Second, it clearly links international communication generally with international advertising, showing that the research agenda of one cannot be separated from the other. The MacBride Report critiques the disproportionate media and communications wealth of the developed world, and urges a "new international information order" within which international advertising would play a part. The report serves as a common reference point for policy makers who can influence advertising penetration within nations.

The communications industries generally are acknowledged as an area in which the success of Western cultural and economic hegemony continues, in contrast to failures of the more traditional industrial base on the one hand, and the high technology industries on the other. A Canadian academic is quoted in the *The Nation* as claiming "Other people make better cars, better electronics. Our schoolchildren are stupider, and so on. But the one thing the world envies is the miracle of Hollywood. It's very comfortable to focus on something the United States has and everybody wants" (*The Nation*, 1990, Editorial, p. 509). International communications scholar Schiller (1989) said that "[t]he global push of transnational capital in the information–cultural sphere has been remarkably successful to date" (p. 133). He continued:

No activity, national or international, is exempt from the corporate sponsor – not even, apparently, the worldwide programs of the United Nations . . . corporate sponsorship could be magnificently expanded from Grand Prix and Olympics events to the United Nations itself. . . .

But it is not only U.S. television programming that carries the virus of transational corporate culture. Politics, sports, tourism, language, and business data flows transmit it and reinforce it as well. (Schiller, 1988, pp. 133–134)

Another example of Western (and particularly U.S.) hegemony in the communications industry is the growing attention to media-dominated political campaigns. (*Advertising Age*, 1990; Bichovsky-Little, 1988; Knight, 1987). Political advertising is an acknowledged subfield of advertising research; politicians from other cultures avail themselves of U.S. advertising talent. Thus, advertising is used to communicate about almost every facet of political-economic, social, and cultural life both within the United States and internationally. Although the Canadian academic singled out Hollywood, implying a discussion of the film industry, his comments are equally relevant in terms of U.S./Western advertising. Along with film, journalism, and publishing, advertising comprises the culture industries.

Schiller's comments suggest explicitly that communication of all sorts is effective advertising of a global economic order and a way of life. Thus, it makes little sense to separate advertising research from the broader field of mass communication research. The separation that is maintained through a number of disciplinary and bureaucratic structures is perhaps more related to the establishment of territorial expertise than it is any kind of real delineation between separate fields of practice.

Even more than in the academic literature, advertising trade literature acknowledges that the growth in international advertising is linked to political–economic developments. *Adweek* begins a cover story on *Marketing to the Year 2000: The Chameleon Decade* with the statement that "[n]ot since the colonial powers of Europe themselves cast covetous eyes at other continents has a land mass been viewed with such hungry expectation." (Alter, Simurda, Berry, & Stelly, Jr., 1989) The article continues with an analysis of what the changes in both Western Europe (EC) and Eastern Europe will mean for both markets and advertising. Another factor that will increasingly have an impact on international advertising research is the continued interest of the so-called "Second World," (i.e., the socialist countries) in developing freer market systems. Also of interest are political developments in South Africa in light of Nelson Mandela's release from prison, and the increased likelihood of talks between the apartheid government and the African National Congress, the impact of the Democracy Movement in China, and shifts in governments in Latin America. The fact that political and economic change is so closely linked with advertising issues also indicates that an awareness of the theoretical underpinnings of the research must be carefully articulated.

International advertising research, however, lags behind both the political debates and the advertising industry's awareness. For example, Tse, Lee, Vertinsky, & Wehrung (1988) preface their research with the question "does culture matter?" (p. 81). This question identifies the crux of the matter, the main problem around which the theoretical arguments within international communication research have centered. The study identifies four cultural norms by which decision making in marketing can be measured. Similar kinds of cultural norms are also identified in Frith's (1989) American Academy of Advertising paper "Cultural Imperialism or Cultural Empiricism? A Critical Perspective" and in Frith and Frith's (1989) "The Stranger at the Gate: Western Advertising and Eastern Cultural and Communication Values." The first article is an empirical, data-based research piece; the second, a critical essay, and the third, a descriptive essay. But although written from different perspectives (positivist/culturalist) and with different goals (industry oriented/critical), all three remain uninformed of the theoretical literature in the area of international mass communication research while attempting to make contributions to an understanding of a major form of international mass communication — advertising.

The cultural norms that all three papers identify derive from Daniel Lerner's concepts regarding the modern and traditional mentalities of cosmopolites (from the West) and peasants (from the East). None of these studies, however, acknowledge Lerner as a source; the authors are apparently unaware that Lerner delineated these concepts in the early 1960s and that his perspective has been all but discredited by international communication scholars and by political-economic realities. Lerner, writing about modernization in developing countries adopted a system of bipolar oppositions to describe the differences between the modern and the traditional. The concept of bipolar oppositions fit nicely into the development decade's (i.e., the 1960s) political-economic thrust of growth. Culture does matter; advertising as a consciousness industry is involved in both creating culture and reflecting it. Thus, although international advertising research has an unarticulated theoretical underpinning, that unawareness of the theoretical literature leads to soft or even misleading conclusions.

A review of the international advertising research confirms the lack of theoretical grounding (see Appendix at the end of this chapter). Although interest in international advertising as a legitimate field of inquiry is increasing, responding to the changing world economic order, the field has not turned to international communication research for its theoretical base. I suggest that international advertising researchers must re-evaluate the usefulness of scientific discourse in understanding international advertising communication. Social-psychological research that is industry driven, will continue to yield insights into some aspects of advertising, but is limited in terms of its application to the international situation. Surveys and experiments tend to be culture specific; Gordon Miracle (1990) discussed some of the problems associated with administering questionnaires across cultures in his ongoing work on advertising in Japan, Korea, and the United States.

I am certainly not the first within advertising research to suggest that alternative perspectives lead to fruitful research results. In 1969 Bogart suggested that the focus on the individual, microlevel (whether of ads or individuals) obscures important critical issues:

My argument is that self-interested, short term perspective decisions by individual advertisers add up to large-scale collective controls that profoundly affect the whole . . . cultural and political experience. . . . Advertising research must inevitably be limited in its intellectual aspirations so long as its concerns are microscopic, so long as the field essentially reflects an engineering, "how-to-do-it" approach to the solution of particular advertising problems. . . . (p. 10–11)

However, recent reviews of advertising literature in general show that this kind of "engineering, how-to" research, the kind which seeks to solve only specific, short term problems, continues to dominate the field. Pavlik and Ulanet, conducting a content analysis of conference proceedings of the American Academy of Advertising (1977–1984) support the hypothesis that advertising research focuses primarily on the individual primarily because the research is "industry driven." Yale and Gilly's study concurs.

Interestingly, although advertising research remains for the most part fixed in the social–psychological (positivist, scientific) paradigm, marketing research operates in two distinct paradigms, positivism and interpretivisim. Hudson and Ozanne (1988) summarized the differences between the two paradigms and suggested: "By juxtaposing ways of seeking knowledge, we can learn and reflect on the strengths and weaknesses of both research approaches. This reflection is critical if we are to improve the ways in which we study consumers" (p. 508)

Although this is not to suggest that there needs to be an abandonment of the social–psychological perspective, it seems imperative to encourage the development of other research paradigms as well. International communication is of growing importance and advertising's crucial role worldwide must be examined in terms of its broad social, political–economic, and cultural implications as well as its narrower "product-defined" aspects. Thus international advertising research, along with advertising research in general, should move toward asking the more complex, apparently critical research questions that are made possible only through alternative theoretical paradigms.

PARADIGMS OF INTERNATIONAL COMMUNICATION RESEARCH

There are two major, mainstream paradigms within international communication research literature: the modernization perspective, also called the "dominant paradigm" (within which Lerner's work, mentioned earlier, falls) and the cultural imperialism perspective, also called the "new paradigm." A third perspective, postmodernism, is beginning to be applied to the study of international communication. All three have important implications for international advertising research. Each paradigm suggests its ontology or world view, its epistemology or research questions and levels of analysis, and, by implication, what sorts of answers the paradigm can yield. Thus an awareness of theoretical paradigm or perspective and an understanding of both its uses and limitations provide invaluable information to both the researcher and the "consumer" of the research (i.e., policy makers, social analysts, advertising professionals, "ordinary" consumers).

The "Dominant Paradigm"

Everett Rogers described the first dominant paradigm of international communication, which originated in the late 1950s and early 1960s, as assuming that there is a one-way flow of information from the developed to the developing worlds (see Fig. 1.1). International communication was conceived of as a top-down sharing from the dominant world economic powers to the underdeveloped Third World. International communication was perceived as linked to social change, both short and long term, with diffusion of innovations being one of the important models of persuasion. Much of this literature analyzed information campaigns in terms of how both information and adoption of innovations dispersed throughout communities.

To link international communication with social change (and specifically economic development), required an understanding of development in concrete terms as behavioral and psychological, introducing psychological variables (motivation, perception, emotion, attitudes) into the study of economic development along with measures of gross economic data, and operationalizing these criteria quantitatively. As Rogers suggested: "mass communication was . . . thought to be a very powerful and direct force for development. . . . a kind of magic multiplier for development . . ." (Rogers, 1976, p. 226). And communication "effectiveness" could be measured by observing changes in the criteria. The key concepts in this paradigm were *growth*, *development*, and *modernization*.

It is perhaps not surprising that much of the international advertising research literature implicitly adopts this paradigm, although usually without acknowledging the debt. McQuail (1983), describing the body of literature on diffusion of innovations, said:

the model of information diffusion envisaged four stages: information; persuasion; decision or adoption; confirmation. . . . The diffusionist school of thought tends to emphasize organization and planning, linearity of effect, hierarchy (of status and expertise), social structure (thus personal experience), reinforcement and feedback. (p. 194)

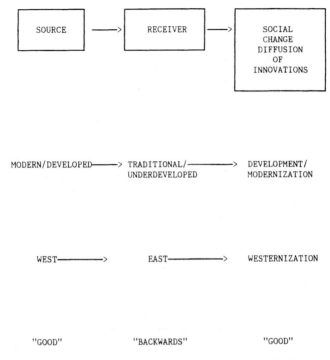

FIG. 1.1   Dominant paradigm of international communication.

It seems clear why this paradigm provides an unspoken support to much international advertising research, based as it is on a model of communication that is essentially top-down and persuasive. Also, because this is a perspective that is based on specific notions of economic development (i.e., Western capitalism and the "free market"), it is congenial to the perspective that sees advertising as simply an aspect of marketing, a relatively limited cultural form, which at most "reflects" the larger culture within which advertising is embedded.

The "New Paradigm"

The so-called dominant paradigm of international communication research, with its focus on gross national product and per capita incomes as measures of economic success, and its emphasis on diffusion of innovations, although appropriate to a strictly market-oriented perspective, offers little insight into "reasons why"; its results are often descriptive in spite of the use of increasingly sophisticated statistical methods. The emergence of a "new paradigm" of international communication research was in part, a direct response to the lack of analytical research (see Fig. 1.2). Rogers described the passing of the dominant paradigm, critiquing it as ethnocentric, overly reliant on crude economic measures, unable to articulate structural variables, and generally inappropriate for the newer more complex communications needs of the mid-1970s. In essence, he suggested that culture does matter. He described the new paradigm as redefining "development" in terms of a kind of "self-development" (a cultural awareness). Along with that, the concept of international communication itself is problematized, with an emphasis on the structural and social-system level elements and impediments to communication.

Development within the newer paradigm refers to expanding choices. Choices suggest alternatives that are then operationalized for research purposes in terms of access via networks of social roles, classes or institutions. Controling that access to choices and promoting the sharing of it according to approved guidelines became the special political concern of development.

Not without reason, the challenges to the dominant paradigm came primarily from Third World researchers and politically committed Western researchers. Thus, the newer paradigm, not tied as the earlier one was to economic growth, seems less appropriate and certainly less hospitable to advertising research. And yet, the critique of the dominant paradigm is a convincing one, especially in its acknowledgment of the importance of culture to an understanding of the issues of international communication. The UNESCO MacBride Report, which is generally sympathetic to the underlying assumptions of the newer paradigm and which is generally supportive of the Third World call for a "new international information

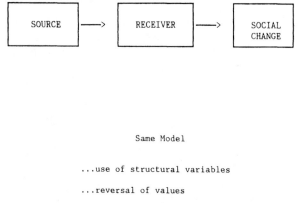

FIG. 1.2.   New paradigm of international communication.

order," also concedes that advertising is an important part of international communication. And furthermore, the notion of development as "choice" is suggestive for advertising researchers whether industry-oriented or critical.

Other researchers have described the shifting theoretical terrain within international communication research. Critical researcher John Sinclair (1987), in his book on international advertising, described the shift in paradigms:

> Contrasting approaches have been noted amongst theorists concerned with the effects of transnationalisation. . . . "Modernisation" theorists have enthused about the "propaganda" for "a whole modernized way of life" offered by commercial media . . . while theorists closed to a "cultural imperialism" approach have been more concerned with what they think of as the "cultural homogenization" of the world . . . and the "export of consumerism. . . ." The "ideological effects" of advertising . . . are seen to be instrumental in securing monopoly markets for transnational manufacturers of light consumer goods . . . as well as implementing "a mechanism for political mind control". . . . (p. 157)

Boyd-Barrett, a lecturer at Open University in England, identified three paradigm shifts in international communication research: the missionary approach, which is roughly analogous to the "dominant paradigm"; the pluralist approach, which is roughly analogous to the "new paradigm"; and what he termed the *totalistic* approach, also analogous to the new paradigm, which holds that "there could be no real understanding of the media unless priority was given to an understanding of the fundamental relationship between 'developed' and 'developing' economies, 'the international socio-politico-economic system that *decisively determines* the course of development within the sphere of each nation." (Boyd-Barrett, 1982, p. 175) Boyd-Barrett showed how each of these approaches is aligned with movements in sociological theory, the first with structural functionalism, the second with neo-Weberianism, and the third with neo-Marxism. Boyd-Barrett continued by noting that, in terms of theory, the totalistic perspective acknowledges the important role of advertising and marketing within generalized information and mass media activities globally, linking those kinds of industries to developments in related industries such as satellite communication, and the commercialization of innovations in the defense and aerospace industries.

Boyd-Barrett suggested that the totalistic approach opens up or problematizes certain aspects of international communication but he also critiqued the approach for the following reasons. First, its political position is unquestioningly and perhaps aggressively in line with what he termed the *nationalist-Marxist* alliance (i.e. the movement of "Third Worldism"). Second, it is often ahistorical and reductionist. And third, it takes a simplistic, unidirectional approach to dependency, which assumes thatWestern media steamroll cultures into subordination. Thus, although the totalistic approach enlarges the area of concern, and theorizes aspects of the communication process that the other paradigms accept as unproblematic, it does not overcome the limitation of viewing the "rest of the world" (i.e., the "rest" as opposed the the West) as a blank stage upon which the West is the primary actor.

What the new paradigm accomplishes most effectively is the recognition that there is in fact a "transnational" order in both economics and communication, and that any attempt at understanding international communication, including advertising, must theorize both the macro-order and the micro-order. Boyd-Barrett (1982), unlike many researchers who take a cultural perspective, recognized the "need for an emphasis on micro-analysis of media impacts at small group and individual levels to engage with and to illuminate the present emphasis on macro-analysis of media and multinational structures" (p. 193). But important for advertising research specifically is also the macro-analysis, which often only tangentially addresses advertising issues. A problem with the new paradigm or what is also termed *critical* research is that the research, as Boyd-Barrett pointed out, is so specifically engaged with its political program that it fails to question tenets of that program. Thus, advertising is aligned with "bad" capitalist expansion — and perhaps justifiably — but that perspective, like the dominant paradigm before it, theorizes the world as a dichotomy; the bipolarization, good and bad, is simply reversed.

Postmodernism

The older dominant paradigm of international communication might be characterized as a liberal perspective (Boyd-Barrett's missionary approach), with the succeeding newer paradigm characterized as a critical perspective (Boyd-Barrett's Weberian or Marxian approaches). Both perspectives, liberal and critical, share a specific discourse of mastery, although they locate and theorize power differently. But to a large extent, both tend to operate in terms of underlying dichotomies, the mastery of the major discourses of the Western world (i.e., male–female, rational–irrational, intellectual–emotional, good–evil, modern–traditional, and so forth). That explains why critical advertising research such as Frith's remains conflicted; although she takes a more sympathetic approach to other cultures, she merely reverses the dichotomies in terms of their value. Thus, rather than construct emotional or collective as traditional/backward, she sees those as "authentic" values. But the conflict is that the notion of "authenticity" is compromised in an age of almost instant international communication and a world economic order in which interdepency is a political–economic reality.

It is necessary to explore the underlying ontology and epistemology or world view and knowledge system of both perspectives before it is clear as to why each one, useful as they may be in answering some questions, cannot provide the whole picture. The liberal paradigm holds that the "real" world can be known directly through sense perceptions; that is why quantitative methods can be applied, because counting depends on the assumption that what the researcher actually perceives is what he or she wants to measure. This perspective contrasts with that of the interpretive approaches in which it is held that reality is unknown directly and that what may be observed and interpreted are the *effects* of reality, a perspective that suggests historical or textual analysis.

The paradigms also theorize differently on a number of dimensions: the nature of power, the nature of society, the nature of communications media, the nature of the relationship between the media and society, the nature of the relationship between media and change, and the nature of ideology (see Table 1.1). Within the liberal paradigm, power is understood as diffused and society is composed of groups with competing interests. The communications media are seen as reflecting reality, or perhaps distorting it for specific purposes. The relationship of the media to the society is that of a corrective where the media has social responsibility to act as a watchdog or fourth estate, a position that includes even advertising. The relationship of the media to social or behavioral change is seen as potentially positive; thus, if advertising is not responsible it must be brought into line used for prosocial purposes. And finally, ideology is understood as beliefs along a political spectrum, but it is not theorized in any special way as a social practice to be controlled.

In contrast, critical cultural studies (poststructuralism), the paradigm from which postmodernism emerges, proposes that power is hegemonic. *Hegemony*, a concept developed by the Italian theorist Antonio Gramsci, suggests that an elite shapes the social common sense understanding of reality. Society is composed of a ruling elite who maintain their power with the consent of the many. Media is understood as a defining constellation of institutions, where the hegemony is represented in such as way that it appears natural; thus the nature of the relationship of media to the society is one of reproduction and the legitimation of the status quo. The media can help shape consensus. And ideology is theorized as a reproductive practice; it is not just a system of beliefs or vague consciousness, but a tool in the social jockeying for power.

TABLE 1.1

Emerging Paradigm of International Communication

Paradigm	World View	Ideology	Power	Nature of Social Formation	Nature of Media	Media: Social Formation	Media: Change
Post-modernism "Emerging Paradigm(s)"	reality nonexistent; or regimes of meaning;	inappropriate since it corresponds to a betrayal of "truth"	hegemonic	monopoly of power by few thru concentration; possible to ignore the many	infinite play of signifiers without causal tie to signified; simulation	regenerative; genealogical; and memory-less	deterrence

Given these different understandings and underlying assumptions, it is clear that the research questions, methodologies used, and results derived will differ depending on the paradigm within which the researcher operates. International advertising research has been conducted almost primarily within the liberal perspective. The notable exceptions include the work of Judith Williamson, Gillian Dywer, Raymond Williams, Noreen Janus, and Jean Baudrillard. Of these, most are critical culturalists; Jean Baudrillard is considered a postmodernist. All take a highly critical view toward advertising and apparently are either rejected out of hand or perhaps unread by advertising researchers. Yet their research is highly suggestive, both for criticism and for industry-related needs in the complex international environment.

An alternative perspective to both the liberal and critical approaches is postmodernism. Art critic Hal Foster distinguished between two positions on postmodernism, one which is essentially a neoconservative position (a reaction to the excesses of Modernism), the other derived from a poststructuralist (European responses to Structuralism) position. The postmodernism discussed here is the latter; but it is still necessary to understand the modernism to which it is named and which both positions stand in opposition to.

Modernism is the perspective with which our society has enunciated its dominant values and within which liberal and critical research is conducted. According to Habermas (1983) it was the project of the Enlightenment to develop the principles of science, morality, and art "according to their inner logic." "The project of the Enlightenment consisted in [the] effort to develop objective science, universal morality and law, and autonomous art coording to their inner logic . . . [for the purpose of] the enrichment of everyday life — that is to say, for the rational organization of everyday social life" (p. 9).

As Habermas, who in fact argued for the recovery of modernity, shows that this perspective is historically specific; it organizes and directs relations of power and discourse in particular ways that then operate to influence the kinds of questions we ask and the answers at which we arrive.

Postmodernism works to problematize categories and concepts that remain fixed and immutable in Modernism, that is, for both liberal and critical research. It liberates the research from some of the constricting conditions of the scientific discourse, most particularly the condition that a phenomenon is "real" only if it can be measured and that if it cannot be measured it is not real. The need within scientific discourse for operationalizing social phenomenon in quantifiable ways is particularly problematic for international communication research. But more importantly the insistence on qualification exists within a discourse of mastery, suggesting that without the specific understanding of statistical methods, knowledge is inaccessible. Postmodernism is a position that is defined as an oppositional one to modernism, oppositional to both liberal and critical perspectives. Postmodernism, by problematizing the categories of knowledge, by blurring the distinctions between forms of expression, concerns itself with the interstices between power and knowledge, destructuring the object of analysis and decentering the subject.

Postmodernism is a theoretical perspective or position, a term of historical periodization, and a critical practice. The term is associated with Charles Jencks who used it to describe a school of architecture; its appropriation by both neo-conservatives and neo-Marxists is explained by the need within both positions to help chart out the apparent contradictions of late 20th century life.

"Postmodernism is characterized as a conflict between new and old modes – cultural and economic, the one not entirely autonomous, the other not all determinative . . . the agenda [is to] disengage the emergent cultural forms and social relations" (Foster, 1983, p. xi). In other words, a postmodern perspective can examine advertising at both the cultural and economic levels, simultaneously acknowledging that the spheres exist together. Postmodernism is also a kind of periodization that distinguishes the modern world, the period of industrialization and colonial-imperialism, from the postmodern world of postindustrialism and economic consolidation. The postmodern period is one in which class structures and political-economic arrangements are substantially different from the modern period. As critical practice, postmodernism is associated with semiotics and deconstruction, which locate power as existing within discourses and which attempt to rethink the importance and autonomy of human agency in the face of those structuring discourses that help mold and shape our ability to understand.

In mass communication research a postmodern perspective opens up ways to understand contradictions, for example, to understand how the political and cultural hegemony of the West can exist alongside economic hegemony of Japan and the Pacific Rim. Advertising is one of the prime "products" of a postmodern world, where the production of consumable objects is being increasingly abetted by the production of productions, that is, the production of markets with specific knowledge and needs. Advertising research in an era of multinationalism and the increasing success of monopoly capitalism, and the rhetoric of freedom and democracy, must be able to deal explicitly with profound contradiction, rather than rewrite contradiction as "outlayers" or as unaccounted variance.

CONCLUSION: INTERNATIONAL ADVERTISING RESEARCH & INTERNATIONAL COMMUNICATION THEORY

What do these theoretical perspectives have to do with advertising research, and specifically, how do they contribute to advertisers' and researchers' understanding of international communication to consumers. First, the critique of the current state of international advertising research reveals that international communication theory has been disregarded. Thus, many of the concepts that contribute to the first dominant paradigm of international communication are commonly but naively applied in both social-psychological and culturally oriented advertising research. That these concepts, and their underlying assumptions, have been questioned and expanded, and in some cases discredited or replaced in international communication research, suggests that conclusions reached may not be helpful in understanding advertising's relationship to the international market place or the consumer.

The critical research that has emerged from the school of British cultural studies and European research traditions provides a more theoretically articulated understanding of advertising. But this school apparently does not consider advertising of primary importance on their agenda, nor do critical researchers who do focus on advertising such as Judith Williamson (1978) or Gillian Dyer (1982) tend to communicate with mainstream advertising researchers or practitioners. Furthermore, these researchers tend to see advertising as "bad," believing that it contributes to the perpetuation of the bipolarization of our understanding of cultural phenomena.

My argument is that international advertising is a legitimate and important area of international communication research, and should be theoretically situated as such. Theory can then inform both critical research and practice, while at the same time helping researchers to gain access to the meaning of advertising at the international level. Heretofore unasked questions must be addressed such as: Does advertising work to sell products? Does advertising sell a way of life? What is the "real" work of advertising? And perhaps most importantly, just What is "advertising"? What is the object of analysis?

A postmodern perspective is suggested as an alternative to either the older dominant paradigm or the new paradigm, because it enables a richer, more complex critique. This is due in part to postmodernism's refusal of the "dominant narratives" of modernism (i.e., West vs. East, male vs. female, developed vs. underdeveloped, etc.) and its flexibility as a critical practice (engaged with, rather than extracted from, its object of analysis). As art critic Craig Owens (1983) commented;

> postmodernism [is] a crisis in Western representation, its authority and universal claims — a crisis announced by heretofore marginal or repressed discourses. . . . As a radical critique of the master narratives of modern man . . . [it] is a political and epistemological event — political in that it

challenges the order . . . of society, epistemological in that it questions the structure of its representations. (p. xiii)

Critics that identify with the postmodern understand that as critics/ researchers, we ourselves cannot be outside the politics of representation. This is an understanding that is not addressed within the boundaries of social-psychological research, where the position of the researcher does not assume any importance but is privileged by "his" authority—the appropriate degree, the appropriate measurement techniques, the replicability of the research design are *theorized* as providing guarantees. The postmodern critic theorizes the position of the researcher as well as the object of the research as existing within the terms of social relations, which are always relations of power. Jack Solomon (1988) wrote about the apparent contradiction of maintaining a critical stance toward the researcher's position:

in spite of its contradictions, semiotics is founded on a firm reality: the reality of power. That, finally, is what semiotics is all about: the power we have to define and enforce our own conceptions of reality. Because it is in the interest of those who hold power to conceal the fact that *they* have defined the "facts" of social reality, we need semiotics to unmask them . . . it enables us to question authority, to challenge the status quo. (p. 235)

Postmodern criticism is also freer in its form, not tied to the dictates and restrictions of positivism. For example, some of the same perspectives and techniques commonly applied in the creation of advertising messages, including international advertising messages—such as semiotics, popular art forms, collage/montage, pastiche—are also techniques employed in postmodern criticism. Advertising research has heretofore been addressed primarily to other advertising researchers within academia or to industry specialists who try to solve specific problems. Advertising is a small field defined by expertise and exclusive to the experts. Postmodern critique maintains a more democratic approach to the concept of research through its methodology, and is especially appropriate to a practice, advertising, which is an industry in its own right and a link in the chain of marketing, connecting it to the production process of almost every other industry and making it a form of popular art. Furthermore because advertising operates through ideas, attitudes, motivations, dreams, desires and values, giving them cultural form, it embues words and images with culturally bound meaning. Advertising, thus, should not be understood as simply one or the other (i.e. as part of industry or as part of culture), nor does the term "culture industry" cover the bases for the researcher. Advertising threads through cultures at every level; my argument is that a research perspective that is fully operational must also be able to operate with the same degree of flexibility. At the same time "culture" itself must be understood as being "in the making"; culture is a process, not an achievement. Postmodernism, because it denies the linear, master narrative, representational understanding of history (time and space), permits an analysis that threads through practices of all sorts.

What would a postmodern critique look like? It would look like interdisciplinary scholarship combined with popular art, which is to say, the critique could be understood not only by a few hundred research "experts," but by both academics across disciplines and by interested "lay people," that is, by the creative workers in advertising (copywriters, artists) and by consumers themselves who also have a stake in the results of advertising research. In terms of international advertising this seems particularly important, because the political-economic and cultural stakes are high, and the likelihood for both expense and error are correspondly high. The specific look of the critique would depend on the object of analysis, that is, where in the "circuit of communication (producer–texts –audience–lived culture)" (Johnson, 1986/1987 p. 42) a researcher decides to concentrate.

A postmodern critique would acknowledge that "culture is made in relationship to structures of dominance" (Fiske, 1989, p.2) and that the advertisement (text), though it may be the focus of interest, is "read" by the audience in light of a number of other cultural forms, several of which may be of prime importance in understanding how a particular ad or campaign will be produced and interpreted. So a postmodern critique might look as it does in John Fiske's analysis of popular culture as text (although Fiske himself tries to evade the notion of a *post*-modern). Another way it might look is like Jean Baudrillard's writing in *Simulations* (1983) a scathing critique of popular culture and acedemia, or in his *In the Shadow of the Silent Majorities* (1978), a critique of subjects/audiences, both of which are written in a highly idiosyncratic style, but have nonetheless proven to be extremely suggestive for researchers in disciplines ranging from political science to media studies. Another example of a postmodern critique is that found in John Berger's (1984) *And Our Faces, My Heart, Brief as Photos*, a work that combines essay, poetry, and art criticism to chart a powerful analysis of late 20th-century culture.

I began by claiming (a) that international advertising research, as it has been practiced, tends to ignore the theoretical developments within the broader field of international communication research; (b) that this encourages the kind of situation-specific research that Bogart criticized in 1969; and (c) that furthermore it permits researchers to remain fuzzy about how their unacknowledged assumptions or ontology structures both the questions asked and the conclusions reached. My first suggestion is that researchers establish the link to international communication theory, which will lead to theory-driven research; in this way, researchers and their audience will have a clearer understanding of the underlying purpose of advertising research and how that purpose affects the product research results.

My second suggestion is that postmodernism, understood as a theoretical perspective deriving from poststructuralism, enhances researchers' abilities to understand the highly complex (postmodern) international communication situation, and that as a practice, postmodernism allows researchers to ask different kinds of questions and to communicate results in a fresh, ultimately, and more accessible way.

Whichever paradigm a researcher adopts, it is only through a rigorous understanding of the theoretical underpinnings of the research that a coherent body of knowledge can emerge. International advertising research, thus far, lacks that coherence.

REFERENCES

Advertising Age (1990, March 5) President Carlos Menem's campaign. *Advertising Age*.

Alter, Simurda, Berry, & Stelly, Jr. (1989). Marketing to the year 2000: The chameleon decade. *Adweek*, pp. 56-65.

Baudrillard, J. (1978) *A l'ombre des majorites silencie uses ou la fin du social suivi de l'extase* [In the shadow of the silent majority]. Paris: Denoel/Gonthier.

Baudrillard, J. (1983). *Simulations*. New York: Semiotext(e).

Berger, J. (1984). *And our faces, my heart, brief as photos*. New York: Pantheonl.

Bogart, L. (1969). Where does advertising research go from here? *Journal of Advertising Research*, 9(1), 3-14.

Bichovsky-Little, H. (1988, March 3). "Naked Appeal". *The New Statesman*, pp. 25.

Boyd-Barrett, J. O. (1982). Cultural dependency and the mass media. In M. Gurevitch, T. Barnett, J. Curren, & J. Woollacott (Eds.), *Culture, society and the media* (pp. 174-195). London: Methuen.

Dyer, G. (1982). *Advertising as communication*. London: Metheun.

Fiske, J. (1989). *Reading the popular*. Boston: Unwin Hyman.

Frith, K. T. (1989). Cultural imperialism or cultural empiricism? A critical perspective. Paper presented at the 1989 Annual Conference of the American Academy of Advertising, San Diego, CA.

Frith, K. T., & Frith, M. (1989). The stranger at the gate: Western Advertising and Eastern cultural and communication values. Paper presented at 1989 Annual Conference of International Communication Association, San Francisco, CA.

Habermas, J. (1983). Modernity—an incomplete project. In H. Foster (Ed.), *The anti-aesthetic: Essays on postmodern culture* (pp. 3-17). Port Townsend, Western Australia: Bay Press.

Hachten, W. A. (1987). *The world news prism: Changing media, clashing Ideologies*. (2nd ed). Ames, IA: Iowa State University Press.

Hudson, L. A., & Ozanne, J. L. (1988). Alternative ways of seeking knowledge in consumer research. *Journal of Consumer Research*, 14, 508-521.

Johnson, R. (1986/1987). What is cultural studies anyway? *Social Text*, 16, 38-80.

Knight R. (1987, June 15). In the telly's eye: An American-style British Campaign. *US News of World Report*, p. 10-11.

McQuail, D. (1983). *Mass communication theory: An introduction.* Beverly Hills, CA: Sage.

Miracle, G. (1990). research in progress [Rep.] American Academy of Advertising conference, Orlando, Florida.

The Nation. (1990, April 16). Field of dreams. *The Nation,* pp. 509.

Owens, C. (1983). The discourse of others: Feminists and Postmodernism. in H. Foster (Ed), *The anti-aesthetic: Essays on postmodern culture.* Port Townsend, Western Australia: Bay Press.

Rogers, E. M. (1976). Communication and development: The passing of the dominant paradigm. *Communication Research, 3*(2), 213–240.

Sinclair, J. (1987). *Images incorporated: Advertising as industry and ideology.* London: Croom Helm.

Solomon, J. (1988) *The signs of our time. Semiotics: The hidden messages of environments, objects, and cultural images.* Los Angeles: Jeremy P. Tarcher.

Tse, D. K. Lee, K., Vertinsky, I., & Wehrung, D. A. et al. (1988) "Does culture matter? A cross-cultural study of executives' choice, decisiveness, and risk adjustment in international marketing. *Journal of Marketing, 52,* 81–95.

UNESCO. (1984) *Many voices, one world (the MacBride report).* Paris: Author.

Williams, R. (1980). Advertising: The magic system. In *problems in materialism of culture.* (pp. 170–195) London: Verso.

APPENDIX: SELECTED INTERNATIONAL ADVERTISING LITERATURE

Cook, W. A. (1988). "Marketing: Magnifying the small and the large of the world. *Journal of Advertising Research, 8*(9), 7.

Farmer, R. N. (1987). Would you want your granddaughter to marry a Taiwanese marketing man? *Journal of Marketing, 51,* 111–116.

Gilly, M. C. (1988). Sex roles in advertising: A comparison of television advertisements in Australia, Mexico and the United States. *Journal of Marketing, 52,* 75–85.

Hong, J. W., Muderrisoglu, A., & Zinkhan, G. M. (1987) Cultural differences and advertising expression: A comparative content analysis of Japanese and U.S. magazine advertising. *Journal of Advertising, 16,* 55–62.

Mueller, B. (1987). Reflections of culture: An analysis of Japanese and American advertising appeals. *Journal of Advertising Research, 6*(7), 51–59.

Okechuku, C., & Wang, G. (1988). The effectiveness of Chinese print advertisements in North America. *Journal of Advertising Research, 10*(11), 25–34.

Plummer, J. T. (1986). The role of copy research in multinational advertising. *Journal of Advertising Research,* 10(11), 11–20.

Rice, M. D., & Luz. (1988). A content analysis of Chinese magazine advertisements. *Journal of Advertising, 17*(4), 43–48.

Rosen, B. N., Boddewyn, J. J., & Louis, E. (1988) "Participation by U.S. Agencies in International Brand Advertising: an Empirical Study," in *Journal of Advertising, 17*(4), 14–22.

Shane, S. (1988). Language and marketing in Japan. *International Journal of Advertising, 7,* 155–161.

Sherry, J. F., Jr., & Camargo, E. G. (1987). May your life be marvelous: English language labelling and the semiotics of Japanese promotion. *Journal of Consumer Research, 14,* 174–188.

Stewart, D. W., & McAuliffe, K. J. (1988). Determinants of international media purchasing: A survey of media buyers. *Journal of Advertising,* 17(3), 22–26.

2

The Role of Cultural Value Orientations in Cross-Cultural Research and International Marketing and Advertising

John A. McCarty
American University

Over the past several years there has been an increase in interest in the relationship of values to consumer behavior. In general, the focus of this interest has been on *personal values* (values that individuals hold that presumably affect their behavior). Research has shown relationships between values and purchases in particular product classes (e.g., Homer & Kahle, 1988; Howard, 1977; McQuarrie & Langmeyer, 1985), as well as factors affecting the choices for a variety of products and services (e.g., Pitts & Woodside, 1983, 1984; Vinson, Scott, & Lamont, 1977). Personal values have typically been measured by paper and pencil value inventories such as the Rokeach Value Survey or Kahle's LOV Scale (e.g., Kahle & Kennedy, 1988; Munson, 1984; Pitts & Woodside, 1983, 1984; Rokeach, 1973). Other approaches to the study of values and their relationships with behavior have been used, however, including qualitative techniques (e.g., Reynolds & Gutman, 1984).

It is important to note that this concern with personal values originated, to some extent, from an interest with cross-cultural issues (e.g., Munson & McIntyre, 1979). Personal values were considered to be an important arena with which to compare the consumption of individuals in different cultures. Although the early interest in values was fueled by cross-cultural concerns, research on values and consumer behavior has moved away from these cultural issues in recent years. Current investigations in this area have tended to focus on personal values and their relationship to consumer behavior; in general, these studies have dealt with this relationship within a single culture.

The purpose of the present chapter is quite simple, yet fundamental. It is

23

this author's contention that the investigation of values is indeed important in the study of cross-cultural consumer behavior, however, it is likely that the more fruitful path in this area will be to concentrate on cultural value orientations rather than personal values. Although personal values may be important in understanding variability across individuals within a culture, cultural value orientations will likely be of greater importance in understanding variability in consumer behavior across cultures.

To understand this distinction more completely, it is useful to discuss the nature of culture, values, and the differences between personal values and cultural value orientations.

THE NATURE OF CULTURE

There have been numerous definitions of culture that have been used by anthropologists, sociologists, and psychologists over the past several decades. Indeed, the definitions of culture were so numerous that Kroeber and Kluckhohn (1963) classified the definitions that had been used up to the time of their writing. Although various definitions of culture have emphasized different aspects of the concept, it is clear that several themes have emerged across many of the definitions.

Culture is Adaptive

First, many of the definitions have emphasized that culture is a group's adaptation to the environment. That is, cultures develop as a response to the physical and social environment with which a particular group must deal. Therefore, culture is "human constructed" and develops as a response to specific problems encountered by the group. Cultures differ primarily because different groups are exposed to different physical and social environments. Even if the environments of two groups are relatively similar, the approaches taken to adapting to the environment may be unique in each of the groups.

Culture is Shared

A second theme is that culture is shared by members of a group. Therefore, on the one hand, culture is not idiosyncratic to an individual and, on the other hand, it is not common to all humankind. Culture is something that members of a group have in common. A useful way of thinking about this is to consider the three levels of mental programming that people possess as suggested by Hofstede (1984). There are some things that are *universal* and therefore shared by everyone. Mental programming at this tier is not dependent on cultural learning; much of this mental activity is innate and/or instinctual. Emotions and the expression of them are examples of mental programming at this universal level. At the other extreme is the *individual* level of mental programming. This refers to the mental activity that is unique to an individual. Most of what is referred to as a person's personality is at this tier. An individual's personality is unique to him or her in that no two people share exactly the same set of dispositions, traits, and so on. A person may have some things in common with others, but the similarities across individuals are not a function of membership in a particular cultural group. This type of mental programming would include, among other things, how introverted, authoritarian, or emotional a person is. Within a particular cultural group, some individuals may be similar regarding their level of introversion but different from others with regard to that trait. Similarly, the attitudes that a person holds are at this level of mental programming. Some of a person's attitudes may be similar to those of another person, but it is unlikely that any two individuals think exactly alike on all issues. Furthermore, it is unlikely that all members of a common cultural group have a similar point of view regarding a particular attitude domain. In the United States, for example, people differ dramatically on a great number of political attitudes.

The *collective* level of mental programming includes those things that are held by some but not all humans. Furthermore, there is consistency across members of a particular group in terms of what is held in common. Language is an example of this sort of mental programming; most of the things that are considered as part of a group's culture also constitute mental activity at this tier. Therefore, culture is mental programming that is shared among members of a group, yet is different from the programming that is held by members of other groups.

Culture is Learned

A third theme that is apparent in many definitions of culture is that it is learned. A member of a cultural group is not born with an understanding of the culture, rather, it is learned through one of two processes. For an individual who is born in the culture, he or she learns the culture through socialization. A person is socialized by parents, peers, the media, and the educational and religious institutions of the culture. Although this socialization process is often explicit, it is generally very subtle. That is, a culture will sometimes make explicit statements about the core cultural beliefs, as when the teachings of the United States stress the belief of freedom. Other cultural teachings may be far more implicitly transmitted. The explicit statements of a culture are often subtly shaded. "Turning the other cheek" when one has been wronged by another is an explicit cultural teaching in the

United States, but most people subtly learn that they should not let others exploit them and that a certain amount of looking out for oneself is considered wise.

The alternative process by which culture is learned is through acculturation. Acculturation is the process where an individual entering a culture learns about the new culture. Acculturation is complex because it involves the learning of the new culture by a person who has been socialized most of his or her life in a different culture. Because a person is entering the new culture and has an awareness of this, acculturation is a more active and conscious process than is socialization. When a person enters a new culture, he or she can choose to adopt the new culture or resist it in favor of the culture of birth.

The Subjective Culture

A useful construct in the consideration of culture is the notion of *subjective culture*, originally suggested by Osgood (1964) and further developed by Triandis, Vassiliou, Vassiliou, Tanaka, and Shanmugam (1972). The subjective culture involves the perceptions of the culture by members of the cultural group. This concept is particularly useful when the data collected by a researcher are the psychological responses of individuals. It should be noted, however, that the aspects of a culture are often subtle and implicit; therefore, the subjective culture of a particular person in a culture may or may not reflect the subtleties of the culture. For example, in the United States it is part of the culture to profess many high ideals, although members of the culture act more pragmatically in many instances. One person's subjective culture may include ideals as well as a subtle understanding how those ideals are not always practiced. Another person's subjective culture may believe that the ideals are indeed held and practiced as stated.

CULTURE, VALUES, AND VALUE ORIENTATIONS

Clyde Kluckhohn (1951), an anthropologist, and Milton Rokeach (1973), a social psychologist, have been particularly important in developing the value construct in their respective disciplines. More recently, Kahle (1983), among others, has been influential in the development of the values concept in the consumer behavior domain. Values have been considered as an important element in describing individual motivations, as well as a basic element in the description of culture and the differences between cultures (e.g., Kluckhohn, 1956; Kluckhohn & Strodtbeck, 1961).

Rokeach (1973) considered values to be relatively enduring beliefs that individuals possess; he also argued that these beliefs are prescriptions for behavior. In this regard, Rokeach's conception of values tends to focus on the personal values of the individual. Kluckhohn (1951) defined a value as "a conception, explicit or implicit, distinctive of an individual or characteristic of a group, of the desirable which influences the selection from available modes, means, and ends of actions" (p. 395). Kluckhohn further indicated that values represent what one *should* do in a situation and not necessarily what one may desire to do. Values, therefore, tend to have a positive quality to them: they are generally what is perceived as correct, just, fair, and so on.

It is this prescriptive aspect of values, however, that has caused great difficulty with them as theoretical antecedents of behavior. There are a great number of influences on the behavior of individuals in a particular situation. Values as standards of behavior must compete with other internal motivations of the individual as well as situational demands and constraints. Whether one will act according to his or her values may vary from situation to situation. Furthermore, individuals and/or groups may hold what Kluckhohn (1951) referred to as utopian values. These are values to which a person or group may pay lip service, but the person or group rarely acts as these values would indicate. Clearly, the inherent nature of values as ideals or standards is such that their relationship to behavior is tenuous.

There has been some degree of confusion in the use of the concept of values. This confusion is due in part to the fact that the term *value* has been used in a variety of definitions; these definitions include ones that refer to basic cultural beliefs, some that include both cultural and individual beliefs, and definitions that focus on individual motivations. Therefore, important distinctions between cultural beliefs and individual values have not always been made. It is useful to clarify some of these uses of the values concept.

Personal Values

Personal values are values that individuals believe that they hold as motivating factors in their life. Individuals often conceptualize these values as basic principles in their life and may indeed use the term value to describe these basic motivators. As Kluckhohn (1951) indicated, however, values can be implicitly held in the sense that they are at such an abstract level that they are not "clearly and habitually verbalized," but the ability of a person to potentially verbalize them as motivation is important to be considered as values. The self-concept is a useful construct when considering the role of personal values in the life of an individual; it would generally be expected that personal values will be a fairly central part of a person's sense of self. What individuals value and believe to be the prime motivators in their life are fairly central to the concept they have of the kind of persons they are.

The fact that most values have a positive quality to them is not surprising because most people want to have a positive self-concept and believe they are driven by good motivations. Values need not relate specifically to the self (e.g., an exciting life) to be a part of the self-concept. A person may value a world of beauty and this may be a part of the self-concept in the sense that the person would think "I am the kind of person who values beauty in the world." Personal values, according to Rokeach (1973), tend to relate to desirable end-states (e.g., an exciting life, salvation, a world of beauty) or modes of conduct that help one to achieve these end-states (e.g., ambition, self-control). It is important to note that although values may be a part of a person's self-concept, he or she may or may not act on them because the values are of the utopian sort. One's self-concept and how one actually acts may not always coincide.

The Individual and Cultural Nature of Values

Part of the confusion in the use of the values concept rests with the fact that personal values are generally part of the cultural teachings. Most personal values are cultural in the sense that they are learned through the socializing institutions of a society and, hence, can be part of the collective level of mental programming. Kluckhohn (1951) argued that all values are at some level a product of the culture in which a person is a member, but it is likely that each person gives a private interpretation to the values that he or she learns from the culture. Personal values, therefore, are cultural and, at the same time, individual. There could be great variability across cultures in the extent to which personal values are consistent across people within a culture. This level of variability may depend on how explicitly the values are taught by the culture and how central they are to a culture.

At one extreme there are the values that are taught explicitly by the culture; these are often the "conceptions of the desirable," that is, they are what the culture teaches as what one ought to do. These explicitly taught personal values may be closely tied to the basic beliefs of the culture. It would generally be expected that the personal values that a culture teaches in an explicit fashion would show little variation across the individuals in the society in terms of being stated as values. Individuals might, however, vary greatly on how much they act as these values suggest. The belief in these culturally taught values would therefore be a part of the collective level of mental programming.

At the other extreme are personal values that might show a great deal of variation across people in the culture in terms of whether they are expressed as values. This variation might be related to a number of causes. First, the value might be communicated by the culture in a very implicit fashion, thus allowing for a wide latitude in individual interpretation of the value.

Secondly, different socializing agents of the cultures may provide different points of view with regard to certain values. What one particular individual may believe with regard to the value would depend on which socializing force was most powerful in his or her life. For example, the Rokeach value of social recognition may be given different levels of importance by different socializing agents in the culture of the United States. A third reason why some personal values may show variability within a culture is that personal values are often tied to individual motivations and needs. In cultures where there is a fair amount of individual self-determination and heterogeneity among the population, personal values may differ across people because of different needs. These values that show individual differences across people in a culture are a part of the individual level of mental programming because any consistencies across people are not particularly tied to group membership.

Personal values, therefore, are values that are held by individuals. They may vary in the extent to which they are tied to the core teachings of the culture and, hence, vary in the extent to which they are "cultural." The term *cultural values* should be used to refer to personal values that are very prevalent in a particular culture.

Cultural Value Orientations

Personal values, regardless of the extent they are cultural, should be distinguished from *cultural value orientations*, a different concept with which the term value has been used. A value orientation, according to Kluckhohn (1951), is "a generalized and organized conception, influencing behavior, of nature, of man's place in it, of man's relation to man, and of the desirable and nondesirable as they may relate to man–environment and interhuman relations" (p. 411). The concern here is in cultural value orientations, although Kluckhohn indicated that value orientations can be at the individual level.

Cultural value orientations form the foundation upon which the culture rests; they are the basic beliefs around which the culture is organized. According to Kluckhohn and Strodtbeck (1961), there are basic problems with which all societies must deal, and cultural value orientations relate to these basic problems. These basic problems, as the definition of value orientations suggests, relates to human relationships with others and with the environment. It has been argued that culture is an adaptation to the environment, so it would seem that cultural value orientations assist the group as a whole in this adaptation process. Therefore, although personal values will often relate to individual motivations, cultural value orientations focus on the needs of the collective.

Cultural value orientations are often such a basic part of the culture that they may not always be identified as a value at the individual level. They are often beliefs that are taken for granted and, therefore, are not necessarily salient to individuals as important guiding beliefs for their own life. Rokeach (1973) argued that they should be referred to as basic philosophical orientations rather than values because individuals may not necessarily hold a position on one of them as a desirable state of affairs. For example, the culture of the United States believes in mastery over nature. It is clear that the culture acts in such a way as to deal with whatever problems nature presents. California is not abandoned as a place to live because of the probability of earthquakes, rather, there is a constant effort to build buildings and so on that can withstand such disturbances. Although the culture as a whole may hold a value orientation of mastery over nature, it is not necessarily true that such an orientation is salient to an individual as his or her value. Mastery over nature is important to the culture as a whole, but not necessarily a part of an individual's self-concept.

Cultural Value Orientations and Individual Behavior

Although cultural value orientations are not necessarily salient to an individual as a guiding belief, these orientations do have influences on individual behavior and these influences may be strong and pervasive. There are multiple ways in which these values can influence individual behavior and, in many ways, basic cultural value orientations may have influences on individual consumption behavior that are stronger and more fundamental than that of personal values. Presumably, personal values affect consumption behavior to the extent that one's values affect that person's behavior. To date, however, little research has shown strong and consistent relationships between personal values and behavior. This lack of relationship is likely related to the nature of personal values. As suggested in many of the definitions of values, values are conceptions of what one should do and, thus, they compete with other dispositions that motivate an individual as well as a variety of situational influences.

Cultural value orientations, on the other hand, may have a far more pervasive influence on individual consumption behavior. It would seem that cultural value orientations could influence consumption in at least three ways as indicated in Fig. 2.1. Cultural value orientations may be internalized by the individual as his or her personal values, or they may develop in the individual as other types of internal predispositions to behavior. As previously suggested, many values are learned through the institutions in the culture that socialize the members of the culture. These values, which are taught through this socialization process, may often be closely related to the core beliefs of the culture. For example, the United States is a very individualistic culture (Hofstede, 1984) where an emphasis is placed on the

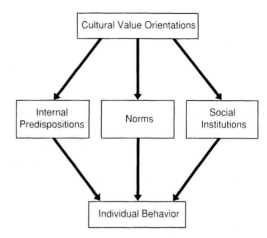

FIG. 2.1. The influence of cultural value orientations on individual behavior.

individual relative to the group. This cultural orientation may be internalized as personal values such as self-determination and/or independence. As Triandis (1989) indicated, the term used for a person who is individualistic is *idiocentric*. In a similar fashion, the core cultural value orientations may influence other elements of an individual's personality. Therefore, a person may act very individualistically and independently because it is a trait that he or she has acquired, even though this trait is not identified as a personal value by the person.

Whether or not cultural value orientations are internalized by individuals as predispositions, the behavior of individuals may be affected by these cultural beliefs either through norms or through the nature of social institutions. Norms prescribe the appropriate behavior in particular situations. As Triandis (1977) stated, "Norms are beliefs that certain behaviors are correct, appropriate, or desirable and other behaviors are incorrect, inappropriate, immoral, or undesirable" (p. 8). Norms are a part of the culture and often quite specific to a culture. The core value orientations of a culture can influence the norms that are present in that particular society. Therefore, norms will likely be consistent with the value orientations of the culture. Because cultural value orientations differ across societies, norms will also vary greatly across cultures. The sanctions against breaking a norm in a society can be quite severe.[1] Therefore, an individual will often consume in a manner prescribed by the norms of the consumption situation in that culture, regardless of what his or her individual beliefs may be. That

---

[1]Triandis (1989) stated that cultures vary on the dimension of tightness versus looseness. In tight cultures, the sanctions against breaking norms is quite strong and norm violation is more rare than in loose cultures where there is far more individual latitude. Therefore, cultures will vary on the extent to which norms will influence individual behavior.

is, the norms dictate what the appropriate behavior is in the situation and individuals are obliged to behave accordingly. For example, in the culture of the United States one is expected to tip a waiter or waitress for the service provided at a restaurant. The norm or custom is to tip 15% of the bill for acceptable service. Even though a person may not believe in tipping for service, he or she will often engage in the behavior because of the strength of the norm.

The social institutions that exist in a culture can profoundly affect individual behavior, and these institutions can develop in a manner that is consistent with the cultural value orientations. Simply stated, individuals must consume in the ways prescribed by the institutions in the culture. For example, the distribution system that develops in a culture largely determines the way that a group consumes. Regardless of personal desires to the contrary, in the culture of the United States people must buy most packaged goods through grocery store chains or other large retailers. Most grocery items are prepackaged in specific sizes. In other cultures, the distribution outlets may be quite different and affect consumption accordingly. In France, smaller stores are prevalent and there is less consumption of convenience foods compared to the United States because these small stores do not have the shelf space to stock them (Douglas, 1978, cited in Robertson, Zielinski, & Ward, 1984). Therefore, in a given culture certain products may be unavailable to consumers because of the nature of the institutions, and individual consumption behavior is affected accordingly.

CULTURAL VALUE ORIENTATIONS AND CONSUMPTION

Cultural value orientations can have a profound influence on consumer behavior and aspects of the marketing endeavor. Consequently, a knowledge of the value orientations of a particular culture would seem to be important in the design of marketing and communication programs. In this regard, the investigation of cultural value orientations, rather than personal values, will provide a more fruitful path to understanding the important aspects of a culture. Several examples of cultural value orientations and how they relate to consumption, advertising, and marketing are now presented to illustrate their potential importance.

Individualism-Collectivism

One of the most essential arenas with which a cultural group must deal is humans' relationships with one another. The value orientation dimension of individualism versus collectivism has been discussed by many with regard to the issue of how individuals relate to one another (Bellah, Madsen,

Sullivan, Swindler, & Tipton, 1985; Hofstede, 1984; Kluckhohn & Strodt-beck, 1961; Triandis, 1989; Triandis, Bontempo, Villareal, Asai, & Lucca, 1988). Individualistic cultures tend to place emphasis on the individual relative to the group, whereas collectivistic cultures tend to subordinate the individual to the group. This is particularly true for goals. In individualistic cultures, individual aspirations are considered as more important than group goals; in collectivistic societies, the group's goals are either more important than individual motivations or the ambitions of individuals are synonymous with group goals (Triandis, 1989). Individualism implies that it is acceptable or indeed expected that an individual can stand out from the group. Individual initiative is rewarded and expected. In collectivistic societies, individuals cooperate with the group; individuals tend to have an identity only as members of the group.

Not surprisingly, a culture's level of individualism affects the relationships of members of the group. In collectivistic cultures, the relationships between members of the group are more nurturant and intimate than such relationships in individualistic cultures (Triandis, 1989). Furthermore, there is more interdependence of the group members and a concern about the welfare of the group in collectivistic cultures. As Triandis points out, however, this concern may only be among and for group members. Collectivism should not be considered to be synonymous with a general concern for one's fellow humans. Members of a collective may feel nurturance and concern for other members of the collective, yet feel that it is acceptable to exploit those who are not members of the group.

Generally speaking, the more advanced a culture, the more it tends to be individualistic, and it appears that cultures evolve into individualism from more collectivistic pasts (Triandis, 1989). Most research on individualism versus collectivism across cultures consistently shows that the United States is a very individualistic culture (Hofstede, 1984). As Triandis (1989) suggested, the major antecedents of individualism are affluence and the complexity of a culture. The United States is a very complex, affluent culture. Other countries that are very individualistic include Great Britain, Australia, Canada, Netherlands, and Italy (Hofstede, 1984); all of these cultures are relatively affluent and complex. Collectivistic cultures include Peru, Venezuela, Chile, and Taiwan. Interestingly, Japan seems to be an exception in that it is a culture that is relatively collectivistic, although it is also a relatively affluent and complex society.

According to Triandis (1989), individuals within a culture can vary on the extent to which they feel individualistic or collectivistic. The terms used when describing individuals are *idiocentric* (an individualistic orientation) versus *allocentric* (a collectivistic orientation). Research within the United States has shown that idiocentric individuals tend to be more concerned with achievement but are more alienated than allocentric individuals. In spite of variations within a culture among individuals, it would generally be expected that cross-cultural differences would be greater than the variance within a culture.

The individualism in the United States is clearly apparent in much of the advertising. In an analysis of advertisements from the United States and Japan, Belk and Bryce (1986) found that U. S. ads did indeed reflect more individualistic themes than did the ads of Japan. There are many advertisements that reflect individual achievement, winning, and getting ahead. Advertising for the *Wall Street Journal*, for example, stresses that the newspaper is essential for those who want to get ahead in the business world. In contrast, advertising in Japan reflects a sense of harmony (Engle, Blackwell, & Miniard, 1986), as would be expected in a collectivistic culture.

Masculinity-Femininity

A second dimension on which cultures vary is masculinity versus femininity; this dimension, like individualism versus collectivism, deals with how people relate to one another. As Hofstede (1984) stated, this dimension relates to the extent to which the attributes commonly associated with one sex or the other are considered more popular or favored. Therefore, the dimension is not a question of what is considered to be masculine attributes and feminine attributes, rather it relates to the issue of a society's emphasis. Hofstede indicated that most research from the social sciences has shown a consistency across cultures as to what is considered masculine and what is feminine. Masculine behavior is, in general, associated with assertiveness, dominance, achievement, and aggression; feminine behavior is associated with nurturance, humility, helpfulness, and affiliation. The dimension on which cultures do vary, therefore, is the extent to which these two sets of attributes are dominant within the culture. Therefore, highly masculine cultures tend to consider assertiveness and achievement to be more important than nurturance, whereas highly feminine cultures value nurturance and affiliation.[2]

According to Hofstede (1984), the degree of masculinity of a culture can have a pervasive effect on the society. Masculinity correlates positively with need for achievement. Highly masculine countries also tend to display more differences in the sexes; these countries will tend to have fewer women in professional and technical jobs than highly feminine countries. Interest-

---

[2]The dimension of masculinity versus femininity appears similar to the individualism versus collectivism dimension in some ways. That is, collectivistic thinking is associated with affiliation and helpfulness among group members. Femininity is related to affiliation and helpfulness. Although somewhat related, the dimensions are different in their basic emphases. Furthermore, some cultures are collectivistic, yet highly masculine (e.g., Japan).

ingly, masculine countries tend to have higher traffic speeds and more traffic deaths, higher job stress, and more industrial conflict compared with more feminine societies (Hofstede, 1984). Countries that are very high in masculinity, according to Hofstede (1984), include Japan, Austria, Italy, Switzerland, and Mexico. Societies that are low on masculinity include Sweden, Norway, Denmark, and Chile. The United States is relatively masculine, although it is surpassed on this dimension by several other industrial countries, including Germany, Great Britain, and Japan.

At the level of individuals, the masculinity versus femininity dimension has been investigated by Bem (1974). Individuals can be classified as masculine, feminine, androgynous, or undifferentiated, depending on whether they favor male personality characteristics, female characteristics, a mixture of both male and female (androgenous), or neither (the undifferentiated). There are presumably individual differences across people within a society with regard to the dominance of the characteristics, even though the culture as a whole may be more masculine or feminine.

It would be expected that a society's position with regard to masculinity and femininity would influence their consumption patterns. One arena where this dimension has been suggested to influence consumption is family decision making (Robertson et al., 1984). It is reasoned that males may be more dominant in family decisions in the Hispanic subculture, whereas females are more dominant in the African American subculture. It is suggested that this relates to the matriarchal nature of the Black subculture and the patriarchal nature of the Hispanic subculture. Although the discussion of Robertson et al. related to subcultures within the United States, similar patterns may emerge when countries of different cultures and family structures are investigated. For example, Mexico would likely be similar to the Hispanic subculture of the United States with regard to family decision making.

Time Orientation

Cultures can differ in their perception of time (Kluckhohn & Strodtbeck, 1961). Some cultures have a past orientation where there is great respect for tradition and doing things the way they have always been done. Other cultures regard the present as most important. As Kluckhohn and Strodtbeck stated: "They pay little attention to what has happened in the Past and regard the Future as both vague and unpredictable. Planning for the Future or hoping that the Future will be better than either the Present or the Past simply is not their way of life" (p. 14). Still other cultures are future oriented. These cultures may respect the past and live in the present, but there is a premium placed on the future and they change to meet the future.

According to Kluckhohn and Strodtbeck, the United States is a very future oriented society. It is a culture that is generally looking to the future as being better than the present. Typically, members of the culture plan for the future and look forward to it. It seems that this future orientation is apparent in the advertising in the United States and the consumption behavior of individuals in the culture. Although advertisements may occasionally provide a feeling of nostalgia, it is often the case that consumption is oriented with the future and change in mind. Furthermore, the importance of fast food in the culture of the United States is related to this future orientation. Many feel a need to eat quickly so that they can get on with the day. The time orientation may be very different in other cultures and it is likely that much of the future oriented advertising of the culture in the United States would be confusing and misunderstood in other countries. In contrasting the advertising of the United States with that of Japan, Mueller (1987) found that Japanese advertising had a greater tendency to reflect tradition. Her research did not, however, show differences between these two cultures on appeals to modernity.

Humans' Relationship with Nature

Yet another value orientation that has implications for advertising and consumer behavior is how a cultural group believes that they relate with the world around them (Kluckhohn & Strodtbeck, 1961). It is the belief of some societies that humans can not control the forces of nature and that they are powerless to change the course of natural events. This subjugation-to-nature stance is typical of less advanced cultures. A different stance held by some cultures is that humans live in harmony with nature. As Kluckhohn and Strodtbeck indicated, this point of view sees no separation of humans with nature or the supernatural. One is simply an extension of the others. A third point of view, typically held by more advanced societies, is that humans can master nature. For these cultures it is not enough that the events of nature are understood and planned for; it is believed that steps can be taken to change them toward more favorable outcomes for the group. As Kluckhohn and Strodtbeck stated:

> Natural forces of all kinds are to be overcome and put to the use of human beings. Rivers everywhere are spanned by bridges; mountains have roads put through and around them; new lakes are built, sometimes in the heart of deserts; old lakes get partially filled in when additional land is needed for building sites, roads, or airports; the belief in man-made medical care for the control of illness and the lengthening of life is strong to an extreme. . . .(p. 13)

Triandis (1984) suggested that the value orientation of mastery over nature versus subjugation to nature can be represented at the level of individuals as a feeling of internal versus external locus of control (Rotter, 1966). Individuals who have an internal locus of control feel that they control their lives to a great degree and can shape their future. Alternatively, those who have an external locus of control feel that they have little control over the events in their lives and can not change the course of events affecting them. These individuals feel powerless to forces beyond their control.

A society's belief about their relationship with nature will have a fundamental effect on the types of products that are available and the way that these are marketed. The culture of the United States, for example, is a culture where mastery over nature is held as a core belief. This belief is apparent in a variety of products and services. Vehicles are available to transverse virtually every type of terrain. The equipment of these vehicles such as snow tires, windshield wipers, and so on allow driving in any kind of road condition and weather. In a different domain, all sorts of products are available to the home dweller for use in the lawn and garden such as weed killer, pest spray, and fertilizer. For the most part there is a product available that will assist with any problem encountered on a person's land. In yet another arena, a variety of medications can be purchased to relieve most ailments that a person can have.

The promotion and advertising of products in the United States tends to reflect this mastery over nature orientation. Belk and Bryce (1986) found that U. S. print advertising was more likely to stress actively changing the environment than adapting to it, compared to advertising in Japan. Examples of advertising stressing such mastery can easily come to mind. Advertisements for cold and flu remedies often emphasize the ability of the medications to keep you going when you have such an ailment, effectively mastering the situation. Numerous advertisements for automobiles show how particular vehicles can get you through the most adverse weather conditions.

Activity Orientation

Kluckhohn and Strodtbeck (1961) identified three possible orientations that a society can have with regard to activity. Two of these, *being* and *doing*, are the traditional stances that have been identified by philosophers; they added a third stance with regard to activity: *being-in-becoming*. As the name suggests, a doing orientation indicates a culture value placed on acting and doing. A being orientation, on the other hand, suggests that a premium is placed on experiencing life deeply, an orientation toward reflection about life and one's actions. The doing versus being distinction is, simply stated, a distinction between acting and reflecting. The being-in-becoming orientation suggests an evolutionary process that an individual is to go through in his or her life. That is, one should evolve into a better individual and reach a higher level of self-understanding.[3]

According to Triandis (1984), the activity orientation that a culture has can have a pervasive effect on the activity of individuals. Individuals in doing cultures score higher on scales of aggression, autonomy, dominance, and achievement compared with people in societies with a being orientation. Also, people in doing societies typically have shorter reaction times than people in being countries and, if asked to estimate a minute of time, those in a doing culture will underestimate whereas those in being cultures will overestimate.

At the level of the individual, the doing versus being distinction might relate to the individual difference variable of private self-consciousness (Fenigstein, Scheier, & Buss, 1975). Individuals who have a high level of private self-consciousness tend to examine their motives and reflect about themselves a lot, whereas those who are low in private self-consciousness tend not to engage in self-reflection. Although self-consciousness is an individual difference variable that probably exists in all cultures, it is likely that the cultural stance on the doing versus being orientation relates to the prevalence of this trait.

It would be expected that a culture's orientation with regard to activity would be reflected in the themes used in advertising. The United States, for example, is a very doing oriented culture, and a doing theme has generally been more prevalent in the advertising than a being theme (Belk & Pollay, 1985). Advertisements in the United States typically show people as active rather than reflective, although this would obviously relate to product category, as certain products would relate more to one theme than another (e.g., advertising for leisure time activities vs. for business products). In a study of three Chinese cultures (People's Republic of China, Hong Kong, and Taiwan) by Tse, Belk, and Zhou (1989), the level of being themes versus doing themes was consistent with the differences in activity orientations of these three cultures.

GENERAL RESEARCH ISSUES AND IMPLICATIONS

The intent of this section is not to provide an elaborate discussion of cross-cultural methodology, rather, broad issues regarding the investigation of value orientations across cultures is the focus. The thorough investiga-

---

[3]The activity dimension discussed by Kluckhohn and Strodtbeck is somewhat different than being, doing, and having as used by Belk and Pollay (1985). Belk and Pollay's use of these relates particularly to what products will do for an individual rather than dealing with the activity level of individuals per se.

tion of cultural value orientations is essential when considering marketing and advertising in other cultures. To date, however, our knowledge of the variation in cultures is mostly anecdotal (Douglas & Craig, 1983). Several key points have been made with regard to cultural value orientations that bear on the method of assessing them. First, because cultural value orientations are basic beliefs of the culture, they are often very abstract. These basic beliefs are usually implicitly and subtlety communicated to cultural members through socialization. Therefore, these beliefs may be known by the members of a society, but group members may not easily be able to explain or discuss the ideas. Secondly, it was noted that value orientations differ from personal values in that value orientations are not necessarily held by the individuals as personal values. Value orientations are important to the culture as a whole, but not necessarily salient to individuals as guiding principles. Value orientations may be internalized by individuals as personal values, but they may also affect behavior through other forms of predispositions such as traits, behavioral tendencies, habits, and so on. Several examples of value orientations as individual predispositions are given in the previous section (e.g., internal-external locus of control, private self-consciousness). Furthermore, value orientations may not be internalized by individuals at all; these core beliefs may affect behavior through norms or social institutions. Third, because personal values are often utopian ideals of the culture, these values may be widely held by individuals but not routinely acted upon. These utopian values may or may not accurately reflect core cultural value orientations.

This suggests that the investigation of personal values may or may not provide a researcher with insights about the value orientations of a culture. In some cases, personal values may simply not be relevant to the core beliefs of a culture. Other approaches to the study of value orientations will likely be necessary. Moreover, because of the complex nature of value orientations, it is probable that a multimethod approach to their investigation is warranted. As Spates (1983) observed,

> This is dictated by the subjective nature of values and the different social settings in which they emerge. Single techniques—even grounded ones— cannot provide complete portraits. For example, an analysis of a community newspaper may show values A and B to be dominant while an interview with community members may indicate X and Y are preferred group values. While a multitechnique approach is expensive and time-consuming, the discrepancies created by past data make it a prerequisite for adequate value work of the future. (p. 44)

One of the approaches that can certainly be a part of this multitechnique approach is the study of the individuals in a culture. Two possibilities for studying individuals would be to: (a) investigate the subjective culture of individuals and (b) study individual predispositions that are likely to relate to particular value orientations of the culture. As mentioned, the subjective culture is the way that individuals perceive their culture. Therefore, the investigation of the subjective culture in a society is a matter of individuals reporting about aspects of their social environment. In a sense, this method is treating the respondents as informants about the culture; it is the informant's insights about what is generally true of members of his or her group that are important, rather than the informant's own point of view. In this approach, not only are the individual beliefs of the respondents studied, but also their perceptions of norms, role relationships, and antecedents and consequences of behaviors (Triandis et al., 1972). For example, through interview and survey techniques, respondents can relate the normative influences in a culture and can do so regardless of whether individual respondents are motivated to comply with such norms. The report of such norms can provide the researcher with an insight to the value orientations in a particular culture.

It has also been suggested that cultural value orientations can be internalized by individuals as beliefs, personal values, traits, and so on. One approach to understanding the basic beliefs of a culture would be to survey the beliefs and predispositions of individuals in the culture. Given the abstract nature of value orientations, it would be difficult to directly ask individuals to describe them. Kluckhohn and Strodtbeck (1961) did, however, advocate a relatively straightforward approach to tapping value orientations. Through an interview situation, they posed a variety of life situations to respondents who were forced to choose among the alternatives; each of the alternatives represented one of the stances that could be taken with regard to a particular value orientation dimension. For example, one of their life situations dealt with how three different farmers planted crops and took care of them, which pertained to the value dimension of humans' relationship with nature. One farmer's behavior exemplified harmony with nature, another's exemplified subjugation with nature, the third description expressed mastery over nature. Respondents were asked which approach they felt was best, which was the next best, and which would most people (in their culture) think was the best. Consistency in the responses of many individuals in a culture would provide a sense of the cultural orientation toward its relationship with nature.

These life situations would need to be tailored to the particular culture studied (the cultures that Kluckhohn and Strodtbeck investigated were all rural cultures where farming was a way of life), but if designed correctly, this approach could provide relatively direct information about the value orientations of a group.

In a similar vein, Triandis, Leung, Villareal, and Clark (1985) developed a scale to measure individualism (idiocentric) and collectivism (allocentric) at the individual level; their scale has been tested in both China and the United States (Hui, 1988). The measurement of individuals on the idiocentric-allocentric dimension should provide some indication of the degree to which a culture tends toward individualism or collectivism. Although there would be variability within a culture, it would generally be expected that a greater percentage of individuals in an individualistic culture would respond to the scale in an idiocentric fashion compared with individuals in a collectivistic culture.

Other dispositional states could be used as surrogate measures of the value orientations of a culture. It would be expected that if a value orientation is relatively strong in a culture, this could lead to a prevalence of certain personality types in that culture. As mentioned, Rotter's (1966) construct of locus of control probably relates to the value orientation dimension of humans' relationship with nature. If a culture has a high percentage of individuals who have an internal locus of control, this should indicate that the culture has a belief in mastery over nature. Similarly, private self-consciousness may prove to be useful as a surrogate measure for being versus doing; to date, however, this individual difference measure's relationship to the activity orientation has not been investigated.

The content analysis of the media in a society has often been considered as a method of understanding a culture. Cultural values have been investigated via the study of the fiction of a culture (Albrecht, 1956) and biographies (Lowenthal, 1944). In a cross national study, Wayne (1956) analyzed magazine pictures in the Soviet Union and the United States for an indication of values in these two cultures. Virtually all advanced societies have a variety of media that can be content analyzed for value orientation themes.

Advertising can be a significant source of information about a culture and the value orientations of a society. The examples mentioned in the discussion of specific value orientation dimensions have indicated this to be true. Several cautions should be addressed, however, with regard to the current advertising of a culture as an indication of value orientations. First, the culture as presented in advertising may be a distortion of reality, as suggested by Belk and Pollay (1985). After reviewing the available evidence, they concluded that advertising tends to reflect an image of the good life rather than the mundane reality of many people's lives. Although it is unclear whether a picture of a society's value orientations are distorted by their advertising, it is possible that advertising may provide an inaccurate picture of the core beliefs of a culture. Secondly, it should be emphasized that the advertising for products in a particular country may have been the work of a marketer in a different culture. Many products are marketed internationally, and the advertising may be handled by an advertising agency of the country where the product is produced. Therefore, the advertising may reflect a different culture's conception of the value orientations of the culture where the advertising is being seen or read. The accuracy of that conception is a matter of how well the particular marketer has investigated the culture. Third, as Belk and Pollay (1985) noted, advertising can either change lifestyles or reflect current lifestyles. Particularly in developing societies, the advertising may not reflect the current value orientations but the orientations of a society that the culture is progressing toward. As cultures progress, they tend to become more individualistic, believe more in mastery over nature, become more future oriented, and so on. Therefore, current advertising may reflect the evolving value orientations of the culture. Finally, advertising may reflect value orientations that are consistent with the nature of the product, regardless of the orientations of the culture. For example, a product that helps a person get something accomplished may stress a doing orientation, as this is consistent with the nature of the product.

Other approaches to the investigation of a culture have been suggested, including observation, physical trace measures, and archival research (Douglas & Craig, 1983). As previously emphasized, the understanding of a culture's core beliefs will require a multimethod approach so that the subtleties of the beliefs are understood.

PRACTICAL IMPLICATIONS

International marketing is a task of monumental difficulty. Cultures differ on a variety of dimensions that will affect the marketing effort, including wealth and its distribution, levels of literacy, and linguistic heterogeneity (Douglas & Craig, 1983). These factors are important to consider in the early stages of deciding whether a product should be marketed in a particular country. For example, the wealth of a country and how the wealth is distributed among its population may determine whether marketing a particular product is viable at all in that country.

If it is determined that a product should be marketed in a country, then an understanding of the cultural value orientations of that society is necessary. The value orientations of a culture may affect the way a product is packaged, positioned, promoted, and distributed. The understanding of the core beliefs are particularly important with regard to the positioning and promotion of a product. For example, fast food restaurants are particularly important in a doing oriented culture but the speed at which one gets their food may be unimportant in a being oriented culture. In a being culture, the experience of dining in a restaurant may be more important. A fast food restaurant would make little sense in a culture that values the experience of eating. Knowledge of the activity orientation would be useful in the considerations of how to position the restaurant chain.

Marketers have likely advanced beyond the obvious cross-cultural blunders caused by language differences and custom. More subtle blunders are still possible and mistakes that relate to implicitly held beliefs may not be so easy to discern. Through a multimethod research process, the core value orientations of a culture can be investigated such that a product or service can be marketed in the most advantageous way in a particular society.

SUMMARY

This chapter clarifies the meanings of several concepts that use the term value, but are different entities. Personal values are beliefs held by individuals and are generally conceptions of the way one ought to act. These personal values may show a great variation among members of a culture, particularly in very loose, heterogeneous cultures such as the United States. Some personal values are part of the teachings of a society; there may be less variation among members of a society with regard to these culturally taught values. The term cultural values, therefore, can be used to describe personal values that are widely held by members of a society. Personal values, whether idiosyncratic or cultural, should be distinguished from cultural value orientations. Value orientations are the core beliefs of the culture and deal with human relationships with one another and with the world around them.

This chapter stresses that a knowledge of the value orientations of a society will be important for those who wish to market goods or services in that culture. Value orientations can affect consumption in profound and basic ways, and a marketing and communication plan will need to coincide with these basic beliefs. A multimethod research approach will be a useful in the investigation of the value orientations of a culture.

REFERENCES

Albrecht, M. C. (1956). Does literature reflect common values? *American Sociological Review, 21*, 722–729.

Belk, R. W., & Bryce W. J. (1986). Materialism and individual determinism in U. S. and Japanese print and television advertising. In R. J. Lutz (Ed.), *Advances in consumer research* (Vol. 13, pp. 568–572). Provo, UT: Association for Consumer Research.

Belk, R. W., & Pollay, R. W. (1985). Images of ourselves: The good life in twentieth century advertising. *Journal of Consumer Research, 11*, 887–897.

Bellah, R. N., Madsen, R., Sullivan, W. M., Swindler, A., & Tipton, S. M. (1985). *Habits of the heart: Individualism and commitment in American Life*. Berkeley: University of California Press.

Bem, S. L. (1974). The measurement of psychological androgyny. *Journal of Consulting and Clinical Psychology, 42,* 155-162.

Douglas, S. P. (1978). Cross national comparisons and consumer stereotypes. In *European business in international business* (pp. 263-281). Amsterdam: North Holland.

Douglas, S. P., & Craig, S. (1983). *International marketing research.* Englewood Cliffs, NJ: Prentice Hall.

Engle, J. F., Blackwell, R. D., & Miniard, P. W. (1986). *Consumer behavior* (5th ed.). Chicago: Dryden Press.

Fenigstein, A., Scheier, M. F., & Buss, A. H. (1975). Public and private self-consciousness: Assessment and theory. *Journal of Consulting and Clinical Psychology, 43,* 522-527.

Hofstede, G. (1984). *Culture's consequences.* Beverly Hills: Sage.

Homer, P., & Kahle, L. R. (1988). A structural equation test of the values–attitude–behavior hierarchy. *Journal of Personality and Social Psychology, 54,* 638-646.

Howard, J. A. (1977). *Consumer behavior: Application and theory.* New York: McGraw-Hill.

Hui, C. H. (1988). Measurement of individualism–collectivism. *Journal of Research in Personality, 22,* 17-36.

Kahle, L. R. (Ed.). (1983). *Social values and social change: Adaptation to life in America.* New York: Praeger.

Kahle, L. R., & Kennedy, P. (1988). Using the list of values (LOV) to understand consumers. *Journal of Services Marketing, 2,* 49-56.

Kluckhohn, C. (1951). Values and value orientations in the theory of action: An exploration in definition and classification. In T. Parsons & E. Shils (Eds.), *Toward a general theory of action* (pp. 388-433). Cambridge: Harvard University Press.

Kluckhohn, C. (1956). Toward a comparison of value emphasis in different cultures. In L. D. White (Ed.), *The state of social sciences* (pp. 116-132). Chicago: The University of Chicago Press.

Kluckhohn, F. R., & Strodtbeck, F. L. (1961). *Variations in value orientations.* Evanston, IL: Row, Peterson & Company.

Kroeber, A., Kluckhohn, C. (1963). *Culture: A critical review of concepts and definitions.* New York: Vintage Books.

Lowenthal, L. (1944). Biographies in popular magazines. In P. F. Lazarsfeld & F. N. Stanton (Eds.), *Radio research 1942–43* (pp. 507-548). New York: Duell, Sloan & Pearce.

McQuarrie, E. F., & Langmeyer, D. (1985). Using values to measure attitudes toward discontinuous innovations. *Psychology and Marketing, 2,* 239-252.

Mueller, B. (1987). Reflections of culture: An analysis of Japanese and American advertising appeals. *Journal of Advertising Research, 27*(3), 51-59.

Munson, J. M. (1984). Personal values: Considerations on their measurement and application to five areas of research inquiry. In R. E. Pitts & A. G. Woodside (Eds.), *Personal values and consumer psychology* (pp. 13-33). Lexington, MA: Lexington Books.

Munson, J. M., & McIntyre, S. H. (1979). Developing practical procedures for the measurement of personal values in cross-cultural marketing. *Journal of Marketing Research, 16,* 48-52.

Osgood, C. (1964). Semantic differential technique in the comparative study of cultures. *American Anthropologist, 66,* 171-200.

Pitts, R. E., & Woodside, A. G. (1983). Personal value influences on consumer product class and brand preferences. *The Journal of Social Psychology, 119,* 37-53.

Pitts, R. E., & Woodside, A. G. (1984). Personal values and market segmentation: Applying the value construct. In R. E. Pitts & A. G. Woodside (Eds.), *Personal values and consumer psychology* (pp. 55-67). Lexington, MA: Lexington Books.

Reynolds, T. J., & Gutman, J. (1984). Laddering: Extending the repertory grid methodology to construct attribute–consequence–value hierarchies. In R. E. Pitts & A. G. Woodside (Eds.), *Personal values and consumer psychology* (pp. 155-167). Lexington, MA: Lexington Books.

Robertson, T. S., Zielinski, J., & Ward, S. (1984). *Consumer behavior*. Glenview, IL: Scott, Foresman.

Rokeach, M. (1973). *The nature of human values*. New York: The Free Press.

Rotter, J. (1966). Generalized expectancies for internal versus external locus of control of reinforcement. *Psychological Monographs, 80* (1, Whole No. 609).

Spates, J. L. (1983). The sociology of values. In R. H. Turner & J. F. Short (Eds.), *Annual review of Sociology* (Vol. 9, pp. 27–49). Palo Alto: Annual Reviews, Inc.

Tse, D. K., Belk, R. W., & Zhou, N. (1989). Becoming a consumer society: A longitudinal and cross-cultural content analysis of print ads from Hong Kong, the People's Republic of China, and Taiwan. *Journal of Consumer Research, 15*, 457–472.

Triandis, H. C. (1977). *Interpersonal behavior*. Monterey, CA: Brooks/Cole Publishing Company.

Triandis, H. C. (1984). A theoretical framework for the more efficient construction of culture assimilators. *International Journal of Intercultural Relations, 8*, 301–330.

Triandis, H. C. (1989). The self and social behavior in differing cultural contexts. *Psychological Review, 96*, 506–520.

Triandis, H. C., Bontempo, R., Villareal, M. J., Asai, M., & Lucca, N. (1988). Individualism and collectivism: Cross-cultural perspectives on self-ingroup relationships. *Journal of Personality and Social Psychology, 54*, 323–338.

Triandis, H. C., Leung, K., Villareal, M. J., & Clark, F. (1985). Allocentric vs. idiocentric tendencies: Convergent and discriminant validation. *Journal of Research in Personality, 19*, 395–415.

Triandis, H. C., Vassiliou, V., Vassiliou, G., Tanaka, Y., & Shanmugam, A. (1972). *The analysis of subjective culture*. New York: Wiley.

Vinson, D. E., Scott, J. E., & Lamont, L. M. (1977). The role of personal values in marketing and consumer behavior. *Journal of Marketing, 41* (2), 44–50.

Wayne, I. (1956). American and Soviet themes and values: A content analysis of pictures in popular magazines. *Public Opinion Quarterly, 20*, 314–320.

3 Implications of Social Values for Consumer Communications: The Case of the European Community

Lynn R. Kahle
University of Oregon

Sharon Beatty
University of Alabama

John Mager
Eastern Washington University

Culture often manifests itself in political decisions and consumer decisions. These decisions are driven by the individual values that members of the culture hold. Studying political and value structures often provide more efficient and accurate windows to culture than studies of peripheral habits. This chapter examines changing culture by investigating the changing political structure and values in Europe.

Most of the major countries of Western Europe have been moving toward economic cooperation for several decades via what has been known as the Common Market, the European Economic Community, or more recently simply the European Community (EC). The chosen 12 current EC participants are listed in Table 3.1, which in addition provides the population and Gross National Product (GNP) of each listed country. Table 3.1 also shows the relations among the EC, the military North Atlantic Treaty Organization (NATO), and the European Free Trade Association (EFTA). Several neutral countries have not participated in the EC, such as Austria and Switzerland, as well as the northern-most countries of Finland, Sweden, Norway, and Iceland. Austria and Turkey would explicitly like to join the EC (Yemma, 1988), and the EFTA, at worst, has cooperated with the EC. At best, some anticipate unification of the EC and EFTA. Other NATO countries, such as the United States, will most likely not become EC members any time soon, raising questions about the continuing significance of NATO. Some have advocated completely decoupling the EC from the United States to form an anti-Stalinist, anti-capitalist type of socialism (e.g., Palmer, 1988).

The EC is gradually moving toward functioning as a super country. The

TABLE 3.1
Selected Countries' Population, Gross National Product, and Membership
Status in Major European Economic and Military Alliances

Country	Pop. (mil.)	GNP (bil.)	EC	NATO	EFTA
Belgium	9.9	$ 111	Yes	Yes	No
Denmark	5.1	101	Yes	Yes	No
France	55.8	724	Yes	Yes	No
W. Germany(BRD)	60.2	898	Yes	Yes	No
Greece	10.0	37	Yes	Yes	No
Ireland	3.7	29	Yes	No	No
Italy	57.4	368	Yes	Yes	No
Luxembourg	.4	6	Yes	Yes	No
The Netherlands	14.7	190	Yes	Yes	No
Portugal	10.2	29	Yes	Yes	Yes
Spain	39.8	188	Yes	Yes	No
United Kingdom	56.6	504	Yes	Yes	No
EC TOTAL	323.8	3185			
Iceland	.3	3	No	Yes	Yes
Norway	4.2	64	No	Yes	Yes
Austria	7.6	95	No	No	Yes
Finland	4.9	97	No	No	Associate
Sweden	8.4	109	No	No	Yes
Switzerland	6.5	171	No	No	Yes
Canada	23.3	367	No	Yes	No
Turkey	55.4	52	No	Yes	No
US	247.5	4500	No	Yes	No
E. Germany(DDR)	16.7	367	No	No	No
Japan	123.2	1900	No	No	No
U.S.S.R.	287.0	2300	No	No	No

Note. Adapted from *The World Almanac and Book of Facts 1990.*

EC has as permanent governmental structures the Council of Ministers, the European Parliament, a Commission, and a Court of Justice. The current structures began functioning on July 1, 1967, although the groundwork dates back to 1951. The countries want to coordinate social developments, to integrate economies, and eventually to bring about political union. Sixty African, Caribbean, and Pacific nations are affiliated with the EC, and it has had free trade agreements with the EFTA since 1973. The world-wide significance of a unified EC is evident from the figures in Table 3.2. Clearly the unified EC will play in the same league as Japan and the United States.

In June, 1985, the Commission of the EC issued a White Paper, "Completing the Internal Market," which proposed 279 changes to increase economic union. Of the 279 proposals, the council has adopted most, although some of the proposals are currently in various states of ratification, and many of the remaining proposals are among the most controversial. The target was to complete ratification of these changes by the end of 1992, at which time sales and value-added taxes, product specifications,

TABLE 3.2
Relative Sizes in 1987 of Western Economic Powers

Dimension	EC	Japan	U.S.
Population (mil)	323	122	244
GDP (tril ECUs)	3.669	2.058	3.869
World's exports	20%	12%	14%
Social cost as % of GDP	25%	18%	16%

Note. Adapted from Beatson (1990a), and Emerson et al. (1988)

transportation regulations, monetary units, and tariffs became equal for all participating nations. Goods, money, workers, and services pass internal EC borders freely. The EC will experience greater internal competition and will be better positioned to compete in and even lead the globalizing economy. The EC will maintain its social commitments evidenced in the last line of Table 3.2, which may both help and hurt its economic fate. Recently the leaders of the 12 nations called for political union by 1992 as well (Whitney, 1990).

These changes may have profound effects on how Europeans conduct business, although no one is exactly sure what all of those effects will be. Estimates range from a 0.3% to a 4% increase in output simply from improved efficiency (Yemma, 1988). North American pessimists see the changes as leading to the blockading of "Fortress Europe," creating a nearly impenetrable economic union of former trading partners who will establish protectionist barriers to outsider participation. The Table 3.2 data regarding the importance of European exports would argue against a Fortress Europe mentality because exports are too important in EC countries (Worlock, 1990), and most relevant communiques from the EC headquarters dismiss this consequence of integration, too. Optimists see the 1992 changes as simplifying and standardizing western European business practices, as eliminating long-outdated local traditions and restrictions, and as launching an enormous opportunity toward more efficient marketing.

For the most part, European big business and large North American multinational corporations have provided the push toward 1992 (Laurent, 1988). These forces from the political right have cooperated with forces from the political left, who want greater international understanding and tolerance, to work toward a goal grounded in realism but idealistic enough to shape dreams. Modern communications have homogenized European culture to some extent, paving the way for left and right to travel together toward increased cooperation. The road, however, still has potholes and steep hills.

As with all predictions about the future, we can only look at where the present is heading and guess where it might arrive. Anyone who claims to know the future for sure is either God or not honest, and we have more aspirations toward honesty than deification. With the rapid changes in Europe that are taking place apart from the development of the EC, we must view economic unification as only one force for change out of many. Numerous forces other than the "1992 changes" will also alter Europe. Certainly the reunification of East (Deutsche Demokratische Republik; DDR) and West (Bundes Republik Deutschland; BRD) Germany is modifying the nature of the continent, as are the rapid other changes in Eastern Europe set in motion by the Soviet Union's admission that the Cold War is over and by its economic and political difficulties. Western Europeans trust the Soviets and the East much more now than 10 years ago, with the correlated decline in reliance on the United States for economic and military security. We should not underestimate the significance of transportation and information technology changes in the reshaping of Europe, either. On the other hand, cultural, political, geographic, and linguistic barriers did not all suddenly evaporate on January 1, 1993. Some of the targeted economic changes were not even in place, and others will not respond to new policies as anticipated. But let us at this point assume for the sake of edification that the targeted economic changes are indeed occurring as planned.

THE NEW ECONOMY OF THE EC

The White Paper proposed the planned changes clearly enough. Let us look at each of the broad classes of targeted changes more carefully.

1. Fiscal Barriers Ended.   For example, excise taxes and value-added taxes are not to be levied anew each time a product passes another border. Tariffs and quotas had presumably already been removed, although a few still remain, for example in agricultural and steel products. These internal tariffs ended. Direct state control of interest rates and lending quotas ended.

Government subsidies of industry receded and usually ceased. Subsidies from the governments are being heavily discouraged by the EC Commissioner for Competition. The EC has ordered over $1 billion in subsidy paybacks in 26 cases since 1981 (Kapstein, 1989). More will certainly follow.

2. Technical Barriers Are Being Removed.   Divergent technical norms for goods and services essentially ended. Health and safety standards in the work place are synchronized. Foreign companies are allowed to establish subsidiaries more easily, and foreign company bids do not receive discriminatory treatment in government procurement. Countries within the EC are able to bid freely on government procurement, and outside countries can win procurement bids if they can provide at least a 3% saving over EC competitors. Trademarks, patent, and intellectual property rights now extend throughout the EC.

Protection of intellectual properties involves many issues, not just traditional trademark, copyright, and patent issues. For example, who controls computer data documents, screen displays, and software (Worlock, 1990)? A proposed copyright law in the EC would give more control over software interfaces to the companies who write them, thus giving a boost to large computer manufacturers and creating more difficulty for small software companies (Verity, 1990).

Consider an example of how technology change will be an inevitable part of the new Europe. Currently, Europeans cannot use "beepers" to page one another across national borders. The United States has at present eight times as many beepers as the EC. In December 1992, a common paging system became available, allowing increased paging and presumably increasing sales greatly (International Herald Tribune 1990, p. 4). This change is not a revolutionary one, but it exemplifies how technology transfer has increased with standardization of technical specifications and how it will increase access to people.

Regulations did not disappear in 1992, they only became more uniform. Tobacco ads, for example, are generally banned on European television, but in print they may take many forms. In an effort to integrate the laws, all tobacco advertising of any type may be banned (Rosenbaum, 1990). The European Parliament passed legislation, yet to be ratified, banning print, broadcast, and event sponsorship advertising of tobacco products.

3. Physical Frontier Barriers Have Been Removed.   Vehicles now do not have to stop for customs inspection at each border, for example. Because excise taxes and technical specification differences ended, the prior justifications for strangling the transportation industry in red tape disappeared. Laws against backhauling, which prevent truckers from returning with full loads, ended, for example. Currently trucks cross the United States at an average of 64 kph, whereas prior to 1992 they crossed the EC at an average of 12 kph, in spite of very liberal speed limits on, for example, the German Autobahnen. These changes should speed up transportation considerably. Increased competition in air transportation should result from reduction of regulations and subsidies (James, 1990).

Calingaert (1988) suggested that several changes are especially important for North Americans, and we must monitor how these changes are occurring.

1. The terms and conditions of participation for foreign service providers have major implications both for American companies operating in Europe currently and for companies desiring to operate there in the future. The vital financial and information technology services warrant special atten-

tion. Quraeshi and Lyqmani (1990) suggested that protectionism, openness of directives, and the view of reciprocity top the list of US concerns.

2. Synchronizing regulations and standards changed them, but it is too early to tell how exclusionary new regulations and standards will be (Calingaert, 1988). North Americans should monitor testing and certification regulations, and we should also focus on how local content rules are fashioned.

3. Public procurement laws allow foreign competitors to bid on public projects, reducing the number of local sweetheart deals. This fact may be especially important in construction, communication, and power equipment sales. These fields are ones in which the United States excels, but it is too soon to tell whether the new laws will include open competition only for other EC countries or for all countries. Bids from non-EC countries will have to be at least 3% lower than EC bids to win contracts.

Most of the other changes, according to Calingaert, have a more general influence on North Americans, Japanese, and Europeans alike: common legal framework, capital liberalization, border controls, freedom of movement, and tax harmonization influence everyone more or less equally.

4. These Changes Are Increasing Internal Competition. Thereby, they will reduce prices while increasing efficiency. If each country currently has two or three major suppliers, removal of internal market barriers could suddenly create 20 or 30 competitors. The current pace of European mergers and acquisitions, however, suggests that three or four major competitors may more often be the norm. In the grocery business, for example, many European tastes are becoming more homogeneous, thus leading to border-jumping by many brands before 1992. As with supermarkets in the United States, European retailers are tempted to stock only the top brands (Toy, 1989). The same type of oligopoly may emerge in the EC's currently-fragmented airline industry (Toy, 1990).

Related laws that are not part of the White Paper also influence European trade, especially the rules of origin and local content (Business International Corporation, 1989). Rules of origin give a product its nationality, which in turn determines EC tariffs. Local content regulations define whether a product is an EC product, based on the value of EC inputs relative to its total value.

Local (e.g., European) content laws become especially complex in the information and entertainment industries. An example of a recent local-content law that influences communication is the rule that at least 50% of all EC television programming, except news, sports, and game shows, must be of EC origin "where practicable" (Business International Corporation, 1989). Currently 70% of all nondocumentary shows, films, serials, and soap operas are imported, and over half of those imports come from the United States (Reimer, 1989). Because the United States has a larger homogeneous audience and allows far more commercials, it can produce exportable entertainment more efficiently than Europe. The new ruling is increasing joint ventures between United States and EC entertainment companies, and it may also necessitate EC-wide government subsidies on the entertainment industry. Some perceive these rules as politically, but not legally, binding (Wentz, 1989b).

CORPORATE STRATEGY IN THE NEW EUROPE

Strategically, many international companies are planning to manufacturer (or to ally themselves with a manufacturer) in western Europe, in case local content and origin laws exclude countries outside of the chosen 12. Mergers and acquisitions top the priority list of many corporations. Japan has doubled its investment in Europe in the past 2 years (Business International Corporation, 1989). American investments in the EC have risen sharply in recent years (Melcher, 1988; Reimer, 1990), as have European investments in America (Holden, 1989). Strategic alliances are also becoming more commonplace, such as the "intensive cooperation" between Daimler Benz, West Germany's largest company, and Mitzubishi, Japan's top manufacturing and trading conglomerate (Gross, 1990). Buyouts, mergers, acquisitions, franchising, joint ventures, and redirecting investments all are dominating international activity aimed at strengthening European companies. The new companies that emerge in Europe will be bigger, stronger, and more international.

Companies will need to adapt their strategies to the new environment. Friberg (1989) suggested that the four most basic challenges will be to reduce overcapacity, build scale, recognize international competition, and work to homogenize local tastes — a goal especially relevant to advertising. The objective will be to operate as efficiently as possible in a much larger, mass market. European business leaders are becoming more democratic, pragmatic, global, entrepreneurial, creative, and aggressive (Templeton & Sharles, 1989) as they adapt to this new environment.

U.S. companies have traditionally tried to treat Europe as a single market; hence, North Americans may have an advantage in this regard. On the other hand, Americans have been slow to conceptualize the implications of changes in Europe. Perhaps because many U.S. companies are already satisfied with their successes in Europe, or perhaps because the United States is less internationally oriented than other countries, the major changes have not yet influenced behavior as much for U.S. companies as for Japanese and EC companies.

One exception to the lack of U.S. savvy is the recognition that pan-European market niches will be more viable in the future (Business International Corporation, 1989). Pan-European marketing will soon be the norm for most large and middle-sized companies. Strategies will be developed and niches identified with the entire EC in mind. Retailer integration across national boundaries will certainly occur as well.

Different types of companies will necessarily respond differently to the changes because different structural characteristics will imply different outcomes (Buigues & Jacquemin, 1989). Magee (1989), for example, suggested quite different strategies for established multinationals, corporations with one European subsidiary, businesses that export to Europe, and business with no interest in Europe.

No one can predict all of the consequences of the changes taking place, but the changes will reverberate throughout society. Labor worries that manufacturing's new capital investments will seek locations with low wages and benefits. For example, wages and benefits are nearly double in former West Germany what they are in Spain (Comes & Kapstein, 1988). Unrest and frustration could result if this trend does indeed emerge.

To provide one example of an American company in its quest to adapt, consider General Motors (GM). GM Europe was established in Zurich in 1986 to coordinate all of GM's European subsidiaries. GM developed a mid-sized car with suspension rugged enough to handle German Autobahnen and smooth enough to please the French. Options allow the austere Northern Europeans and the flashy Southern Europeans to obtain what they want. Without all details of technical standards, GM has had to take some risks, such as assuming catalytic converters will be required on all EC cars. GM has tried to integrate its advertising, too, with Lowe International planning its United Kingdom and West German launch, and with McCann-Erickson, Zurich adapting its campaign for other European countries (Cote, 1989).

ADVERTISING IN THE EC AFTER 1992

Unification Benefits

Fewer but larger companies will be willing and able to spend larger amounts of advertising money in attempts to create mass markets. This should create a positive environment for advertising. Companies will pursue niches that transcend national boundaries more aggressively. For example, lifestyles transcend borders. German and British yuppies are more alike than yuppies and blue collar workers within either country. "Businessmen all over the EC have similar lifestyles" (Beatson, 1990a p. 16). Advertisers will reach for lifestyle niches more than political niches.

Another potential consequence of EC changes will be an increase in pan-European advertising, and evidence corroborates this as a trend. "Many advertisers are consolidating spending by brand or product category with a single agency and launching products with a pan-European rollout. More than $1 billion in pan-European advertising has been awarded to agencies since 1988" (Wentz, 1989a, p. 42). The direction of EC rulings should increase the ease of cross-frontier advertising (Wentz, 1989b).

Pan-European advertising will benefit from removal of technical specification barriers because one product will be available for all EC countries. Thus, preparation of catalogues and product descriptions will not change (except for translations) from country to country. Likewise, uniform legal requirements will end the need for legal opinions about controversial activities from each country. Recent relaxing of laws on television advertising in Europe has boosted advertising expenditure growth in Europe to double what it is in the United States (Reed, 1989). The Interpublic Group may be the best-positioned American company to cash in on this change because it already earns 35% of its profits in Europe. Murdoch is also well-positioned for internationalization of media markets.

Unification Challenges

Although advertisers hope to develop pan-European ads, the task will not be easy. This goal will partly suffer from the lack of pan-European media outlets. One forecast is that by 1995, only 10% to 20% of media will be pan-European (Business International Corporation, 1989). Reed International plans to expand its international efforts in Europe (Wentz, 1989c). Maxwell Communication circulates a newspaper called *The European*, which is a weekend newspaper designed to inform Europeans about what is going on in Europe. It anticipated an initial circulation of 350,000 in Europe, and it eventually hopes to reach a world-wide audience (*Advertising Age*, Feb. 26, 1990, p. 41).

Media that already have outlets in several EC countries, such as the *Reader's Digest*, promote this virtue to potential advertisers. A recent *Reader's Digest* ad from the *New York Times Magazine* with the headline "Ready for 1992" noted that *Reader's Digest* already has 15 European editions. It claims to be the number one magazine in Europe. The copy provided an important clue to its plans: "As Europe's internal barriers disappear, *Reader's Digest* will continue tailoring each edition to serve readers' native cultural and language differences. Our editors — who live and work in the countries they serve — speak their readers' language, know their customs and are intimately familiar with their interests and concerns."

Not everyone sees a trend toward pan-European advertising, however. Beatson (1990a) believed that cultural characteristics, although blurring, are nevertheless strong enough to require a predominance of local advertising. Language and culture will inhibit truly international ads, as will the current lack of truly international brands and the lack of truly international product usage (Collins, 1989).

Language certainly remains a barrier. Although English – often American English – is widely used, most countries want to preserve their own linguistic heritage. Machine translations will increase in popularity over the years, but the quality of these translations still falls short for many formal purposes (Worlock, 1990). Of the 70 machine translation systems available today, the best translate only roughly. Some specialized tasks can be performed with about 95% accuracy, but we can expect EC electronic companies will focus considerable effort on improving translation machines (Guttman, 1990).

Another solution to the language problem is the visual or nonverbal advertisement (Beatson, 1990b). Graphic visual depiction often expresses a concept without words. Music can also aid in nonverbal communication, even if message recipients share no language.

Cultural tastes vary from country to country. For example, the *Benny Hill Show* has achieved popularity in the United Kingdom, the Netherlands, and Scandinavia, but it has not been particularly appreciated by German, Swiss, or Belgian viewers (Collins, 1989). Unification will not end unique national characteristics.

Product usage often differs from country to country (Mussey & Laurel, 1989). For example, laundry habits and washing machines differ from Northern to Southern Europe. The cost of energy varies widely from one country to another, leading to product and demand differences. Identical ads are pointless if products or services are unavailable, unattractive, or impractical in certain places.

Agencies face the difficult task of eliciting employee cooperation in any attempt at pan-European advertising. European advertising executives often subscribe to the "Not Invented Here Syndrome" (Mussey & Laurel, 1989), which implies that agency officials object to creative strategies and executions imposed on them from elsewhere. International cooperation must occur at the individual employee level as well as the governmental level.

Technology

Technology change will influence advertising. The technologies especially important for pan-European advertising are information technologies. Communication among businesses is easier with computers and fax machines. Television is benefiting from satellite and cable systems, although penetration has not come as rapidly in Europe, perhaps because of local regulations. The United States currently has about double the telephone usage of the EC. In the EC, voice telephony currently accounts for 85% to 90% of transmissions, with up to 10% derived from facsimile and up to 5% from telex (Emerson, Aujean, Catinat, Goybet, & Jacquemin, 1988). It is expected that within 20 years the transmission of data will exceed voice transmission in the EC. The imminent introduction of Integrated Services Digital Networks (ISDNs) will greatly improve EC communications. In fact, the EC has been slow to modernize in anticipation of the 1992 technical synchrony. When specifications are established and implemented, the EC could well race toward the most modern telecommunication system in the world, leapfrogging over the Asians. Europe currently has state-run telecommunication monopolies, similar to but more controlled than the United States prior to the divestiture of AT&T. Increased competitiveness and multiple players seem almost certain to loom over the horizon in the near future.

Television technology will change in Europe, just as it has changed in the United States. Already in the United Kingdom we are witnessing an intense battle over satellite. British Satellite Broadcasting (BSB) is launching a 5-channel system to compete with incompatible technology with Rupert Murdoch's 4-channel Sky Television (Melcher, 1990). Sky costs subscribers $30 per month plus $17 for premium movies. BSB costs consumers $26 per month. Sky spent $45 million advertising itself last year, and it received considerable favorable publicity in other Murdoch-owned media. BSB plans to spend $164 million on advertising in the next 3 years (Kelly, 1990). After its first year, Sky is losing $3 million per week in spite of having 1.1 million subscribers. There is a question regarding whether both Sky and BSB can survive. Cable TV may also become a competitive factor, although for now experts apparently believe that the cost of laying cable, which must all be underground in Britain, will limit cable's growth (Melcher, 1990). The penetration of both cable and satellite varies widely from country to country (Collins, 1989). Many U.S. companies, such as baby-bell U.S. WEST (Symonds, 1989), have aggressively pursued cable opportunities in Europe.

In Ireland TV3 launched a new competitor for Irish entertainment (Craig, 1989). A new radio network will also lure ad revenue from the current competitors there.

Scandinavia has been the last outpost of commercial-free television, but a 2-year-old satellite channel, TV3, has been broadcasting to affluent Scandinavia from London, in order to circumvent Scandinavian laws. In February, it was viewed by 33.4% of TV homes in Sweden, 37.3% of TV homes in Denmark, and 36.2% of TV homes in Norway. It has met with significant success, perhaps breaking even by 1991 (Wentz, 1990). It has had the political effect of relaxing Scandinavian laws on advertising, in order to prevent further defection of advertising revenue. On Sept. 15, 1990, Nordisk TV4 began cablecasting in Sweden. It allows 6 minutes of ads per hour. Norway allowed radio advertising in 1989 for the first time since 1945, and it will likely soon have a commercial television channel. Most Norwegians can receive Swedish broadcasts; hence developments in Sweden influence Norway. In Denmark TV2 will likely increase its advertising from the current limit of 15 minutes per day (Wentz, 1990).

Because Spain and Portugal only recently (1988) joined the EC, advertising there has been growing rapidly. In 1989 Spain's advertising increased by 24% after inflation, and it increased by 12.7% in Portugal, compared to 2.8% in the BRD (Spect, 1989). More open television will change advertising in Spain, too (Goodman & Specht, 1989). One channel started to broadcast in December 1989, and two more are expected soon (Spect & Daley, 1990).

Research

Pan-European marketing research has become easier. A.C. Nielsen Co., for example, has traditionally allowed subsidiaries in each country to set up unique methodologies because international research was too difficult (Cote & Hill, 1989). For example, lemon-flavored Perrier could be classified as a mineral water in France but a soft drink in Italy. Bottle sizes might vary. In one country sales are in francs, in the other lira. Now it is possible to have integrated European databases.

VALUES AND ADVERTISING IN THE GLOBAL ECONOMY

We know that relating products to values is one of the more effective means of advertising. Personal values have consistently shown a clear and noteworthy relation to consumer and other behavior (e.g., Almond & Verba, 1963; Baum, 1968; Beatty, Kahle, Homer, & Misra, 1985; Becker & Conner, 1981; Feather, 1984; Grube, Weir, Getzlaf, & Rokeach, 1984; Henry, 1976; Hensehl, 1971; Homer and Kahle, 1988; Rokeach, 1973; Rosenberg, 1957; Wickert, 1940; Williams, 1959, 1979). In order to discover the extent to which values differ and therefore imply different approaches to advertising, we need to ask how values differ from country to country.

Table 3.3 summarizes data on the List of Values (LOV) as administered in several different countries. The data for the BRD, Norway, and the United States come from national samples of previously published research

TABLE 3.3
Social Values in Several Countries

Value	France	BRD	Denmark	Norway	U.S.	U.S.S.R.	Japan
Self-fulfillment	30.9%	4.8%	7.1%	7.7%	6.5%	8.8%	36.7%
Sense of belonging	1.7	28.6	13.0	33.4	5.1	23.9	2.3
Security	6.3	24.1	6.3	10.0	16.5	5.7	10.9
Self-respect	7.4	12.9	29.7	16.6	23.0	10.1	4.7
Warm relationships with others	17.7	7.9	11.3	13.4	19.9	23.3	27.6
Fun & enjoyment in life/excitement	16.6	10.1	16.8	3.6	7.2	9.7	7.5
Being well respected	4.0	6.1	5.0	8.4	5.9	8.5	2.1
Sense of accomplishment	15.4	5.4	10.9	6.8	15.9	10.1	8.3
TOTAL	100.0%	100.0%	100.0%	100.0%	100.0%	100.0%	100.0%
N	175	1008	239	457	997	321	387

Note. Adapted from Beatty et al., (1990), Grunert and Scherhorn (1990), Kahle, Beatty, and Homer (1989), Kahle, Poulos, and Sukhdial (1988).

(Grunert & Scherhorn, 1990; Kahle, Beatty, & Homer 1989; Kahle, Poulos, & Sukhdial, 1988). The other data (Beatty, Yoon, Grunert & Kahle, 1991) come from convenience samples of students and their parents, except the U.S.S.R. data, which are from a convenience sample of adult education students. All of the difficulties of international survey data characterize these results, including linguistic issues such as translation and connotative meanings, methodological issues such as the differences in divergent types of surveys, and sampling issues such as how one obtains adequate and comparable samples in different countries. It is even possible that the values from which one chooses are indeed different in, for example, Denmark and Japan; hence, one should offer different lists from which to choose values in different countries. In short, these data are more suggestive than definitive, more heuristic than conclusive.

Nevertheless, the data do have a certain face validity and are instructive inasmuch as they have any external validity. Contrary to what one might expect, the respect values are weak in Japan, but self-fulfillment is quite strong. Self-fulfillment is a value humanists have introduced to the West from the East; hence, its prevalence in Japan is not too surprising. Germans turn out not to be puritanical workaholics (cf. Grunert & Scherhorn, 1990; Meuhlermann, 1987), inasmuch as they emphasize fun and enjoyment in life more and accomplishment less than other countries. The supposedly stoic Danes also value fun more than the norm. The French, as well as the Americans, place far more emphasis on fulfillment and accomplishment than the Germans. The image of the obsessed Nazi probably tells less about contemporary Germany than the image of the Bavarian beer hall patron. Grunert and Scherhorn attributed German concern about security to

Germany's location on the eastern edge of Western Europe. The next survey of German values will present a fascinating test of that hypothesis because, presumably, concern about Eastern Europe as a threat to security has diminished greatly in the recent past. The U.S.S.R. and Japan have been characterized as ruthless in U.S. media, but the data show warm relationships with others to have great appeal in these two countries.

One need look no further than the first two columns to see the difficulties facing the EC. EC partners France and Germany have at least a 5% difference in all values except the relatively unimportant being well respected. Sense of belonging and security are the most important values in Germany, together comprising the values of over half the population. These two values are endorsed by only 9% of the French sample. Nearly half of the French endorse either self-fulfillment or warm relationships with others as most important, a far cry from the 12.7% of Germans who endorse this value.

These differences among countries, even limiting the scope to EC countries, are much greater than we have observed within the U.S. regions (Kahle 1986; Kahle, Liu, & Watkins, 1992). They suggested a tremendous amount of diversity and a great need to tolerate diversity. The tolerance will be necessary for the community to hold together. Germans and French, for example, will need to respect their diversity as much as, say, the other British people tolerate the Welsh or the other Spanish people tolerate the Catalans. Much of the splintering in Eastern Europe is resulting from groups who do not want to participate in a community whose activities in the past have shown little respect for their unique contributions.

These value differences also suggest that merely removing regulations will not immediately increase the ease of communications among all Europeans. Value-based advertisements will still be splintered throughout Europe, even if legal complexities do not require diversity. Sales presentations still need to consider unique local values. For example, appeals to sense of belonging will still primarily be targeted at Germany and Norway rather than France and Denmark.

OTHER SOURCES OF CHANGE

Consider some of the things about Europe that have not changed: language, preferences, habits, culture, climate, incomes, and many other variables that influence consumer desire for certain products. The difficulties in achieving the 1992 goals run deep in the fabric of Europe. "The social, cultural, and even linguistic repercussions may pose more of a threat than real economic issues" (Laurent, 1988, p. 357). The changes are all on the supply side, yet market acceptance will, in the end, rule.

In spite of the stated goals and the very real progress toward political unification, Europe still seems quite a distance from true coordination, in the United States sense. Most people in the United States probably have a greater loyalty to the United States than to their own particular state (e.g., California or New York), but we are probably several generations away from a Europe in which, for example, French consider themselves to be more European than French.

Europe is facing many demographic trends similar to the trends in North America. For example, the average age is increasing (Templeman, 1989). Women are participating in the work force to a greater extent. European trends in marriage mirror North American trends. These changes are independent of economic regulation.

Changes to the East require monitoring. Eastern Europeans may provide new markets with pent-up demand, and they will provide low-cost labor. Many countries in Eastern Europe expect to move rapidly from a planned economy to a market economy. The next decade in Eastern Europe may resemble the decade after World War II in NATO countries. The infrastructure will have to be rebuilt, from telephones to pollution control devices. And consumers will want many of the products they have been denied. Yet pentup demand associated with decades of political suppression could undermine Eastern Europe's economic progress. Ironically, Western European countries that have allowed independence are seeking unity while Eastern European countries that have experienced forced unity have sought fragmentation.

With German reunification now a reality, many wonder whether Germany will be too dominant in the EC. France and the United Kingdom have roughly the same population as the BRD, but the BRD already had more economic power than the other two major EC powers. With the DDR attached, the German economy is roughly double the size of France's (Templeman, Peterson, & Sharles, 1989). Redefining business, political, and military relations will provide a fascinating series of stories from Eastern and Western Europe over the next decade. The German value for sense of belonging seems especially pertinent here. If Germans see themselves as belonging to the EC, they may emphasize continental cooperation.

Consider, for example, the German beer industry, one of our favorites (International Business Corp., 1989). In 1516 Germany began observing the *Reinheitsgebot*, requiring that beer be manufactured only of pure ingredients. In 1987 the EC overturned that law, allowing all manner of beverages to be called beer and to be sold in Germany. As the world's leading beer-drinking nation on a per capita basis, Germany would seem a prime candidate for foreign brewer penetration. Germans, however, prefer pure, German beer. In spite of the now-open market, German habits have not substantially changed. German beer brands, of which there are nearly 4000, command nearly genetic brand loyalty in the domestic market, are perceived as having high quality, control channels of distribution tightly, and quite frankly are unlikely to suffer from competition with foreign brands that are considered inferior by consumers. In fact no foreign brewer has obtained significant market share in Germany since the EC removed the "barriers." The point is that ultimately consumer lifestyles and tastes will direct economic outcomes more than policy. Policy only allows options, it does not insure what choices are made.

REFERENCES

Almond, G. A., & S. Verba (1963). *The civic culture.* Princeton, NJ: Princeton University Press.

Baum, R. C. (1968). Values and democracy in empirical Germany. *Sociological Inquiry, 38,* 176-196.

Beatson, R. (1990a, April 2). The Americanization of Europe? *Advertising Age,* p. 16.

Beatson, R. (1990b, April 9). Reaching united Europe won't be a simple task. *Advertising Age,* p. 31.

Beatty, S. E., Yoon, M. H., Grunert, K. G., & Kahle, L. R. (1991). Alternative measurement approaches to values: Ratings versus rankings in a cross-cultural context (Working paper). University of Alabama, Tuscaloosa.

Beatty, S. E., Kahle, L. R., Homer, P., & Misra, S. (1985). Alternative measurement approaches to consumer values: The List of Values and the Rokeach Value Survey. *Psychology & Marketing, 3,* 181-200.

Becker, B. W., & Connor, P. E. (1981). Personal values of the heavy user of mass media. *Journal of Advertising Research, 21,* 37-43.

Buigues, P., & Jacquemin, A. (1989). Strategies of firms and structural environments in the large Internal Market. *Journal of Common Market Studies, 28,* 53-67.

Business International Corporation (1989). *Gaining a competitive edge in the new Europe: strategic responses of non-European companies to 1992.* New York: Author.

Calingaert, M. (1988), *The 1992 challenge from Europe: Development of the European Community's Internal Market.* Washington, DC: National Planning Association.

Collins, R. (1989). The language of advantage: Satellite television in Western Europe. *Media, Culture and Society, 11,* 351-371.

Comes, F. J., & Kapstein, J. (1988, December 12). Reshaping Europe: 1992 and beyond. *Business Week,* pp. 48-51.

Cote, K. (1989, June 5). Uncertain future plagues marketers planning for 1992. *Advertising Age,* p. 42.

Cote, K., & Hill, J. S. (1989, June 5). As world shrinks, Nielsen expands. *Advertising Age,* p. 52.

Craig, C. (1989, October 2). Private Irish TV faces hard start. *Advertising Age,* p. 38.

Emerson, M., Aujean, M., Catinat, M., Goybet, P., & Jacquemin, A. (1988). *The economics of 1992: The E. C. Commission's assessment of the economic effects of completing the internal market.* Oxford: Oxford University Press.

Feather, N. T. (1984). Protestant ethic, conservatism, and values. *Journal of Personality and Social Psychology, 46,* 1132-1141.

Friberg, E. G. (1989). 1992: Moves Europeans are making. *Harvard Business Review, 67,* 85-95.

Goodman, A., & Spect, M. (1989, August 21). Spain airs TV license drama. *Advertising Age*, p. 45.

Gross, N. (1990, March 19). A waltz of giants sends shock waves worldwide. *Business Week*, p. 59-60.

Grube, J. W., Weir, I. L., Getzlaf, S., & Rokeach, M. (1984). Own value system, value images, and cigarette smoking. *Personality and Social Psychology Bulletin, 10*, 306-313.

Grunert, S. C., & Scherhorn, G. (1990). Consumer values in West Germany: Underlying dimensions and cross-cultural comparison with North America. *Journal of Business Research, 20*, 97-107.

Guttman, C. (1990, March 23). Europe's last word in machine translation. *International Herald Tribune*, p. 20.

Henry, W. A. (1976). Cultural values do correlate with consumer behavior. *Journal of Marketing Research, 13*, 121-127.

Holden, T. (1989, October 16). France's beachhead in America. *Business Week*, p. 48-49.

Homer, P. M., & Kahle, L. R. (1988). A structural equation test of the value–attitude–behavior hierarchy. *Journal of Personality and Social Psychology, 54*, 638-646.

James, B. (1990, January 26). Who will gain if EC takes over airways? *International Herald Tribune*, pp. 13, 17.

Kahle, L. R. (1986). The Nine Nations of North America and the value basis of geographic segmentation. *Journal of Marketing, 50*, 37-47.

Kahle, L. R., Beatty, S. E., & Homer, P. M. (1989). Consumer values in Norway and the United States: A comparison. *Journal of International Consumer Marketing, 1*, 81-91.

Kahle, L. R., Poulos, B., & Sukhdial, A. (1988). Changes in social values in the United States during the past decade. *Journal of Advertising Research, 28*, 35-41.

Kahle, L. R., Liu, R., & Watkins, H. (1992). Psychographic variation across United States geographic regions. In J. F. Sherry & B. Sternthal (Eds.), *Advances in Consumer Research* (Vol. 19, pp. 346-352). Ann Arbor, MI: Association for Consumer Research.

Kapstein, J. (1989, June 19). "Subsidy" becomes a dirty word. *Business Week*, p. 48.

Kelly, S. (1990, February 26). Dogfight to the death? *Advertising Age*, p. 39.

Laurent, P. (1988, November). The European Community: Twelve become one. *Current*, pp. 357-360.

Magee, J. F. (1989). 1992: Moves Americans must make. *Harvard Business Review, 67*, 78-84.

Melcher, R. A. (1990, February 5). The Battle of Britain is taking its toll on the media barons. *Business Week*, pp. 38-39.

Meuhlermann, H. (1987). Bildung, Generationen und die Konjuncturen des Werts Leistung [Organization, generations, and the trends of the valued achievement]. *Kolner Zeitschrift fur Soziologie und Sozialpsychologie, 16*, 272-287.

Mussey, D., & Laurel, W. (1989, July 31). Saatchi stresses Pan-European plans. *Advertising Age*, pp. 2, 34.

Palmer, J. (1988). *Europe without America?* Oxford: Oxford University Press.

Quraeshi, Z. A., & Lyqmani, M. (1990). *Europe 1992: Issues and prospects*. Paper presented at the Annual Meeting of the Academy of Marketing Science, New Orleans.

Reed, S. (1989, October 16). Seeking growth in a smaller world. *Business Week*, pp. 94-95.

Reimer, B. (1989, March 27). Europe may slap a quota on *General Hospital*. *Business Week*, pp. 46-47.

Rokeach, M. (1973). *The nature of human values*. New York: Free Press.

Rosenbaum, A. (1990, March 19). Tobacco ad ban for EC members clears first hurdle. *Advertising Age*, pp. 3, 68.

Rosenberg, M., (1957). *Occupation and values*. Glencoe, IL: Free Press.

Spect, M. (1989, June 5). Southern Europe heats up for '92. *Advertising Age*, p. 47.

Spect, M., & Daly, A. (1990, January 15). Spain gets into channeling. *Advertising Age*, p. 47.

Symonds, W. C. (1989, August 14). American cable is lassoing foreign markets. *Business*

Week, pp. 70-71.

Templeman, J. (1989, March 13). Grappling with the graying of Europe. *Business Week*, pp. 54-56.

Templeman, J., Peterson, T., & Sharles, G. E. (1989, November 27). The shape of Europe to come. *Business Week*, pp. 60-66.

Templeman, J., & Sharles, G. E. (1989, December 18). Taking over the helm of Germany, Inc. *Business Week*, pp. 66-67.

Toy, S. (1989, June 26). The race to stock Europe's common supermarket. *Business Week*, pp. 80-82.

Toy, S. (1990, January 29). Will the EC let Air France spread its wings? *Business Week*, pp. 48-49.

Verity, J. W. (1990, May 7). Defense against pirates or death to the clones? *Business Week*, pp. 138-140.

Wentz, L. (1989a, June 5). Agencies brace for new Europe. *Advertising Age*, p. 42.

Wentz, L. (1989b, October 15). EC pleases TV advertisers. *Advertising Age*, p. 56.

Wentz, L. (1989c, August 14). Reed takes on Europe. *Advertising Age*, p. 28.

Wentz, L. (1990, April 16). Commercial TV set to grow. *Advertising Age*, p. 39.

Whitney, C. R. (1990, April 29). Evolution in Europe: From community to federation, Europe alliance seeks closer ties. *New York Times*, p. 8.

Wickert, F. (1940). A test for personal goals-values. *Journal of Social Psychology*, *11*, 259-274.

Williams, R. M., Jr. (1959). Friendship and social values in a suburban community. *Pacific Sociological Review*, *1*, 3-10.

Williams, R. M., Jr. (1979). Change and stability in values and value systems: A sociological perspective. In M. Rokeach (Ed.), *Understanding human values: Individual and societal* (pp. 15-46). New York: Free Press.

The World Almanac and Book of Facts. (1990).

Worlock, D. R. (1990). The information industry's two 1992 tasks. *European Affairs*, *4*, 93-99.

Yemma, J. (1988, June 27). Europe 1992. *Christian Science Monitor*, pp. 1-2.

II SUBCULTURAL ISSUES

4

Advertising to the "Other" Culture: Women's Use of Language and Language's Use of Women

Barbara B. Stern
Rutgers, The State University of New Jersey

> Culture is male. . . . What it does mean (among other things) is that the society we live in like all other historical societies is a patriarchy. And patriarchies imagine or picture themselves from the male point of view. There is a female culture, but it is an underground, unofficial, minor culture, occupying a small corner of what we think of officially as possible human experience. Both men and women in our culture conceive the culture from a single point of view—the male (Russ 1972, p. 4).

Men and women occupy separate cultural spheres as well as separate biological ones. Cultural differences between the sexes occur in all known societies (Gilly, 1988) and are made manifest in language, the shaper of human reality. Shulamith Firestone (1971) in *The Dialectic of Sex* argued that "the sex role system divides human experience; men and women live in these different halves of reality; and culture reflects this" (p. 165). Marketing and advertising researchers have studied several cultural domains in reference to women: stereotypes of women in advertising (see Courtney & Whipple, 1983; Gilly, 1988), feminine themes and values (Marchand, 1985; McLuhan, 1951), and pictorial depictions of gender roles (Goffman, 1979). The focus is ordinarily on visual images and depictions of typical characters, settings, and occupational roles. Most advertising studies rely on content analysis and count denotative elements in the visual imagery to assess depictions of women (see Ferguson, Kreshel, & Tinkhan, 1990, for review). Although some research efforts have incorporated more connotative message elements, these are characteristically conducted outside of the advertising discipline (Williamson, 1978). Even advertising studies of "latent" content, requiring not simply observation of what is "manifest" in the visuals but also interpretation of what the images mean, do not ordinarily focus on language (Ferguson et al., 1990). Although feminist critics since Robin Lakoff (1975) have identified a dichotomy between male and female language, the impact of genderization on the language used in advertising messages has not yet been widely studied. Yet research on advertising verbals is necessary, for language is the vehicle through which culture is transmitted. This chapter thus adopts the perspective of feminist language-based criticism — the discipline that focuses on women's experience as a proper subject for study in its own right (Register, 1975). It draws specifically on feminist literary criticism to examine advertising's words in order to clarify how women use language and how language uses women (Lakoff, 1975). The purpose is to adapt another methodology from a different discipline to enrich our understanding of the nature of role portrayals. Literary criticism can contribute to advertising research by rendering women's language visible. In so doing, it may assist advertisers to design persuasive appeals with greater verisimilitude to position or reposition products more effectively to men's and women's markets.

This chapter begins by discussing some cultural differences between men and women that give rise to three qualities characteristic of women's language: propriety, hesitancy, and verbal excess. It next describes the influence of sex-specific language on advertising dialogue and male/female role portrayals. Last, it discusses two contributions that awareness of women's language can make to better advertising. First is the creation of realistic scenarios for dramatic advertisements, those in which characters speak (Wells, 1989). Second is the development of copy language for product positioning where male and female characters speak and/or are spoken about. The chapter views advertising as one kind of creative text (see Stern, 1989) and relies primarily on feminist literary criticism as the interpretive filter. It is limited to the verbal parts of advertising, and thus excludes elements such as pictures, scenery, or music. Additionally, it does not deal with other cultural factors such as age, race, or social class likely to interact with sex.

LANGUAGE AND WOMEN'S CULTURE

Examination of women's language as a special and separate entity begins with an overview of the pervasiveness of male norms in a patriarchal society (see de Beauvoir, 1953). The gender asymmetry that characterizes male-dominant society (Ortner, 1974; Staton, 1987) went unquestioned for millenia. It was not until the 1960s that feminist critics brought to light the hidden assumptions of male-centered culture in which *female* is defined by negative reference to *male* as the human norm (Abrams, 1988). For most of human history—read by feminists as "his story"—women internalized civilization's reigning patriarchal biases and accepted the cultural constructs defining masculinity and femininity (Abrams, 1988). Although debate continues as to whether men and women are different, and if so, why (Deaux & Major, 1987), consensual beliefs about the stereotypical personality traits that characterize and differentiate the average man and woman have remained consistent for nearly 20 years (see Broverman, Vogel, Broverman, Clarkson, & Rosenkrantz, 1972; Deaux & Major, 1987).

Stereotypical maleness and femaleness are built into the patriarchal culture and expressed in the language of both art and life. Language is now widely viewed as basic to the constitution of social life, a dynamic social phenomenon (see Maynard, 1986), rather than a stable neutral medium of communication. Feminist theorists pointed out that language categorizes and structures one's concept of oneself, others, and society, and they amassed evidence indicating the male bias encoded in our linguistic conventions (Berman, 1988). For example, the nouns "man" or "mankind" are used to define all human beings, and the pronouns "he" and "his" often refer to ostensibly gender-neutral nouns such as God, inventor, author, poet—and the advertiser as well (see McConnell-Ginet, Borker, & Furman, 1980). Lacan stated that women's relationship to language must be seen in terms of the traditional cultural construction of language "around the male term [the "phallic" term] . . . or the privileging of that term" (Mitchell & Rose, 1982, p. 54). The gender identification created and maintained in language was based on the male as a normative model of the self, and the female as a deviant "Other," first identified in Simone de Beauvoir's (1953) landmark book, *The Second Sex*. Since that time, feminist critics have brought to light the almost unthinking acceptance of male norms and female opposites hidden beneath the surface.

By the 1960s, feminist researchers had begun to uncover the extent to which male-dominance is so rooted in our terminology that it is accepted as "normal" language (Abrams, 1988). Feminism—also called "women's studies"—has taken as its domain the study of women's "place" in many disciplines (see, e.g., Ellmann, 1968; Millett, 1970; Showalter, 1985). Its foundation is acceptance of women's role as cultural "other" (de Beauvoir, 1953): the largely invisible subculture unexamined for centuries. Feminism was the first organized school of criticism to recognize the presence of women (albeit their official invisibility), the kinship among them, and the differences between this *sub rosa* group and that of the male mainstream (see Register, 1975). Feminist criticism always examines cultural factors, for to understand a woman's point of view (as a character in a novel or in an advertisement), a critic must take into account the social, legal, and economic status of women in society.

In order to do justice to the female point of view, feminist criticism in America began by investigating the concept of an appropriate cultural "place" for each sex (Welter, 1966). Linguists and literary critics set out to expose the hitherto unquestioned assumptions embedded in language as a result of "place" (Lakoff, 1975). American society, like most others, has traditionally assigned a different place—an appropriate sphere of activity—to men and to women. Women historically assumed the role of homemaker and men that of provider (Bullough, 1974). In at least one consumer behavior text, sex-linked traits are treated as subcultural differences (Schiffman & Kanuk, 1991), and the argument is made that since sex roles are culturally determined, gender as a subcultural category is appropriate. Interestingly, this consumer-oriented definition of subculture as a "distinct cultural group which exists as an identifiable segment within a larger, more complex society" (Schiffman & Kanuk, 1991, p. 430) parallels the feminist view of women's culture. In this view, women exist as an identifiable segment within the larger more complex male society that dominates American life.

In post-Industrial Revolution America, the distinction in place became more rigid. By the mid-19th century, the new manufacturing economy and its attendant prosperity led to a more sharply schismatic differentiation between male and female roles than had existed in the past. When men and women both worked at home—a common pattern in society based on an agrarian economy (Beard, 1946)—their experiences were centered in the same sphere, although role differences existed. Once men left the home, however, and went into the work place, their paths diverged: man's place became the factory, later generalized into the "workplace," and woman's became the home. Victorian society solidified the separation, and idealized the woman enshrined within her home as a "lady": pure, dedicated to her husband and children, and untouched by the rough and tumble of the external world. This pedestalization was commonplace in American thought in the 19th century, evident in literature and language as well as in social life. The nature of women's language was, for the most part, circumscribed by the limitations associated with her place in society.

THREE CHARACTERISTICS OF WOMAN'S LANGUAGE

Feminist critics beginning with Lakoff (1975) have set out to specify the impact of place on "woman's language," that distinctively feminine style of speaking and writing. They have focused on sentence structure, diction (word choice), organizational flow, and characteristic images (see Showalter, 1977) to ascertain how women select and combine words in everyday life. This usage is related to the covert messages that culture sends about women's place. Women's speech reflects cultural imperatives calling for niceness, politeness, ladylike expression, and concern for the feelings of others. Women's style is described by Firestone (1971) as "personal, subjective, emotional, descriptive" in contrast to men's "vigorous, spare, hard-hitting, objective" expression (p. 165). Women externalize society's message to be "nice" in their speech, just as men externalize society's permission to be "rough": male talk can be powerful, hard, and intellectual as a result of man's place from childhood on — the ball field, the army, the factory. But women are expected to speak more softly. Three characteristics that mark women's language as special are its propriety, hesitancy, and verbal excess (Lakoff, 1975).

Propriety

Propriety in word choice (diction) and grammar reinforces the dual sexual standard. First and foremost, women are expected to talk "like ladies." This entails avoiding obscene words, curses, and angry expletives. Sexual or scatological terms are taboo for women (see Johnson & Fine, 1985), whereas men who curse are considered "one of the guys." One reason why obscenity is off-limits for women is that words like "fuck" are expressions of anger historically associated with male hostility. When a woman uses an expletive like this or any other, she expresses a degree of rage that threatens the social order, for women are expected to soothe angry words, not hurl them. Powerful Anglo-Saxon curse words are deemed unlady-like, and when women do use curses in literature, they are labeled as either rebels (intellectual bluestockings, defiant temptresses) or outcasts (whores, addicts, illiterates).

In addition to sanitized diction, women are also expected to use hypercorrect grammar and any polite forms of address that the language possesses. The expectation of perfect correctness harks back to women's role as the keeper of the cultural flame: whereas men went off to work and war to protect society, women stayed home to preserve its cherished values for transmission to future generations. Women have traditionally been regarded as guardians of the language, primarily as mothers teaching their children informally, but also in more formal occupational roles as elementary school teachers and librarians. Women were thus conventionally cast as conservators of language deemed proper in reference to dictional choice and grammatical structure.

Hesitancy

Women's language also avoids the taint of impropriety by displaying hesitancy or tentativeness (Lakoff, 1975). This hesitancy is expressed in two ways: a tendency to make assertions using tag-question form, and a reliance on "hedge" or filler words. Women are likely to state things tentatively either by appending a question to a declarative sentence or by turning a statement into a question. For example, a simple declarative sentence reads: "It's a nice day." This is made tentative by a tacked-on question: "It's a nice day, isn't it?" or by the interrogative, "Isn't it a nice day?" Women are thought to avoid commitment to a point of view that declarative statements imply in order to avoid potential conflict with those who might disagree. Conflict, like anger, is unladylike, and women who declare themselves in no uncertain terms are considered at best, unfeminine, and at worst, aggressive "pushy bitches."

A second way to express uncertainty is to circumlocute, and women tend to use filler and hedge words that undercut ideas so that they may be stated, but not sufficiently strongly to provoke disagreement. Empty adjectives, long stripped of substantive meaning, such as "divine, charming, cute" (Lakoff, 1975) are all-purpose descriptors attached to nearly any noun. Additionally, meaningless filler expressions such as "well," "you know," "sort of," or "like" punctuate women's sentences. The avoidance of assertive language is entertainingly demonstrated in a short parody by Veronica Geng (1979, italics added), reporting a conversation overheard in a restaurant:

Valerie: "Their sole amandine sounds *nice.*"

Man: "I would quarrel with that, Valerie, I'm afraid. Though you are free to disagree. I'd like nothing more than to hear you disagree. Show some spine, Valerie, for a change."

Valerie: "*Well, to be honest—maybe* I'm *way out of line* on this one, but I'm *pretty* positive that I *probably* don't want the sole, I *almost* think."

Man: "Among aware, intelligent people there will always be some difference of opinion. You should have the sole Valerie, even if it is wrong choice. Nobody's keeping score."

Valerie: "*Well,* your willingness to discuss this has *meant a lot.* I *really* appreciate it. I *guess* I'll *just* have the gravy."

Verbal Excess

Related to women's use of tentative expressions and filler words is the last characteristic: a tendency to verbal excess. One kind of excess is sheer verbosity: constructions that use more words than necessary to express a thought. This, of course, inevitably accompanies reliance on filler phrases, and is a means of softening direct assertions by circumlocution, or beating around the bush. Another kind of excess is hyperbole or overstatement. Language is hyperbolic when frequent underlining or italicizing of words and expressions occurs, when unremarkable comments end with exclamation points, and when emphatic words are sprinkled throughout. Although advertising in general is often condemned for puffery, it is important to note that some forms of overstatement are more characteristic of women's usage patterns than of men's. For example, women's language often attaches words describing excessive emotions to mundane things. McLuhan (1951) was one of the first to point out that technology provided the "ever intenser thrills" (p. 101) that characterized advertising depictions of the "mechanical bride's" sexuality. This particular kind of excess is still with us, for a 1989 advertisement for Alberto Culver's Bold Hold hair spray says: "Go ahead . . . give your hair a *thrill!*" Here, a hype-word, italics, and an exclamation point are used all at once. Despite the changes that have occurred in the last generation, then, women's language is still deeply etched with ingrained cultural patterns that lend legitimacy to hesitancy and hyperbole.

ADVERTISING AND WOMEN'S LANGUAGE

How Women Use Language in Dramatic Scenarios

An understanding of women's language is necessary for the creation of realistic scenarios in dramatic advertisements — those in which the characters speak to an audience or to each other (see Wells, 1989). These mini-dramas often use everyday speech, and verisimilitude is enhanced when the characters sound "right." One example of a slice-of-life print drama using realistic dialogue is Talbot's announcement (Exhibit A) of the 1989 opening of its main New York store (labels "WOM 1" and "WOM 2" are mine).

Exhibit A: Talbot's Advertisement.

[WOM 1]	"Look at that brick building . . . I've never noticed it before. What do you think it's going to be?"
[WOM 2]	"I think . . ."
[WOM 1]	"It's so classic . . . like this blazer of mine. I've had it for so long. It's starting to wear out. Where do you think I can find a new one?"

Tag-line: A new tradition in classic women's clothing is coming soon to 525 Madison Avenue.

The ad reveals several characteristics of women's language in spoken dialogue. WOM 1 asks naive and self-doubting questions (what is that building? where can I get a new blazer?) and twice repeats the intensive "so," another typical hedge word (Lakoff, 1975). Neither WOM 1 nor WOM 2 completes a thought, for the elliptical periods (". . .") indicate a trailing off of ideas expressed by a long pause. WOM 1 is garrulous—she allows WOM 2 only two words before resuming speech—and her train of thought appears disconnected. She moves from contemplation of a new building to a metaphorical comparison of the building to her blazer, based on the common dimension of "classic." The characters' questions and incomplete thoughts demonstrate the mildly tentative and inoffensive women's language that lends verisimilitude to advertising as well as to literary dialogue. This newspaper ad relies on words alone (there are no visuals) to delineate the characters by letting them speak in a language recognizable by other women, the sex-linked target market for a new women's clothing store.

It is essential for advertisers who seek to create convincing dramatic scenarios to put suitable language into a character's mouth. Verisimilitude requires sensitivity to differences between appropriate language for men and women. An example of typically male language is found in a Perry Ellis ad for men's cologne, the first instance of a speaker using "fuck" in a nationwide print ad (although the word was not spelled out in full) (Stern, Gould, & Barak, 1987). When women do use obscenity, their curses are milder and less sexually explicit. For example, A Paco Rabanne cologne for men ad features an unseen woman talking on the telephone to a scantily dressed man. She describes her fantasy of him "wearing that Paco Rabanne cologne—and damned little else." *Damned* is not a very strong expletive, and is categorized as a profanity rather than a reference to scatological or sexual activity (Johnson & Fine, 1985). The word suggests that the woman is a sexually frank "liberated" partner, whereas something stronger might imply that she is a whore. Advertisers who are sensitive to women's language can strike a note of authenticity in dramas, even those where visual images are not present.

How Women are "Read": Language and Cultural Roles

Women both use and are used by language, for cultural roles, values, and constraints can be read in language that describes and defines women whether or not they speak directly (Lakoff, 1975). Feminist critics point out differences between the way male and female characters are read, for most readers (men and women) interpret the male experience as dominant and the female experience as peripheral or subordinate (Schumacher, 1975). It is important to understand that these norms are almost automatically called into play when people come into contact with male and female characters in a text. Literature—like advertising—is a textual mirror that reveals the realities of the men's and women's lives (see Bishop, 1979; Donovan, 1975). Some advertising critics feel that it is a "distorted" mirror (Pollay, 1986), and feminist theoreticians often adopt a prescriptive agenda for ameliorating what they judge to be predominantly negative stereotypes of women (Register, 1975).

A contribution of feminist literary criticism to decoding how language uses women has been the revelation of the existence of sex-linked readings by pointing out the underlying "masculinist" assumptions. The methodological process at the heart of feminist theory is the simple act of reversing the sex roles of characters to highlight underlying norms (Schumacher, 1975). Feminists suggest that one way to test the assumptions that we take to be the "natural" order of things is imaginatively to reverse the positions of commonly paired binary opposites such as man and woman (Fetterley, 1977). This enables us to see that what we take for natural is socially conditioned. These societal norms are invoked when people "read" about male and female characters. Goffman (1979) summed up the method as follows: "by imagining the sexes switched and imagining the appearance of what results, one can jar oneself into awareness of stereotypes" (p. 2).

Stereotyping pervades literary images of women. Women characters are described in positive terms when they behave appropriately *as women*— when they embody socially approved feminine traits such as kindness, tactfulness, patience, and selflessness (see Richmond-Abbott, 1979). If women embody masculine traits such as aggressiveness, independence, or leadership, they may be judged negatively and stereotyped as "bitch," "ball-buster," and so forth. Feminist critics point out that masculine traits are ordinarily culturally rewarded to a greater extent than feminine traits, but only when men display them (Fox & Hesse-Biber, 1984). Cultural changes in sex roles in the past 20 years have been associated with the change in woman's place from home to work site. Nevertheless, despite the 1970s call for androgyny (see Heilbrun, 1973) and rereadings of cultural texts based on a man's or a woman's conformance to generally valued human traits (autonomy, unselfishness, humaneness), a traditional trait-dichotomy still differentiates the sexes (Gilly, 1988). Even *Ms.* magazine, despite an explicit commitment to nonstereotypic portrayals of women, presents substantial levels of "sexism" in the course of its 18 year history (see Ferguson et al., 1990). With few exceptions, the androgynous or nonsexist ideal did not become popular reality, and men and women characters are still likely to be read differently.

Reading Women in Advertising

Culturally held beliefs about the sexes can also be read in ads, for as McLuhan pointed out (1951): "ad agencies express for the collective society that which dreams and uncensored behavior do in individuals. They give spatial form to hidden impulses, and when analyzed, make possible bringing into reasonable order a great deal that could not otherwise be observed or discussed" (p. 97). Because advertisements present advertisers' views of how men and women can be profitably pictured (Goffman, 1979), they are likely to show the culturally approved version of maleness/femaleness.

Advertisers often devise male/female characters as spokespersons when it is necessary to position or reposition a product on the basis of sex. Marketers now feel that a wide range of products can be targeted to both sexes. Although the Advertising to Women ad agency, for example, positioned itself in the 1970s as an agency for "women's products," its philosophy shifted in the 1980s: "We feel that you can take almost every product that's traditionally marketed to men and now market it to women" (Kent & Fitch, 1985, p. 17). Products that were formerly marketed to men (e.g., Jockey and Calvin Klein underwear) have been repositioned for women, just as products once marketed to women only (Clinique skin treatments, Sebastian hair gel and mousse) have been repositioned for men. The question that arises is, should there be one ad with one spokesperson to appeal to both sexes, or separate ads, one with a male spokesperson and one with a female spokesperson? Strategic decisions as to the superiority of single versus dual approaches can be made more knowledgably if more can be learned about how audiences read the men and women who speak for products and services.

The feminist method of reading by role reversal is well-suited to an advertising example of perfectly matched Merrill Lynch (ML) print ads from the same issue of the same periodical — *The New Yorker*. The ads take up the same amount of space (one page), feature the same product/service, and use the same title ("Financial Consultant") for the spokesperson. The only difference is that one has a male spokesperson and the other a female. The ad thus permits an unusually clear reading of masculinity and femininity, because the reversal has — in effect — been performed by the advertiser. The texts are set forth side-by-side here for ease of comparison (see Exhibit B):

Exhibit B: Merrill Lynch Advertisements.

Male Spokesperson	Female Spokesperson
Picture of Jere Goldsmith (man)	Picture of Saly Glassman (woman)
"I have to earn my reputation every day."	"My clients work hard for their money. So I work hard to invest it right."
"I'm not one to rest on my laurels. My goal is to give you better service than you could get from anyone else."	"I feel my clients deserve nothing less from me than total commitment."
"I start by looking at your long range goals and how much risk makes you comfortable. Together we'll find the best way to meet your basic financial needs, like asset management, credit management, insurance, and tax minimization."	"That's why we sit down together first and talk about your long range goals and what level of risk is right for you. Then we'll see how best to handle your basic financial needs, including asset management, credit management, insurance, and tax minimization."
Jere has the resources to put his own reputation, plus that of Merrill Lynch, behind every recommendation he makes.	With all of Merrill Lynch behind her, Saly has the resources to help you make the right investment decisions.
Want a professional Financial Consultant like Jere Goldsmith, and the strength of Merrill Lynch on your side?	Put a professional Financial Consultant like Saly Glassman, plus the strength of Merrill Lynch to work for you.

Each ad presents a spokesperson, using the individual's own words (in quotation marks), followed by a narrator's comment (last two paragraphs). The ads reveal several underlying assumptions about culturally conditioned male and female norms that result in different readings of Saly versus Jere. To begin, Saly's headline is nearly twice as long (15 words) as Jere's (8 words). She is more talkative and focuses on her clients, whereas he is more laconic and talks about himself. In the headline, Saly emphasizes hard work for her clients, whereas Jere stresses his reputation among peers. Saly's first copy sentence reiterates her nurturance (she uses the words *feel* and *commitment*), whereas Jere's echoes his competitiveness (he will not *rest on his laurels*, a reference to the winners of Olympic games, and his *goal* is *better service*). Next, Saly says that *we* will sit down and talk, whereas Jere says that *I* will start by looking at your goals, and then "we'll" find the best way to manage your finances. The narrator says that Saly needs *all of Merrill Lynch behind her*, but Jere *has the resources to put his own reputation* (*plus that of ML* as an afterthought) behind his recommendations. The narrator then commands the reader to *put* Saly *to work for you*, but asks the reader to put Jere *on your side*.

The ads can be read as illustrations of prevailing mid-1980s norms for masculinity and femininity. Traits related to instrumentality, dominance, and assertiveness are believed to be more characteristic of men, and those related to expressiveness, warmth, and concern for other people are believed to be more characteristic of women (Deaux & Major, 1987). Jere's language reveals aggressiveness, competitiveness, and self-confidence, whereas Saly's reveals nurturance, cooperativeness, and reliance on the strength of ML masculine rivalry, which has long been identified as a popular advertising theme (McLuhan, 1951). Competition for financial success was especially prevalent in the money-oriented 1980s. However, women's progress in the male workplace caused profound changes in the financial services market. Once women embarked on lifelong careers and gained sufficient education to compete for lucrative positions, they began earning salaries that made them a tempting target for financial vendors (Bartos, 1989). ML's marketing strategy, which formerly targeted financial planning to men, now repositioned the services bundle to attract women.

The Saly ads appear to be designed to appeal to women by depicting a female financial consultant who displays traditionally feminine traits such as caring, commitment, and patience. Men and women are thought to differ in their interpretation of the desirability of particular behaviors: women judge communality as more desirable than do men, whereas men judge self-assertive acts as more socially desirable (Buss, 1981). Jere and Saly appear to conform to the stereotypical cultural norms that expect women to be modest and self-effacing and men to be heroic and nonconformist (Deaux & Major, 1987). Although women as financial advisers may now be a commonplace modern role, the language they use relies on traditional concepts of how women are expected to sound.

This may relate to financial industry wisdom, suggesting that women are not as confident in financial management as men and rely more on their advisers. Proprietary research found that women were more likely to respond unfavorably to "hard sell" than to offers of advice and assistance, for they want someone with whom they can "talk about financial services" (Conklin, 1986). Saly personifies the "personal, subjective, emotional, descriptive" style that women are said to prefer (Firestone 1971, p. 165). Thus, the reading of Saly as feminine and Jere as masculine appears to be part of ML's positioning strategy in using a female spokesperson for the new women's market and retaining a male spokesperson for the men's segment.

However, even though male and female consumers read text through the filter of sex-specific concerns, much additional research on stereotyping is necessary. Several questions arise in reference to the creation of effective product appeals in an age of evolving target markets and to the role of advertising as an agent for social change. The question of advertising effectiveness requires more informed understanding of whether women ought to be set apart as a distinct market segment in situations where this does not seem warranted by specific relationships between gender and product (see Astroff, 1991). This requires further examination, for at present it is unclear whether women do indeed respond more favorably to a woman financial adviser than to a man (see Milner, 1991, for review). It is at least arguable that women may read authoritativeness in a male character as preferable, for women may not yet be conditioned to accept their own self-sufficiency (Donovan, 1975). Recent research in social psychology using reader response theory suggests that when readers are faced with a narrator, they have been culturally conditioned to expect the narrator to be male. This is based on previous reading experience (more stories are told by men than women) and on general cultural beliefs (Howard & Allen, 1989).

The issue of cultural conditioning leads to the need for more careful examination of whether (or how) advertising perpetuates/changes sex-role stereotypes. Despite objectively similar roles that can be adopted by men and women nowadays, stereotypes about sex-linked appropriate behaviors in language persevere and are embodied in advertisements (Deaux & Major, 1987). Even though women have entered the work force and educational institutions in record numbers in the past decades, old habits built into the traditional cultural heritage die hard. The construct of appropriate role behaviors (Ferguson et al., 1990) may be changing more slowly than the actual sociocultural changes in role performance. The habit of language — the vehicle for transmitting the beliefs and values that make culture — is one of the most significant definers of sexual identity. Advertisers can benefit from greater sensitivity to the way women use language and are used by it to create messages that talk to the contemporary consumer in a language she understands. However, since advertising seems less an agent of social change than a reflection of the cultural context, its language concretizes societal norms. Nevertheless, both norms and language change over the course of time, and advertisers must keep pace with the ongoing culture to create effective appeals. As Goffman (1979) said,

> By and large, advertisers do not create the ritualized expressions they employ; they seem to draw upon the same corpus of displays, the same ritual idiom, that is the resource of all of us who participate in social situations, and to the same end: the rendering of glimpsed action readable. If anything, advertisers conventionalize our conventions, stylize what is already a stylization. (p. 84)

REFERENCES

Abrams, M. H. (1988). *A glossary of literary terms* (5th ed.). New York: Holt, Rinehart & Winston.

Bartos, R. (1989, June). Marketing to women: The quiet revolution. *Marketing Insights*, p. 61.

Beard, M. R. (1946). *Women as force in history: A study in traditions and realities.* New York: Collier Books.

Berman, A. (1988). *From the new criticism to deconstruction: The reception of structuralism and post-structuralism.* Chicago: University of Illinois Press.

Bishop, N. (1979). Women in literature. In M. Richmond-Abbott (Ed.), *The American woman: Her past, her present, her future (pp. 48–70).* New York: Holt, Rinehart & Winston.

Bullough, V. L. (1974). *The subordinate sex: A history of attitudes toward women.* Baltimore: Penguin.

Buss, D. M. (1981). Sex differences in the evaluation and performance of dominant acts. *Journal of Personality and Social Psychology, 40,* 147–154.

Broverman, I. K., Vogel, S. R., Broverman, D. M., Clarkson, F. E., & Rosenkrantz, P. S. (1972). Sex-role stereotypes: A current appraisal. *Journal of Social Issues, 28,* 59–78.

Conklin, M. (1986, October). Purses and portfolios. *Madison Avenue,* pp. 25–26.

Courtney, A. E., & Whipple, T. W. (1983). *Sex stereotyping in advertising.* Lexington, MA: D. C. Heath.

Deaux, K., & Major, B. (1987). Putting gender into context: An interactive model of gender-related behavior. *Psychological Review, 94,* 369–389.

de Beauvoir, S. (1953). *The second sex,* (H. M. Parshley, Trans.). New York: Knopf.

Donovan, J. (1975). *Feminist literary criticism: Explorations in theory.* Lexington, KY: University Press of Kentucky.

Ellmann, M. (1968). *Thinking about women.* New York: Harcourt Brace Jovanovich.

Ferguson, J. H., Kreshel, P. J., & Tinkham, S. J. (1990). In the pages of *Ms.*: Sex role portrayals of women in advertising. *Journal of Advertising, 19,* 40–51.

Fetterley, J. (1977). *The resisting reader: A feminist approach to American fiction.* Bloomington: University of Indiana Press.

Firestone, S. (1971). *The dialectic of sex: The case for feminist revolution.* New York: Bantam Books.

Fox, M. F., & Hesse-Biber, S. (1984). *Women at work.* Boston: Mayfield Publishing Company.

Geng, V. (1979, February 26). Lobster night. *The New Yorker,* pp. 30–33.

Gilly, M. C. (1988). Sex roles in advertising: A comparison of television advertisements in Australia, Mexico, and the United States. *Journal of Marketing, 52,* 75–85.

Goffman, E. (1979). *Gender advertising.* New York: Harper & Row.

Heilbrun, C. (1973). *Toward a recognition of androgyny.* New York: Knopf.

Howard, J. A., & Allen, C. (1989). Making meaning: Revealing attributions through analyses of readers' responses. *Social Psychology Quarterly, 52,* 280–298.

Johnson, F. L., & Fine, M. G. (1985). Sex differences in uses and perceptions of obscenity. *Women's Studies in Communication, 8,* 11–24.

Kent, D., & Fitch, E. (1985, September 12). Honey, is this your aftershave or mine? *Advertising Age,* p. 17.

Lakoff, R. (1975). *Language and woman's place.* New York: Harper & Row.

Marchand, R. (1985). *Advertising the American dream: Making way for modernity, 1920–1940.* Berkeley: University of California Press.

Maynard, D. W. (1986). A review of John Heritage, *Garfinkel and Ethnomethodology.* 1984. *Contemporary Sociology, 15,* 346–349.

McConnell-Ginet, S., Borker, R., & Furman, N. (1980). *Women and language in literature and society.* New York: Praeger.

McLuhan, M. (1951). *The Mechanical Bride.* Boston: Beacon Press.

Millett, K. (1970). *Sexual politics.* Garden City, NY: Doubleday.

Mitchell, J., & Rose, J. (1982). *Feminine sexuality: Jacques Lacan and the Ecole Freudienne* (J. Rose, Trans.). New York: Norton.

Ortner, S. B. (1974). Is female to male as nature is to culture? In M. Z. Rosaldo & L. Lamphere (Eds.), *Women, culture, and society (pp. 17–42).* Stanford: Stanford University Press.

Pollay, R. W. (1986). The distorted mirror: Reflections on the unintended consequences of advertising. *Journal of Marketing, 50,* 18–36.

Register, C. (1975). American feminist literary criticism: A bibliographical introduction. In J. Donovan (Ed.), *Feminist literary criticism: Explorations in Theory (pp. 1–28.)* Lexington, KY: University Press of Kentucky.

Richmond-Abbott, M. (1979). Stereotypes of men and women in the American culture. In M. Richmond-Abbott (Ed.), *The American woman: Her past, her present, her future (pp. 71–95).* New York: Holt, Rinehart & Winston.

Russ, J. (1972). What can a heroine do? Or why women can't write. In Cornillon, S. K. (Ed.), *Images of women in fiction: Feminist perspectives (pp. 3–20).* Bowling Green, OH: Bowling Green University Popular Press.

Schiffman, L. G., & Kanuk, L. L. (1991). *Consumer behavior* (4th ed.). Englewood Cliffs, NJ: Prentice-Hall.

Schumacher, D. (1975). Subjectivities: A theory of the critical process. In J. Donovan (Ed.), *Feminist literary criticism: Explorations in theory.* Lexington, KY: University Press of Kentucky.

Showalter, E. (1985). *The new feminist criticism: Essays on women, literature, and theory.* New York: Pantheon.

Showalter, E. (1977). *A literature of their own: British women novelists from Bronte to Lessing.* Princeton: Princeton University Press.

Staton, S. (1987). *Literary theories in praxis.* Philadelphia: The University of Pennsylvania Press.

Stern, B. B. (1989). Literary criticism and consumer research: Overview and illustrative analysis. *Journal of Consumer Research, 16,* 322–334.

Stern, B. B., Gould, S. J., & Barak, B. (1987). Baby boom singles: The social seekers. *The Journal of Consumer Marketing, 4,* 5–22.

Wells, W. D. (1989). Lectures and dramas. In P. Cafferata & A. M. Tybout (Eds.), *Cognitive and affective responses to advertising (pp. 13–20).* Lexington, MA: D. C. Heath.

Welter, B. (1966). The cult of true womanhood: 1920–1860. *American Quarterly, 18,* 151–174.

Williamson, J. (1978). *Decoding advertisements.* London: Marion Boyars.

5 Multinational Gender Positioning: A Call for Research

Laura M. Milner
University of Alaska Fairbanks

Aaker and Shansby (1982) noted that there are six major ways of positioning a product: attribute, price-quality, use/application, product class, competitor, and of interest here, product user. Segmentation variables based on user include class, race, age, and sex. Of all these, sex is the most important. Indeed, gender may properly be considered the "alpha" segmentation variable. Before all else, marketers must decide the relevance of gender to their product or service. This will dictate whether they will position their product as masculine, feminine, both, or neither. Debevec and Iyer (1986) noted that "in positioning and repositioning products, advertisers often work to create a gender image for a brand by featuring the targeted gender in an advertisement as a 'typical' user of the product" (p. 12).

The aim of the present chapter is to examine the research relevant to gender positioning around the world and to suggest new avenues for future research. Literature pertinent to the perceived gender of products, the use of gender in advertisements, and the influence of individual differences in gender positioning is reviewed. Investigations focusing on stigmatized products, the use of sex themes in advertising, and differences between countries in gender positioning research are then suggested as possibilities for future research endeavors.

A great number of the studies reported here focus on Americans. This is an unfortunate artifact of focusing on English language research; however, it is also noted that researchers in American universities are quite interested in this topic, and given the importance of the U.S. market for the rest of the world, the decision to include representative studies on Americans was made. For those interested in pursuing a more detailed picture of American literature, Whipple and Courtney (1985) as well as Lysonski (1985) are excellent sources of information on the American population. However, it should be noted that a major limitation of the "American" research reported here is its almost exclusive focus on Anglo-Americans.

LITERATURE REVIEW

Gender positioning research utilizes three approaches (Bellizzi & Milner, 1991). Specifically, the effects of gender on the product/brand, the gender of the promotion, and/or the effects of the gender of the consumer on perception and consumption are examined, sometimes in isolation, sometimes together. Studies on the effects of gender of the product/brand often literally investigate whether products are considered masculine, feminine, neutral, or both (Iyer & Debevec, 1986, 1989; Milner, Speece, & Anderson, 1990). Research on the gender of promotion examines variables pertinent to the sex of the role models and/or voice-over featured in advertisements (Bellizzi & Milner, 1991; Debevec & Iyer, 1986; Kanungo & Pang, 1973; Whipple & Courtney, 1980). Consumer-specific research focuses on such individual differences as gender and personality traits/psychographics like career orientation and attitudes toward women (Barry, Gilly, & Doran; 1985; Debevec & Iyer, 1986; Ducker & Tucker, 1977; Whipple & Courtney, 1980). Multinational research pertinent to promotion gender will be presented first, followed by the relevant research on product gender and individual differences.

Promotion Gender

Sex Role Portrayal Literature.   The vast majority of research on gender of promotion uses content analysis to examine role portrayals in the media. With few exceptions (Caballero, Lumpkin, & Chonko, 1986; Wolheter & Lammers, 1980), female role portrayals are typically the focus. This is true of the literature on the U.S. population (e.g., Busby, 1975; Poe, 1976; Scheibe, 1979; Sexton & Haberman, 1974; Venkatesan & Losco, 1975; Whipple & Courtney, 1985) as well as large amounts of the existing research on other countries (Gilly, 1988; Lysonski, 1985; Razzouk & Harmon, 1986; Robbins & Paksoy, 1989).

There are several reasons for the initial research to focus on role portrayals. One reason is the relative ease of this type of data collection. There are definite advantages to analyzing television and magazine advertisements in contrast to trying to collect primary data from natives within their own countries. These analyses then serve to provide the researcher with insight, albeit cursory, into the roles that the men and women of a particular country are expected to play as well as the proper manifestation of these roles through the correspondingly correct usage of the appropriate products.

Another reason is that, at least in the United States, the feminist movement gave rise to the need to empirically demonstrate that women were negatively stereotyped in the media. Thus were raised the questions of not only what role *does* advertising play in society, but also, what role *should* advertising play in society? Is advertising merely to be a reflection of society, or should it explicity function as a change agent? A great deal of literature exists to indicate that advertisements serve as role models for appropriate behaviors for men and women and that negative role portrayals may have negative consequences both societally and for businesses that portray their target market inappropriately (Fram & Dubrin, 1971; Hawkins & Coney, 1976; Lammers & Wilkinson, 1980; Lasch, 1979; Pollay, 1986; Silverstein & Silverstein, 1974).

Beyond the political and philosophical aspects, however, are the practical applications. In order to study promotion effectiveness on women, research is needed to demonstrate how women are presently portrayed. The fact that women have been the emphasis of the research at least in part derives from the fact that in many cultures, women are the typical buyers of consumables, at which most mass advertising is aimed. However, this should not preclude increased investigation into the portrayals of men, boys and girls, or elderly men and women. Furthermore, researchers should neither presume that the home consumption situation is the only situation nor, as is discussed later, can researchers assume that because one market is the typical buyer that other markets can not be cultivated. To date, little research exists that includes general work settings (Lysonski, 1985; Robbins & Paksoy, 1989), specific industrial situations (McRee, Corder, & Haizlup, 1974; Mosher, 1976; Prather & Fidell, 1975), or the effects of mutiple target marketing approaches (Bellizzi & Milner, 1991; Debevec & Iyer, 1986; Kanungo & Johar, 1975; Kanungo & Pang, 1973; Krohn & Milner, 1989).

There is very little research from any country on advertising to men. There is a literature that focuses on advertising to professions such as medicine and psychiatry, which happen to be male dominated, by examining the portrayals of men and women in advertisements in their journals. Prather and Fidell (1975) found that psychoactive drug advertisements tended to depict women and that nonpsychoactive drug advertisements depicted men. The etiology of the symptoms for prescribing the psychoactive drugs differed for men and women. Women were shown as having emotional problems and men were depicted as having work-related stress. Mcree, Corder, and Haizlip (1974) suggested depicting both men and women in professional journal advertisements in response to their finding that 45% of the psychiatrists in their study felt that doctors' perceptions of women might be negatively influenced by the tendency of advertisers to depict women as the patients in advertisements rather than men.

The research devoted to studying role portrayals of men is limited. Wolheter and Lammers (1980) and Skelly and Lundstrom (1981) found that American men were depicted over time (1958-1978 and 1959-1979, respectively) in work roles less often and decorative roles more often. Lysonski (1983) examined portrayals of American men and women over time (1974-1975 and 1979-1980) in the print media and found that with regard to men, they were "less likely to be depicted in themes of sex appeal, dominant over women, and as authority figures" (p. 49).

Lysonski (1985) replicated the previous study with British print media. He examined role portrayals over time (1976 and 1982-1983) of both men and women in British magazines, the selection of which included magazines for general interest, women, and men. The women's magazines could be subdivided into those aimed at fashion, the home, and young married. The categories for the men included "sports and outdoor," "contemporary," and "professional." Although the results may vary by type of magazine, overall the findings indicated that some female role depiction categories such as "housewife" and "dependency upon men" had decreased but that there had been no decrease in such themes as "physical attractiveness concern" or "sex object" and no increase in such categories as "career-oriented" or "nontraditional" activities. With regard to men's roles, the results indicated that the promotion of "sex appeal" had increased, whereas the theme of "family man" and "activities and life outside the home" had decreased.

Gilly (1988) examined sex role portrayals of men and women as product users and voiceovers in television advertisements for three countries: Australia, Mexico, and the United States. Common characteristics were shared by all three countries. These included the more frequent use of masculine voiceovers. Youth was more often a characteristic of the women than of the men depicted in the ads. Furthermore, women had a higher probability of being portrayed in roles with relationships than men, who were often depicted as independent. Australian ads were the most eqalitarian. In the United States and Mexico, more ads emphasized sex role differences. For instance, Gilly found that women are less likely to appear in male product ads than men are to appear in female product ads. Furthermore, men are more likely than women to be depicted as employed and men are the most frequently portrayed as authorities. In U.S. ads, women are more likely to be seen in the home, and in Mexican ads, women are more likely to be portrayed as frustrated.

Robbins and Paksoy (1989) compared U.S. and German magazine advertisements on model activity (recreational/social, family, miscellaneous), occupation of the models (blue collar, white collar, mixed), model age, and the role of the female models. They found that American ads more often depicted family situations whereas German ads more frequently portrayed blue collar workers. U.S. and German ads typically featured youthful models. Germans were more likely to show women in business and independent situations whereas U.S. advertisers portrayed women in social roles.

Razzouk and Harmon (1986) examined women's role portrayals in Saudi advertisements in a general audience newspaper, a men's magazine, and a woman' magazine. Using Lysonski's (1983) categories, they found that the categories women were most often portrayed in were "homemaker," "physical attractiveness," and "sex object." Ads pertinent to career orientation and nontraditional activities were infrequent; however, ratings for "dependency upon men" were low and being the "voice of authority" was high.

Even with such limited research, there do appear to be some trends. First, there is more research including an examination of the portrayals of men in advertisements in the literature on countries outside of the United States than in American literature. The reasons for this are entirely speculative. Multinational advertisers could be more equalitarian. Maybe men in other countries are more often targets for consumer goods than in the United States and would therefore be depicted more frequently, and thus more likely to be studied. Perhaps researchers on these issues are more eqalitarian. Researchers could also be making an error in assuming that men play an important role in the purchase of consumables. Advertisers could also be making an error in assuming that men play an important role in the purchase of consumables.

It would also appear that physical attractiveness and sex object themes are popular with advertisers promoting in a variety of countries and that overall, women are not portrayed as positively as men in advertisements. However, the settings are not necessarily consistent, nor are the mechanisms that are used in the ads necessarily the same for conveying these messages. For instance, the Unites States and Saudi Arabia share in common the tendency to show women in home/family situations; German advertisers, however, frequently portray women in business settings. Furthermore, Americans are more likely to use men as the "voice of authority" than were Saudis.

Role portrayal research does address the realities of advertising insofar as they investigate how men and women are presently being portrayed in the media. This type of research does not address actual effective promotional appeals for men and women. Experimental research, however, does.

Experimental Literature. The experimental research that is available on gender promotion where role models and voiceovers are manipulated in conjunction with a variety of products, is based on Americans. Furthermore, the results are often mixed and contradictory. For instance, Kanungo and Pang (1973) found some support for model–product congruity hypothesis when their results indicated that men and women rated consumer durables such as cars, a perceived masculine product, more positively when promoted by a man and sofas, a perceived feminine product, more favorably when promoted by a woman. Later, Kanungo and Johar (1975) found that the most effective approach in promoting nondurable products such as coffee, soap, and toothpaste was using men and women together as models.

Debevec and Iyer (1986) found the total antithesis of the model-product congruity hypothesis. Their results indicated that the most favorable reactions were for male spokespersons endorsing female products and female spokespersons endorsing male products.

Similarly, Bellizzi, and Milner (1991) found that the most effective promotion technique in advertising masculine services, such as car repair care, to women was to use female-directed ads (e.g., female voiceover and copy). This was more effective than the traditional male-directed ads (e.g., male voiceover and copy) or the "combo" approach using male and female voiceovers with copy appropriate for both genders in one ad. Furthermore, the men did not indicate any form of backlash in that their attitudes were not substantially different for any of the approaches.

These studies occur over time, and possibly rather than being viewed as yielding inconsistent and contradictory results, they may more accurately be perceived as reflections of effective advertising strategies changing over time. American attitudes toward appropriate sex role behavior have changed since the early 1970s and, as Gentry, Doering, and O'Brien (1978) noted many products are no longer strongly gender identified. However, Debevec and Iyer (1986) and Bellizzi and Milner (1991) did use innovative advertising formats. Most advertisements are still fairly traditional, and perhaps the respondents were reacting favorably to the innovation and novelty of the ads.

Product Gender

Diverging from the promotion gender literature is the research pertinent to gender of the product/brand. As stated previously, these types of studies literally focus on whether products are considered masculine, feminine, both, or neither. Understanding whether a product has gender (and if so, which gender) will more effectively enable an advertiser operating in different cultural contexts to initially position a product or to reposition it. Milner et al. (1990) examined product gender perceptions among Greek students using a line of thinking developed by Iyer and Debevec (1986,

1989) in their application of the psychology literature on androgyny (Bem, 1974). They found that, like Americans (Iyer & Debevec, 1989), Greeks tend to perceive products as either masculine or feminine and not as androgynous or undifferentiated. Furthermore, Americans and Greeks tend to view the gender of products similarly with few exceptions (i.e., electric irons, sneakers, and wine). These overall results would favor globalization of advertising strategies relying on gender; however, the exceptions do suggest potential advertising problems if a strategy is inappropriate for a particular product in different countries.

Iyer and Debevec (1986, 1989) speculated that product promoter, user, and buyer were major dimensions in the formation of product gender. For Americans, they found that gender promoter and purchaser (followed by the statistically significant but less important user) were the major predictors of perceived product gender, whereas for the Greeks, Milner et al. (1990) found that the categories of promoter and user were predictors, but that the categories of buyer and grammatical gender were not. These findings suggest that, overall, product promoter, user, and buyer are the pertinent dimensions that advertisers can utilize in determining the gender of their products, but that there may be cultural differences with regard to the weight each of the components plays.

Having addressed the idea that, at least for two cultures, products do have a perceived gender, another question arises: Can this perception can be changed? The experimental literature suggests that it can. Alreck, Settle, and Belch (1982) manipulated the gender of a neutral product, soap, by using the feminine name, Rainbow, or the masculine name, Tiger. They found that American women preferred the feminine product but were accepting of the masculine product. American men, on the other hand, rejected the feminine product. Debevec and Iyer (1986) found that the gender of gendered products could be impacted among Americans by changing the gender of the promoter. Their results indicated that "the brand of dishwashing liquid (beer) advertised was perceived as more masculine (feminine) when endorsed by a male (female) spokesperson than when endorsed by a female (male) spokesperson" (p. 18).

Individual Differences

Individual differences, other than gender, have not been a very reliable predictor of American reactions to products and promotions. The measures utilized without much success have included sex-role orientation (Caballero, Lumpkin, & Chonko, 1986; Debevec & Iyer, 1986), self-confidence, and feminist attitudes (Ducker & Tucker, 1977; Whipple & Courtney, 1980). The one dimension, however, that has shown signs of utility among Americans and other cultures is career orientations among women (Bartos,

1989; Langer, 1987; McCall, 1977). Barry, Gilly, and Doran (1985) found that homemaker-oriented advertising was preferred by American women who expressed a low desire to work outside the home and that career-oriented advertising was preferred by women with a high desire to work.

To date, the only research on individual differences among multinational consumers is the work by Bartos (1989), which truly is the most comprehensive work developed thus far on multinational positioning to women. Specifically, she examined 10 countries (Australia, Brazil, Canada, Great Britain, Italy, Japan, Mexico, United States, Venezuela, and West Germany) representing four regions (Europe, Far East, Latin America, and North America) using the segmentation categories for women such as *housewives who plan to work in the future, housewives who plan to stay home, working women who consider their jobs "just a job,"* and *women who are career-minded* in conjunction with their family life cycle to suggest ways that a variety of products and services are best marketed to each segment. Interestingly, however, for those countries for which she could obtain data on attitudes toward advertising, (Great Britain and the United States), these categories were not necessarily predictive. More accurately, women from all of the groups were quite tolerant of advertisements aimed toward women as long as they were not too idealistic or unrealistic about women and were not condescending. Contrary to Barry, Gilly, and Doran (1985), other experimental research such as that by Whipple and Courtney (1980) concluded that traditional or progressive advertisements are not necessarily offensive to any group as long as men and women are portrayed realistically and without exaggeration. Similarly, Bellizzi and Milner (1991) did not find significant results in reactions to different advertising stimuli using a modified version of the Bartos (1978) schema.

FUTURE RESEARCH

The call for more research, especially experimental research on populations outside of the United States, is obvious, but at least investigations are beginning to be undertaken in this important area. Furthermore, because the literature is in its infancy, some actions can be taken now that will in the long run add substantial depth to future literature assessments. These actions pertain to both methodological considerations and the content of the studies.

Methodology

Consistent methodology utilization and replication between studies is important. For instance, Lysonski (1985) and Razzouk and Harmon (1986) used the same sex role categories in their study of sex role portrayals in British and Saudi magazines. Such procedures make cross-study as well as cross-cultural comparison much easier and more meaningful. Furthermore, sex role portrayal assessment is a significant methodology for a variety of reasons. In spite of its relative ease as a data-gathering method, it is very effective. Sex role assessments are an excellent mechanism for examining actual advertising practices, and they provide a historical framework to examine role portrayal change over time.

However, native subjects and experimental manipulations must be more frequently utilized in research. The experimental literature, by virtue of variable manipulation, allows for assessing advertising effectiveness strategies. Once the literature becomes more experimental, Whipple and Courtney (1985) have some suggestions. Though originally written for the U.S. literature, their recommendations are still very appropriate to the multinational literature. For instance, they pointed out that external validity problems may be avoided by not relying on student subject populations that utilize forced exposure situations or nonprofessional advertisement stimuli. Furthermore, measures pertinent to not only attitudes, but also intention to buy, should be used. External validity will be enhanced by using manipulation checks as well as random assignment to treatments. Debevec and Iyer (1986) recommended avoiding limited stimulus materials. Therefore, a greater variety of products and/or advertisements should be incorporated into the research. However, as noted previously, researchers are cautioned against an expansion of stimuli without focusing on replicating previous work. Thorelli (1988) noted that the external validity of research done on one country or culture is questionable. Consequently, research must include comparative studies with specific cultural differences being highlighted.

Research Topics

There are ample opportunities to fill in gaps and widen the streams of research that has gone before. Some suggestions as to future research endeavors follow. These are certainly not new ideas, but they are new applications of existing work. These research possibilities into multinational gender positioning are presented using the format of the communication process and include such topics as cultural differences, sex in advertising, and stigmatized products.

The communication process consists of several components. The source is the sender of the message. The message is what is being said. The medium is the mode of transmission. The receiver, or recipient of the message, gives feedback to the source in the form of sales, complaints, and so on. Noise is those things, such as technical difficulty or choice of advertisement model, that may interfere with receipt of the message. For the sake of explanatory convenience, the discussion begins with the recipient.

Receiver. With respect to the recipient of the message, hopefully the consumer, there are a variety of possibilities available for gender positioning research that could be utilized. Two major cross-cultural research projects that seem very applicable in multinational gender positioning are the work by Rena Bartos (1989) and the work by Geert Hofstede (1980, 1982, 1983, 1984a, 1984b). With regard to lifestyle differences, Bartos' (1989) work, which has already been discussed at length, seems quite appropriate. One shortcoming could be the utility of her categorization schema of *career women, just-a-job women, housewives who plan to work,* and *housewives who plan to stay home* in those countries where such choices do not exist. Career typologies would seemingly have limited utility for women in countries such as China, where work is a lifelong expectation. Bartos' categorization of women, however, makes possible a breakdown for men using a mirror image. That is, for housewives who plan to stay home, there must be men who prefer their wives to stay home. Would effective appeals to this type of men vary from effective appeals to men who prefer career women?

Hofstede's work possesses tremendous cross-cultural comparativeness in terms of methodological consistency and number of countries studied, 50 in all. He has identified four dimensions that seem universally applicable to different cultures. These dimensions are power distance, individualism, masculinity, and uncertainty avoidance. Of interest here is the masculinity--femininity dimension.

With regard to the masculinity dimension, Hofstede (1984b) stated:

> Masculinity stands for a preference in society for achievement, heroism, assertiveness, and material success. Its opposite, Femininity, stands for a preference for relationships, modesty, caring for the weak, and the quality of life. This fundamental issue addressed by this dimension is the way in which a society allocates social (as opposed to biological) roles to the sexes.

> Some societies strive for maximum social differentiation between the sexes. The norm is then that men are given the more outgoing, assertive roles and women the caring, nurturing roles. . . .

> Some societies strive for minimal social differentiation between the sexes. This means that some women can take assertive roles if they want to but especially that some men can take relationship-oriented, modest, caring roles if they want to.

> . . . the Masculinity-Femininity dimension relates to people's self-concept: who am I and what is my task in life? (p. 84)

The results of his work with regard to this dimension are featured in Table 5.1. Though originally written for a work behavior context, Hofstede's research seems particularly appropriate for gender-positioning studies. For instance, the extent to which a culture could be characterized as emphasizing the differences between men and women would affect the positioning of a product and the consequent promotion of that product.

Furthermore, the flavor of his writing suggests that his perspective is much more behaviorally oriented and less psychological-trait oriented than other sex stereotype research (e.g., Williams & Best, 1982). His work is more easily utilized in applied situations because it focuses on social differentiation rather than on specific gender-related traits. By way of example, suppose that advertisers are interested in whether men or women in a particular culture cook or whether both men and women do the cooking. If women do not cook, advertisers are interested in the degree of social differentiation between the sexes; that is, how restrictive the no-cooking taboo is. They are less interested in the rationale, or trait explanation, behind why men do the cooking. Whether men cook because it is based on nurturing, or because it is a quantitive process requiring measurements, or because it is the logical extension of the aggressive hunting instinct is of less concern to the advertisers.

However, as a note of caution, although seemingly very applicable and easily utilized, ultimately a bi-polar continuum for classifying such distinctions may be too simplistic. Other more complex measures for such concepts should probably be sought out and utilized as well.

Regardless of their potential limitations, the work by both Hofstede and Bartos furnishes frameworks for providing future research avenues on multinational gender positioning research.

Source. One of the key dimensions used by the source in communicating with the receiver is product. What products are appropriate when examined in the context of gender positioning research? According to Bartos (1989), the traditional product categories marketed to women are food, fashion, grooming, and homemaking but now are beginning to include travel, automobiles, and financial services. Hofstede's research indicates that those countries that are identified as strong gender differentiators would have less gender-usage crossover for traditional products than those countries identified less strongly. Interestingly, Bartos has no data on women for either travel or automobiles in Japan, which is ranked 50 on the masculine index in Hofstede's list of 50 countries.

Traditional male products, other than travel, financial services, personal grooming, and expensive durables like cars and boats, are not that well documented, nor are the strategies for successful promotion. However, at least for American men, efforts are being made by companies such as

TABLE 5.1
Masculinity–Femininity Dimension[1,2,3,4,5]

Country	Index Score	Rank
Argentina	56	30–31
Australia	61	35
Austria	79	49
Belgium	54	29
Brazil	49	25
Canada	52	28
Chile	28	8
Colombia	64	39–40
Costa Rica	21	5-6
Denmark	16	4
Equador	63	37–38
Finland	26	7
France	43	17–18
Germany (FR)	66	41–42
Great Britain	66	41–42
Greece	57	32–33
Guatemala	37	11
Hong Kong	57	32–33
Indonesia	46	22
India	56	30–31
Iran	43	17–18
Ireland	68	43–44
Israel	47	23
Italy	70	46–47
Jamaica	68	43–44
Japan	95	50
Korea(S)	39	13
Malaysia	50	26–27
Mexico	69	45
Netherlands	14	3
Norway	8	2
New Zealand	58	34
Pakistan	50	26–27
Panama	44	19
Peru	42	15–16
Philippines	64	39–40
Portugal	31	9
South Africa	63	37–38
Salvador	40	14
Singapore	48	24
Spain	42	15–16
Sweden	5	1
Switzerland	70	46–47
Taiwan	45	20–21
Thailand	34	10
Turkey	45	20–21

(continued)

TABLE 5.1 (continued)

Country	Index Score	Rank
Uruguay	38	12
USA	62	36
Venezuala	73	48
Yugoslavia	21	5-6
Regions		
East Africa 1)	41	(14-15)
West Africa 2)	46	(22)
Arab Ctrs 3)	53	(28-29)

[1]The higher the index score (rank), the higher the social differentiation between the sexes.
[2]Adapted from Hofstede (1984b).
[3]Ethiopia, Kenya, Tanzania, Zambia
[4]Ghana, Nigeria, Sierra, Leone
[5]Egypt, Iraq, Kuwait, Lebanon, Lybia, Saudi Arabia, UAE

Campbell Soup Company and Proctor and Gamble to reposition traditionally female products like soaps and food toward men (Rosen, 1985). Again, Hofstede's research suggests that marketing traditionally female products to men would be more difficult in those countries classified as masculine than in those countries classified as feminine.

Stigmatized products such as feminine hygiene and birth control products comprise one category of products that is particularly gender linked but that has received virtually no empirical attention. Milner (1990) noted that: "academic research directly assessing the 'stigmatization' or sensitivity of products does not exist. Rather the literature examines irritation factors present in advertisements, and unfortunately this literature is rather limited" (p. 2). The two major studies in the area by Aaker and Bruzzone (1985) and Bauer and Greyser (1968) focused on product class effects, copy execution effects, and individual differences among consumers. Product classes that seem to cause high irritation among consumers by being rated as offensive or annoying include the following: cigarettes, dental supplies, deodorants, feminine hygiene, laxative, liquor, motion pictures, mouth washes, soaps/detergents, and underwear. In their analysis, Aaker and Bruzzone noted that the irritation factor may rise due to copy execution effects. For instance, in their study, 8 of 524 commercials were for feminine hygiene products; these 8 commercials were rated the 8 most irritating commercials of the study. They observed the following:

A variety of creative approaches was used — singing commercials, appealing lifestyle portrayals, testimonials, and straightforward presenters. Since every one of them proved exceptionally irritating, the irritation appears to stem from the product rather the execution. . . . All of the hemorrhoid, laxative, and women's underwear commercials were also in the top 28 except one, which just missed. The mouthwash and breath product commercials, which were rather consistently regarded as irritating, all graphically showed the embarrassing, unpleasant effect of bad breath. Unlike the feminine hygiene commercials, this irritation is likely to have stemed from the execution" (Aaker & Bruzzon, 1985, p. 49).

Furthermore, individual differences seem to heighten advertising irritation scores, although there is conflicting data. For instance, upper socioeconomic people (as defined by income, occupation, and education) were found by Aaker and Bruzzone (1985) to be more irritated by certain advertisements than lower socioeconomic people. They also found that people under 40 were more irritated than people over 40. Bauer and Greyser's (1968) research did not find such demographic variables to be important predictors. Rather they found that men had higher irritation scores than women. Aaker and Bruzzone did not find substantial gender differences. Both studies, however, found that nonusers of a product had higher irritation scores than users. Furthermore, the data by Aaker and Bruzzone indicate that heavy TV watchers have lower irritation scores than light TV watchers.

Unfortunately no multinational data exists on this subject. Bartos (1989), commenting on earlier research (Bartos, 1982), noted that with American women: "the notion of advertising personal products on television was a particularly sensitive one to many women. Since television is a public medium, they resent a personal product being shown on the screen. Another aspect of the resentment against the invasion of privacy is the sense that advertisers focus on intimate aspects of women's lives but not those of men" (p. 263).

Using Hofstede's research, one would presume that personal products that are so gender dependent would not be advertised as publicly in those countries that focus on the polarization of the sexes. However, this is clearly speculation, because a country like the United States, which ranks fairly high in gender differentiation (#36), is also a country that does allow such advertising.

Message and Medium.   Specific investigations into the uses of the media within a gender positioning framework has been limited. The research by Bartos (1989) indicated that television, radio, newspapers, and magazines are highly utilized media vehicles in the countries studied, although the patterns of usage will vary based on country and whether women are stay-at-home housewives, plan-to-work housewives, just-a-job working women, or career women.

In her look at women's perception of advertising in general, Bartos (1989) found that due to its repetitive, "hammering" nature, "women in Italy are quite negative toward advertising, overall" (p. 254). Japanese women tend to use advertisements as information tools and "are quite tolerant and accepting of advertising" (p. 256). However, "consumers in Mexico and Venezuela are intensely critical of the sheer amount of advertising and clutter on television" (p. 257).

Empirical investigations into the interactions between media vehicles and messages have been limited in gender positioning research. As stated previously, Bartos (1989) noted that American women do not appreciate personal products for women being promoted on public mediums like television. Other research has confirmed this and noted that American men do not care for it either (Aaker & Bruzzone, 1985; Hume, 1988). In Australia, Johnson and Johnson recently had to remove two Meds tampons commercial from television. Utilizing a novel approach, they were featuring male spokespersons to try and increase male buying behaviors of the product for the women in their homes. The consumer outrage was incredible: "The complaints came 'from every age group, but a very large proportion were older people, mostly women" (Martin, 1989, p. 34). Milner (1990) noted that: "situations like these raise important questions for manufacturers, advertisers, and broadcasters. For instance, are such high irritation ratings truly specific to the product? Are men the most appropriate promoters of such intimate female products? Finally, are broadcast media being misused in promoting such sensitive products?" (p. 1).

Aaker and Bruzzone (1985) alluded to the possibility of a media interaction with products in their discussion of feminine hygiene products. Recall that they found that feminine hygiene commercials were rated the most irritating commercials. The Bauer and Greyser study did not yield the same results. Aaker and Bruzzone (1985) noted that:

> Feminine hygiene products weren't advertised until the early 70s. At the time of the Bauer and Greyser study they were advertised in women's magazines, where they apparently caused little annoyance. . . . In an effort to explore the hypothesis that irritation levels for feminine hygiene products might decline as viewers got accustomed to seeing them on television, five feminine hygiene commercials were tested in mid-1983. The resulting irritation scores . . . did not support the hypothesis (pp. 49–50).

They did not, however, draw the conclusion that the high irritation effects could be due to media effects; instead, as stated earlier, they suggested that "since every one of them [feminine hygiene advertisements] proved exceptionally irritating, the irritation appears to stem from the product rather than the execution" (Aaker & Bruzzone, 1985, p. 48)

Surely, however, the fact that feminine hygiene advertising causes high irritation on television but not in the print media suggests that there is an interaction between products and mediums. Indeed, the best vehicle for feminine hygiene commercials and other sensitive, intimate, and stigmatized products might not be television, but rather print or possibly radio (a public medium that people often use privately).

Another area of research that seems particularly intriguing in gender positioning research is the use of sex in advertising. A great deal of this research focuses on nudity, usually female nudity, in advertisements. For instance, Steadman (1969), Alexander and Judd (1978), and Judd and Alexander (1983) found a decline in advertising recall for those ads using suggestive formats. Bello, Pitts, and Etzel (1983) found that "controversial sexual content in the commercial failed to improve effectiveness apart from merely making the commercial more interesting" (p. 32). Richmond and Hartman (1982), however, found that the type of sexual appeal used could be a mitigating factor. According to their research, sex appeals can be classified into the following uses: functional, fantasy, symbolism, inappropriate. They found that inappropriate uses of sex in advertisements diminished recall significantly, and that " 'Functional, 'Fantasy,' and 'Symbolic' use of sex appeal have a legitimate and non-offensive role in advertisement creation" (p. 60).

Peterson and Kerin (1977) found that, overall, men react more favorably to female nudity than do women; however, negative reactions were more profound for total nudity than the totally clothed or seductively clad-model conditions. Reidenback and McCleary (1983) found that females reacted more favorably to male models than did men; however, positive reactions were stronger for the seductively clad-model than for the totally clothed and nude male model. They concluded that "too little nudity and too much nudity operate against the liking and belief of an ad. Apparently, there is a level of male nudity (seductive level) which is acceptable" (p. 453).

Using a different approach, Kilbourne, Painton, and Ridley (1985) studied the impact of sexual embeds in magazine advertisements. They found that "embedding was effective in raising attitudinal evaluations of a liquor ad but not a cigaret ad . . . [and] that embedding was effective in increasing GSR measurements for the versions of the ads with embeds" (p. 48).

Although the literature on sex in advertising in general is very small, the literature on sex in advertising in a multicultural context is virtually nonexistent. Goldsmith and Freiden (1988) compared British and Americans reactions to advertisements featuring various levels of (un)dress of a female model. Country of residence was only a factor when "British men and women and American women rated the experiment similarly, while American men expressed a less positive feeling overall about the experiment" (p. 81).

With regard to the use of nudity in advertisements around the world, there is very limited research. Robbins and Paksoy (1989) found no differences between Germans and Americans in terms of nudity in their examination of magazine advertisements; however, Reid, Salmon, and Soley (1984) found that international television commercials contained more nudity than U.S. commercials. Indeed, Americans are known paradoxically for being very sex conscious but also "puritanical" in our attitudes toward sex. As McCary and McCary (1982) noted: "inconsistency between sexual attitudes and behavior is still a characteristic of the American culture" (p. 343). Indeed, this "approach–avoid" attitude is evidenced in the recent decision by many American women's publications to not carry a Nivea ad showing the entire body of nude female (Springen & Miller, 1990); an advertising format that is frequent in Europe.

Unfortunately, the relation between Hofstede's classification of masculine-feminine cultures and acceptance of nudity is an empirical question. One might assume that the greater the distinction that is made between the sexes, the less tolerance there is of nudity; however, this is totally speculative.

Feedback and Noise.   Until lately, there was no research specifically addressing the dynamics of feedback and noise in advertising in a gender positioning context. However, Richard Pollay and Steven Lysonski recently examined perceived advertising sexism and boycott intentions in Denmark, Greece, New Zealand, and the United States (Lysonski, & Pollay, 1990; Pollay & Lysonski, 1990). They found that though awareness of sexism in advertising is high, the potential for boycotting is low, regardless of country.

Following the lines of this research, then, how do men and women express their displeasure with a particular promotion? If not boycotting, what about complaints to the manufacturer or retailer? What are these businesses' responses? Do these responses differ by whether they are catering to men or women?

With regard to noise, one obvious source for commercials would seem to be audience composition of the recipients. For instance, Milner (1990) asked: "do people hate feminine hygiene product commercials because of the product or the fact that the commercials are often put on broadcast mediums with the probability that they will be exposed to these intimate products in groups, possibly mixed sex groups?" (p. 12). The same question could be asked with regard to nudity. Do people like/dislike nudity in advertisements overall, and is the effect impacted by how public the medium is?

CONCLUSION

This review has been more an exercise in "what isn't" and "what could be" than "what has been" and "what is." There are obviously many empirical questions to be asked and potentially answered, although as yet no overwhelming theoretical framework exists. Hopefully, though, future reviews on multinational gender positioning will encompass a great deal more research, both quantitatively and qualititatively.

REFERENCES

Aaker, D. A., & Bruzzone, D. E. (1985). Causes of irritation in advertising. *Journal of Marketing, 49*(2), 47–57.

Aaker, D. A., & Shansby, J. G. (1982). Positioning your product. *Business Horizons, 25*(2), 56–62.

Alexander, M. W., & Judd, B. B., Jr. (1978). The effects of female nudity in advertising on brand recall. *Journal of Advertising Research, 18*(1), 47–50.

Alreck, P. L., Settle, R. B., & Belch, M. A. (1982). Who responds to 'gendered' ads, and how? *Journal of Advertising Research, 22*(2), 25–31.

Barry, T. E., Gilly, M. C., & Doran, L. (1985). Advertising to women with different career orientations. *Journal of Advertising Research, 25*(2), 26–34.

Bartos, R. (1978) What every marketer should know about women. *Harvard Business Review 56*(3), 73–85.

Bartos, R. (1982) *The Moving Target: What marketing should know about women.* New York: Free Press.

Bartos, R. (1989). *Marketing to women around the world.* Boston: Harvard Business School Press.

Bauer, R. A., & Greyser, S. A. (1968). *Advertising in America: The consumer view.* Boston: Harvard University Press.

Bellizzi, J., & Milner, L. M. (1991). Gender positioning of a traditionally male-dominant product *Journal of Advertising Research,* 31(3), 72–79.

Bello, D. C., Pitts, R. E., & Etzel, M. J. (1983). The communication effects of controversial sexual content in television programs and commercials. *Journal of Advertising, 12*(3), 32–42.

Bem, S. L. (1974). The measurement of psychological androgyny. *Journal of Consulting and Clinical Psychology, 42,* 155–162.

Busby, L. (1975). Sex-role research on the mass media. *Journal of Communication, 25*(4), 107–131.

Caballero, M., Lumpkin, J. R., & Chonko, L. B. (1986). Male sex role portrayal preferences: The influence of sex role orientation. *Proceedings of the Annual Meeting of the Decision Sciences Institute, 7,* 855–857.

Debevec, K., & Iyer, E (1986). The influence of spokespersons in altering a product's gender image: Implication for advertising effectiveness. *Journal of Advertising, 15*(4), 12–20.

Ducker, J. M., & Tucker, L. R., Jr. (1977). Women's libers versus independent women: A study of preferences for women's roles in advertisements. *Journal of Marketing Research, 14*(4), 469–475.

Fram, E., & Dubrin, A. (1971). Coping with women's lib. *Sales Management, 106,* 20–21, 60.

Gentry, J. W., Doering, M., & O'Brien, T. (1978). Masculinity and femininity factors in product perception and self-image. *Advances in Consumer Research, 9,* 322–326.

Gilly, M. C. (1988). Sex roles in advertising: A comparison of television advertisements in Australia, Mexico, and the United States. *Journal of Marketing, 52*(2), 75–85.

Goldsmith, R. E., & Freiden, J. B. (1988). Subject reaction to a sex-in advertising experiment. *Proceedings of the Southern Marketing Association,* pp. 79–82.

Hawkins, D. I. & Coney, K. A. (1976). Advertising and differentiated sex roles in contemporary American society. *Journal of the Academy of Marketing Science, 4*(1), 418-28.

Hofstede, G. (1980). *Culture's consequences: International differences in work-related values.* Beverly Hills, CA: Sage.

Hofstede, G. (1982). Cultural pitfalls for Dutch expatriates in Indonesia: Lessons for Europeans in Asia, part 1. *Euro-Asia Business Review, 1*(1), 37-41.

Hofstede, G. (1983). Cultural pitfalls for Dutch expatriates in Indonesia: Lessons for Europeans in Asia, parts 2 & 3. *Euro-Asia Business Review, 2*(1), 38-47.

Hofstede, G. (1984a). The Cultural Relativity of the quality of life concept. *Academy of Management Review, 9*(3), 389-398.

Hofstede, G. (1984b). Cultural dimensions in management and planning. *Asia Pacific Journal of Management, 1*(2), 81-99.

Hume, S. (1988, July 18). "Most hated" ads: Feminine hygiene. *Advertising Age,* p. 3.

Iyer, E., & Debevec, K. (1986). Gender stereotyping of products: Are products like people? *Developments in Marketing Science (Proceedings of the Academy of Marketing Science), 9,* 40-45.

Iyer, E. & Debevec, K. (1989). Bases for the formation of product gender images. *Developments in Marketing Science (Proceedings of the Academy of Marketing Science), 12,* 38-42.

Judd, B. B., Jr., & Alexander, M. W. (1983). On the reduced effectiveness of some sexually suggestive ads. *Journal of the Academy of Marketing Science, 11*(2), 156-168.

Kanungo, R., & Johar, J. (1975). Effects of slogan and human model characteristics in product advertisements. *Canadian Journal of Behavioral Science, 7*(2), 127-38.

Kanungo, R. N., & Pang, S. (1973). Effects of human models on perceived product quality, *Journal of Applied Psychology, 57*(2), 172-178.

Krohn, F., & Milner, L. M. (1989). The AIDS crisis: Unethical marketing leads to negligent homicide. *Journal of Business Ethics, 8,* 773-780.

Kilbourne, W. E., Painton, S., & Ridley, D. (1985). The Effect of sexual embedding on responses to magazine advertisements. *Journal of Advertising, 14*(2), 48-56.

Lammars, H. B., & Wilkinson, M. L. (1980). Attitudes toward women and satisfaction with sex roles in advertisements. *Psychological Reports, 46,* 690.

Langer, J. (1987). A woman is still a woman, but a man now has his doubts. *Marketing News, 21,* 4.

Lasch, C. (1979). *The culture of narcissism.* New York: Norton.

Lysonski, S. (1983). Sex-role stereotyping in advertisements: A reexamination. *Developments in Marketing Science (Proceedings of the Academy of Marketing Science), 6,* 473-476.

Lysonski, S.(1985). Role portrayals in british magazine advertisements. *European Journal of Marketing, 19*(7), 37-55.

Lysonski S. & Pollay, R. W. (1990). Advertising sexism is forgiven but not forgotten: Historical, cross-cultural and Individual differences in criticism and purchase Boycott intentions *International Journal of Advertising, 9,* 319-331.

Martin, G. L. (1989, March 27). Australians blast tampon ads. *Advertising Age,* p. 34.

McCall, S. H. (1977). Meet the "workwife." *Journal of Marketing, 41*(3), 55-56.

McCary, J. L., & McCary, S. P. (1982). *Human sexuality.* Belmont, CA: Wadsworth.

McRee, C., Corder, B. F., & Haizlip, T. (1974). Psychiatrists' responses to sexual bias in pharmaceutical advertising. *American Journal of Psychiatry, 131*(11), 1273-1275.

Milner, L. M. (1990). *Appropriate media choices for advertising stigmatized products to men and women: An experimental investigation.* Unpublished manuscript.

Milner, L., Speece, M., & Anderson, J. (1990). *Product gender perception: The case of greeks Proceedings of the Third Symposium on Cross-Cultural Consumer and Business Studies* (pp. 404-414).

Mosher, E. H. (1976). Portrayal of women in drug advertisements: A medical betrayal. *Journal of Drug Issues, 6*(1), 72-78.

Peterson, R. A., & Kerin, R. A. (1977). The female role in advertisements: Some experimental evidence. *Journal of Marketing, 41*(4) 59–63.

Poe, A. (1976). Active women in ads. *Journal of Communication, 26*(4), 185–192.

Pollay, R. W. (1986). The distorted mirror: Reflections on the unintended consequences of advertising. *Journal of Marketing, 50*(2), 18–36.

Pollay, R. W., & Lysonski, S. (1990). In the eye of the beholder: International differences in ad sexism. Perceptions and reactions. *Proceedings of the Third Symposium on Cross-Cultural Consumer and Business Studies* (pp. 219–331).

Prather, J., & Fidell, L. S. (1975). Sex differences in the content and style of medical advertisements. *Social Science and Medicine, 9,* 23–26.

Razzouk, N. Y., & Harmon, R. (1986). A study of the role portrayals of women in advertising: The case of Saudi Arabia. *Proceedings of the Southwestern Marketing Association* (pp. 325–327).

Reid, L., Salmon, C. T., & Soley, L. C. (1984). The nature of sexual content in television advertising: A cross-cultural comparison of award-winning commercials. *Proceedings of the American Marketing Association Summers Educator's Conference*, (pp. 214–216). Chicago: American Marketing Association.

Reidenbach, R. E., & McCleary, K. W. (1983). Advertising and male nudity: An experimental investigation. *Journal of the Academy of Marketing Science, 11*(4), 444–454.

Richmond, D., & Hartman, T. P. (1982). Sex appeal in advertising. *Journal of Advertising Research, 22*(5), 53–61.

Robbins, S., & Paksoy, C. H. (1989). A comparative study of german and U.S. magazine advertisements: Has global standardization been achieved? *Proceedings of the Southern Marketing Association* (pp. 339–342). Charleston, SC: Southern Marketing Association.

Rosen, J. (1985, March 14). Marketing to men. *Advertising Age*, pp. 15–27.

Scheibe, C. (1979). Sex roles in TV commercials. *Journal of Advertising Research, 19*(1), 23–27.

Sexton, D. E., & Haberman, P. (1974). Women in magazine advertisements. *Journal of Advertising Research, 14*(4), 41–46.

Silverstein, A. J., & Silverstein, R. (1974). The portrayal of women in television advertising. *Federal Communication Bar Journal,* 27(1), 71–93.

Skelly, G. U., & Lundstrom, W. J. (1981). Male sex roles in magazine advertising, 1959–1979. *Journal of Communication, 31*(4), 52–57.

Springen, K. & Miller, A. (1990, April) when ads don't fit the 'image.' *Newsweek*, p. 48.

Steadman, M. (1969). How sexy illustrations affect brand recall. *Journal of Advertising Research, 9*(1), 15–19.

Thorelli, H. B. (1988). Expanding international consumer research: Why and how (Working Paper #5). Center for global business, school of business Indiana University, Bloomington, IN.

Venkatesan, M., & Losco, J. (1975). Women in magazine ads: 1959–71. *Journal of Advertising Research, 15*(5), 49–54.

Whipple, T. W., & Courtney, A. E. (1980). How to portray women in T.V. commercials. *Journal of Advertising Research, 20,*(2) 53–59.

Whipple, T. W., & Courtney, A. E. (1985). Female role portrayals in advertising and communication effectiveness: A review. *Journal of Advertising, 14*(3), 4–17.

Williams, J. E., & Best, D. (1982). *Measuring sex stereotypes: A thirty nation study.* Beverly Hills, CA: Sage.

Wolheter, M., & Lammers, H. B. (1980). An analysis of male roles in print advertisements over a 20-year span: 1958–1978. *Advances in Consumer Research, 8,* 760–761.

6 Advertising, Anthropology, and Cultural Brokers: A Research Report

Roberta J. Astroff
University of Pittsburgh

CULTURAL STUDIES AND MARKETING

Market research in international and multicultural contexts sets out to increase and organize our understanding of other cultures within the framework of marketing's needs and advertising strategies. This process of gathering information about a culture, ordering that information within domestic institutions, and then instituting policy decisions based on that information parallels the ethnographic process in anthropology. Ethnographers go "out in the field" and establish relationships with members of cultures under study ("informants"), attempting to gain knowledge about those cultures' belief systems, values, family structures, economic relationships, and social behaviors. The anthropologists return home (generally to universities) and create a text that both uses the material they have gathered in the field and conforms to some degree to the professional paradigms of anthropological research (Marcus & Fischer, 1986; Richer, 1988).

Substituting "market researchers" and "marketing" for "anthropologists" and "anthropology" gives a description of market research as well. I argue here, then, that the "texts" of market research can be analyzed and understood by analogy to ethnographies. They share the ethnographic text's nature as an "invention, not representation, of cultures" (Clifford & Marcus, 1986, p. 2), and the result of a process of cultural production. Market researchers "produce" a market by identifying, naming, and defining a culture as a market segment. Perceiving cultures and cultural forms as texts and as products are characteristic analytic approaches of the "network" of research approaches and questions known as cultural studies

(Johnson, 1986/1987). Cultural studies center on how social definitions are created, who creates them, and which ones become the dominant, accepted definitions, at least for a while, and how challenges to those definitions arise. Such an approach to the study of national identity, ethnicity, and/or race, a topic of obvious relevance to any study of international and intercultural advertising, must acknowledge that at least part of the construction of such identities takes place within the advertising and marketing industries. Thus the studies that form the basis for this report apply cultural studies concepts to marketing's study of culture. Specifically, the studies examine the narratives in the marketing trade press about U.S. Latino culture. The focus here is not the content of advertisements themselves—the images of minorities in commercials—so much as the *processes* by which advertising and marketing construct ethnic or racial categories.

ETHNOGRAPHIES AS TEXTS

For the last 15 or 20 years, ethnographers have been exploring the implications of those processes in anthropology, examining the relationship of the researchers to the informants, to the institutions that sponsor the research, and to the descriptions that they produce (see, e.g., Asad, 1973; Clifford, 1988; Clifford & Marcus, 1986). It is now commonplace in anthropology, for example, to recognize that an ethnography is a text. Seeing the ethnography as a text is meaningful on several levels. First, a supposedly objective, scientific, and therefore "true" report, when seen as a text produced by certain people under certain conditions, regains its authors, perspective, and narrative. That is, anthropologists have taken note of the structures within which the production of such texts occurs: the relationship of the West to the Rest when a western anthropologist seeks knowledge about other cultures, the cross-purposes of the ethnographer and the informants, the nature of the audience for that ethnography (Clifford, 1988; Pratt, 1986). Secondly, "textualizing" a culture means taking behaviors, traditions, and comments by members of that culture out of the context that produces them, restating them—and reinterpreting them—in the form of a narrative about that culture. As Clifford (1988) noted:

> Data constituted in discursive, dialogical conditions are appropriated only in textualized forms. Research events and encounters become field notes. Experiences become narratives, meaningful occurrences, or examples. . . . A textualized ritual or event is no longer closely linked to the production of that event by specific actors. Instead these texts become evidences of an englobing

context, a "cultural" reality. Moreover, as specific authors and actors are severed from their productions, a generalized "author" must be invented to account for the world or the context within which the texts are fictionally relocated. This generalized author goes under a variety of names: the native point of view, "the Trobrianders," "the Nuer," "the Dogon," as these and similar phrases appear in ethnographies.

By applying this literature to marketing, we can see the narratives that define, construct, and explain the "U.S. Latinos" as ethnographic texts. In these studies, the articles presenting the "new" Latino market to advertisers through the marketing and advertising trade press constitute the "ethnographic text." "U.S. Latinos" become what Clifford called the generalized author. The narratives present the nature and boundaries of this culture, their family structure, economic situation, and behavior, through the filter of marketing interests. Thus I have applied techniques of textual analysis, based on the critiques of ethnography, to articles in *Advertising Age*, *Broadcasting*, and *Television/Radio Age* from 1966 to 1986 promoting the U.S. Latino population as a market; and two major nonperiodical publications: Yankelovich, Skelly and White, Inc.'s *Spanish USA: A Study of the Hispanic Market in the United States* (1981) and Guernica and Kasperuk's textbook *Reaching the Hispanic Market Effectively* (1982). The Yankelovich et al. market survey study and the Guernica and Kasperuk textbook are considered to be landmark studies and are widely cited in the trade press.

This method of analysis uncovers several points of interest to both cultural studies researchers and advertising researchers. It reveals the socially constructed nature of our ethnic categories, particularly, in this case, that of "U.S. Latino." When such categories are shown to be social constructions, rather than "natural" differences, we can begin to ask questions about the interests and values that shaped the category. In addition, by showing the work involved in constructing such categories, this method points to the existence of other possible definitions and constructions.

CULTURAL STUDIES AND THE STUDY OF IDENTITY

Quite a few people in cultural studies have turned their attention in the past few years to the formation of cultural identities—particularly national and racial identities—seen within this research approach as "continually constituted and reconstructed categories" (Schlesinger, 1987). This social process of constructing categories of race and ethnicity, or of "racial formation" (Omi & Winant, 1986) has been defined as: "the process by which social, economic, and political forces determine the content and importance of racial categories and by which they are in turn shaped by racial meanings . . . [the process by which] racial categories are formed, transformed, destroyed, and re-formed" (p. 61).

The authors of that definition are interested in what they call the "racial state." They analyze the civil rights movement, or any movement that seeks to challenge dominant racial ideologies, as a "dual process of disorganization of the dominant ideology and of construction of an alternative, oppositional framework" (p. 127). That is, in many civil rights, nationalist, or ethnic pride movements, there is a process of self-definition, of rejecting an older definition and/or one imposed from outside the group. There is, in fact, a process of constructing the group through what has been called "constitutive rhetoric" (Charland, 1987). In contrast, this is a report on a series of studies that focus on racial and ethnic categories and discourses in the marketplace — generated largely, though not totally, outside of the group being defined — and have located, in contrast, an *incorporative* process in which the advertising and marketing industries redefine cultures in ways that make them marketable (i.e., rearticulate them in order to absorb, assimilate, or at least profit by them). Despite the difference in intent and the actors involved, this is also a process of racial formation — of determining the content and importance of racial and ethnic categories.

Conspicuously absent in this report, so far, is a definition of the key word *culture*. But rather than presenting some pseudo-authoritative definition of such a slippery concept (Williams, 1976), I focus on revealing the implicit and explicit definitions of culture *used* in market research. The situation I focused on here, the construction in the advertising trade press of a so-called "Latino market" and the "sale" of that market to advertisers as viable and profitable, is a remarkable concrete example of the remaking, or attempted remaking, of cultures into market segments.

SPANISH GOLD

These studies (Astroff, 1988/1989, 1989, 1991) are based on the analysis of more than 20 years of ad industry press articles promoting the U.S. Latinos as a profitable market. The definitional work found in the articles forms the heart of the analysis and inspired the comparison to ethnography (see Clifford & Marcus, 1986).

It is a truism in advertising that any population that is to be defined and treated as a market must be identifiable, accessible, measurable, and profitable. That is, they must be made knowable and there must be worthwhile, that is, economic, reasons to know them. Starting in 1966, articles began to appear regularly in the advertising trade press revealing the existence of a domestic market that was untargeted, ignored, neglected, and invisible (those are their terms). The problem, it was argued, was that industry and advertisers had the wrong image of these people, if they saw them at all. And so these articles, aimed at people who make advertising and marketing decisions, embodied a conscious attempt to create a knowable, marketable image of the U.S. Latino population. In their own words, they set out to transform this "invisible giant" into "Spanish Gold."

This is not, however, the story of the successful functioning of a natural free market that, except for artificial obstacles that can be overcome, provides equal access to naturally existing populations. Market recognition is not an automatic, natural, and impartial force. It is not free from, or apart from, these "continually constituted and reconstructed categories." Instead, the market is highly dependent on existing social relations and helps constitute them. Marketing publications provide us with a clear instance of racial formation as they attempt to create a definition of "Latino culture" out of a variety of cultures, classes, races, linguistic affiliations, and national origins. Significantly, it appears that the writers of these articles and their sources reinterpret longstanding, widely held stereotypes about Latinos in order to persuade advertisers to perceive Latinos as a valuable market. The main findings of these studies on the construction of "U.S. Latino" are detailed in the following sections.

Discovering a New World

The most common discourse is one of "discovery." The trade magazines consciously follow Columbus's path, discovering people who had been invisible to the center of knowledge production. Just as Columbus discovered a supposedly "new" world (whose value, according to Europeans, was its use to Europe), advertising industry writers and their sources represent U.S. Latinos as "new" – that is, a previously nontargetted, underused market.

These marketing texts used Latino identity, as a naturally existing category, to distinguish these people from other American consumers, underlining the need for the use of separate media and ad campaigns. That is, before any research was done, Latinos were separated out from the larger market on the basis of race and culture. Despite the difficulties in coming up with a single determining trait or set of traits that clearly delineated a single population, the industry discourse clearly established the existence of such a defineable, separable population.

In what seems to be a violation of the rules of a research-driven industry, the discourse of race and ethnicity I found in the segmentation of the market *first* defined certain minority groups as distinct segments based on existing cultural categories of race or ethnicity; that is, it is "common sense" to know that U.S. Latinos are different from the "general consumer" assumed to be White and English speaking. Researchers, writers, and agency folks then set out to determine the consumer characteristics of those segments. The researchers then discovered differences in consumer behavior that distinguish this group from the "general" (i.e., White, Anglo) market — and these differences are attributed to their "culture." However, at this point, of course, the research showed that not all Latinos are in the same socioeconomic class, the same gender, the same generation, or, by the way, the same culture, and in fact the researchers have to segment the market segment itself according to the same rules that are applied to White English-speaking markets. But these later discoveries did not in any way challenge the perception in the trade press of the market segment as a "natural" category.

Perhaps the most telling illustration of this pattern in advertising texts is the Yankelovich et al. (1981) report. The entire Yankelovich et al. study, intended to be a study of the "true value" of the Latino population as a market, is organized around *country of origin* rather than socioeconomic demographics. Out of 28 tables on U.S. Latino demographics and media use, all but two use national origin, not socioeconomic status or VALS, as category headings. Only in one table — "Hours Spent with the Three Media" (p. 18) — is the same information organized comparatively: one table based on country of origin ("Hispanics by National Groups"), the other on family income ("Hispanics by Income Group"). No other market study examining luxury product ownership, new product openness (p. 13) or "life-styles," would *not* organize such data by socioeconomic statistics, education, gender, and so on. The unstated but clear assumption is that the racial category is the dominant definition of these people — over and above class, education, income, gender, and so on; so much so, that those who do not fit into the dominant cultural categorization disappear. That is, in this set of huge agglomerated racial categories, in which Latinos are compared to "Caucasians" and Blacks, Black Latinos literally do not exist.

Defining the Culture

What was needed at this point in the narrative was a definition of this defining Latino culture. A category of U.S. Latino was constructed out of the Chicanos, Puerto Ricans, Cuban Americans, and "others" that attempted to conflate linguistic, racial, ethnic, class, and regional differences into the one broad category for marketing purposes. It is here, perhaps, that definitional work is most clearly seen, in part because there were conflicting goals, and also because most of their definitions did not work. The Spanish-language television network promoted their role in "unifying Spanish U.S.A.," whereas the specialty ad shops fought to keep their regionally divided turf (Cubans in Florida; Mexican Americans in the West) clearly identified. Their difficulties in defining the group are explicitly stated ("First thing you'll run into is a definitional problem, namely, what is a Hispanic?" [Honomichl, 1982, p. 22]). They first tried to define "Latino" by language, but discovered that there is a bilingual, and sometimes only English-speaking, Latino population. They then tried race (Hispanic vs. Caucasian), conflated with country of origin to talk about what were actually class differences (thus stating that Cubans are "simply white, middle-class people who happen to speak Spanish" [quoted in Sugg, 1982, p. 40]). Because none of these categories is dependable in the analysis of the multilingual, multiracial, multinational Latino communities, the trade press fell back once again on a nebulous "Latino culture."

But this Latino culture was defined largely through the use of traditional stereotypes that were presented as explanations of both Latino consumer behavior and the successes and failures of marketing firms. We are told in these articles (published between 1966 and 1986), for example, that Latinos have rhythm, that "when a Latin hears music, he has to dance to it, he can't just sit and listen. That's why Spanish television, rather than records, is his favorite medium for music" (Rustin, 1972, p. 44); that "for the average Spanish-speaking housewife, shopping is an emotional experience. She is a passionate shopper" in supermarkets (quoted in Weiner, 1978, p. 12); that Latino men buy deodorants and cologne because they all come from the tropics, and "when you come from the tropics, you are more conscious of being offensive" (quoted in Weiner, 1978, p.); and that Latinos are unreliable in new product tests because "it might just be their normal emotional nature showing through" (quoted in Honomichl, 1982, p. 22).

Thus this transformation did not erase stereotypes but rather reapplied them; as Latino ethnic identity was restructured as consumer behavior, elements of the stereotypes were assigned new values. Cultural characteristics that had earlier been seen by the dominant culture as harmful to Latinos — the larger average family and a lower rate of savings, for example — are reinterpreted to construct the culture as producing ideal consumers. Advertisers are repeatedly advised to use radio and television to reach Latinos because "traditionally Spanish-culture [sic] people are not readers. They are an aural and visual people" (Rustin, 1972, p. 21; "Spanish-speaking," 1973). One early article provided research to support this claim, referring to a survey done in San Antonio (Rustin, 1972). That survey showed that on a basis of self-report, Mexican-Americans in San Antonio chose Spanish-language radio over newspapers. The results are attributed to "Spanish culture": not to English-only education, low educational levels, or the fact that there was no Spanish-language daily newspaper in Texas.

The confusions and contradictions are obvious. Any Latin "tradition" of not reading is highly questionable in light of varying rates of newsprint use in different Latin countries and across different socioeconomic classes, and reading is of course a visual process. Nor is it clear why any Latino "compulsion" to dance would lead to a preference for television. Nevertheless, in the analysis of discourses, such confusions and contradictions are indications of the discursive work going on — the attempts to categorize, to make things fit — especially because such contradictions and confusions do not undermine the potency of the discourse for its users. There is to this day in the advertising trade press a persistent recourse to some overarching "Spanish" culture, to which Mexican-Americans, Cuban-Americans, Colombians, Puerto Ricans, and so on, all are said to belong, and which is used to explain media and consumer preferences. To sum up, researchers construct these categories and reify them: that is, make them discrete and static, natural rather than social.

The Production of the Text

The institutions most involved in the processes being analyzed in these studies — advertising and U.S. Spanish-language television, particularly Univision — are overwhelmingly owned and operated by people who are *not* U.S. Latinos. The *only* site of significant participation by U.S. Latinos in this process is as "Latino ad specialists." Latinos are present in the text as active participants only through their authority as "experts" stemming from a double identity as "Latino" in ethnic origins and as advertising cogniscenti. Quoted constantly throughout these trade press articles, Latino ad experts (who are both Latino and presenting themselves as experts in advertising to Latinos) are the only sources of supposed expertise about what the press described as Latino culture.

The comparison of ethnography (or anthropology's cultural study) and marketing research (capital's cultural study, as Johnson [1986/1987] put it) provides us with an anthropological concept that might be useful in illuminating the role played by Latino ad specialists: that of the "cultural broker" or native informant. Of particular use here is some recent work in critical anthropology that identifies the cultural process, and the labor process, that can be seen as transforming cultural identity into a market category, from use value to exchange value (Richer, 1988).

In both ethnography and marketing, researchers attempt to gain information about the culture under study through the services of cultural brokers or native informants.[1] The enthography can thus be considered a

---

[1]The term *native informant* refers to the person with whom the anthropologist in the field establishes a relationship, exchanging goods, status, friendship, and/or money in exchange for information about the informant's way of life. "Cultural brokers," in contrast, appear to mediate between their people and institutions. See Paine (1971), Briggs (1971), Gentemann and Whitehead (1983), and Seymour-Smith (1986).

collective work in that it is produced between two cultures – through joint efforts on the part of the native informant, the anthropologist, and anthropology itself. The anthropological term *cultural broker* refers to people who are links between two cultures and their institutions, in this case, "Latino" culture and marketing. This linking function is carried out by bicultural actors – someone able to straddle both cultures, serving as a communicator between them, processing, shaping, and selecting the information that travels between them. Brokers are thus involved in what has been called "the impression-management of ethnicity" (Paine, 1971).

It is their fluency in both cultures that makes all cultural brokers, and in our case, Latino advertising specialists, valuable. The brokers construct a version of their culture in partnership with the marketing industry, creating a "Latino culture" mediated by the paradigms, theories, needs, and value systems of which advertising as a system is composed.

The final form of the culture that has been so produced is that of a commodity for sale on the advertising market. It is also a commodity in that the brokers, in exchange for their interpretations and constructions, obtain status as specialists in Latino advertising – and all but one Latino quoted on Latino culture in these articles runs a specialty ad shop. It is therefore, obviously, to their economic advantage to construct a marketable image of Latinos and to maintain a limited, controllable degree of difference. That is, Latinos must be presented as a profitable market for the brokers to have an economically viable position in the industry. However, Latinos must also be defined as different and distinct from a larger market, or the brokers themselves have no value as informants and cultural guides.

CONCLUSION

This chapter, then, is leading to a critique of market segmentation, by which I do *not* mean to imply that I think only mass advertising is somehow "correct," but that I am looking at particular instances of how market segments are defined – which, in the case of minority segments, appears to be tautologically. The next step in the larger series of research projects is to examine how social scientific research, and how political movements or identities emerging from Latino communities, define U.S. Latino.

An additional result of this study has been and will be, in later sections of the larger study, a re-evaluation of the medium itself. Advertising researchers appear to be uneasy about the trade press, at times dismissing it and at times citing articles from it (see, e.g., Pitts, [1986]). The business and trade press, generally neglected in media research, can easily be seen as a site in which industry discourses (in this case about cultural identity) are played out and made public. The study of the nature of representations created for specialized — and decision-making — audiences has been neglected in favor of texts produced for mass audiences. There is no reason that the theories, methods, and techniques developed for the analysis of mass media cannot be used to study the construction of images within an industry's press. As a matter of fact, a case can be made that the categories defined in the advertising trade press (directed at advertisers, advertising producers, advertising time and space buyers and sellers), though of course mediated by existing prejudices and business ideologies, will have a relatively strong and direct impact on the media, a principle site of social meaning making. The texts in questions here, advertising trade magazine articles promoting Latinos as a viable television market, set about very consciously to construct new market segments.

Note that, in the context of these studies, the fact that the brokers' constructions of Latino culture are self-serving, or that the trade press is "unscientific," does not erase those images or the discourses thus produced. Nor is this an argument that Latino ad executives are selling out their culture. Nor am I saying there are no differences in our multicultural society. Instead, I am interested in analyzing how and where and by whom cultural identities are produced. The traditional focus in such research has been the individual and the family, or the process of "us-formation" — how the subculture defines itself and its borders, or "they-formation" — the construction of minority groups' identities from outside, from the dominant culture and its institutions. Recent research on identity, though, indicates that this we-they distinction is inadequate and that the process of identity formation draws on multiple sources. This series of studies contributes to the newer literature on an institutional level by showing how institutions, too, draw on multiple sources, "inside" and "outside" population groups, in their constructions of group identities.

Studying market research or trade press articles as a form of ethnography presents a number of issues and questions. Although the labor process of ethnography, as detailed by Richer (1988), and that of marketing appear to be parallel, some anthropologists would no doubt object to the comparison, clinging to social science's claim to objective, neutral knowledge construction. Richer noted, however, that the academic researcher profits, at least in terms of cultural capital, from the production of the ethnographic text, in the form of prestige, promotion, tenure, and, of course, royalties. Similarly, market researchers seek to produce proprietary information that can be sold to marketers, and the goal, of course, is profit for the researchers, writers, publications, marketers, and advertisers. What happens, though, if we compare marketing's writers and researchers to ethnographers?

First, these marketing writers and researchers might have to acknowledge that their "facts" about other cultures have been shaped by the goals, tools, interests, and social location of the researchers and their institutions. That is, marketing's needs, interests, and definitions shape what they "discover." Critical cultural studies state that this is true of all knowledge production. Its implications, though, may vary depending on the use to which that knowledge is put. Critical ethnographers are struggling with ways to let others speak in the text, to diminish their own authority. Marketers, however, stand in a somewhat different position, one that requires further study. The move that has taken place in the trade press' articles is one that now calls for "scientific research" to replace the narratives of native informants. This assumes, however, that "scientific" research is free from its social structures, a now widely contested notion.

Cultural studies sees cultures as processes of constant negotiation and interpretation rather than as static units whose boundaries are easily identified. This notion, which is extremely important in cultural studies and anthropology, may not be of equal importance to marketing as currently structured. That is, those who run promotional campaigns want concrete facts, and may not want to know that concrete facts about cultural formations are in fact snapshots that freeze a moment of continual change. That is, like the ratings industry, advertising relies on a consensual acceptance of such research (Meehan, 1984), and what is important is the possession of such facts rather than their "truth."

REFERENCES

Asad, T. (Ed.). (1973). *Anthropology and the colonial encounter*. London: Ithaca Press.

Astroff, R. J. (1988/1989). Spanish Gold: Stereotypes, ideology, and the construction of a U.S. Latino market. *Howard Journal of Communication, 1*(4), 155-173.

Astroff, R. J. (1989). *Commodifying cultures: Latino ad specialists as cultural brokers*. Paper presented at the 7th International Conference on Culture and Communication, Temple University, Philadelphia.

Astroff, R. J. (1991) *Capital's cultural study*. Unpublished manuscript.

Briggs, J. (1971). Strategies of perception: The management of ethnic identity. In R. Paine (Ed.), *Patrons and brokers in the East Arctic* (pp. 53-73; Newfoundland Social and Economic Papers No. 2). Newfoundland: Institute of Social and Economic Research, Memorial University of Newfoundland.

Charland, M. (1987). Constitutive rhetoric: The case of the *peuple québécois. Quarterly Journal of Speech, 73*(2), 133-150.

Clifford, J. (1988). On ethnographic authority. *The Predicament of culture: Twentieth century ethnography, literature, and art* (pp. 21-54). Cambridge, MA: Harvard University Press.

Clifford, J., & Marcus, G. E. (Eds.). (1986). *Writing culture: The poetics and politics of ethnography*. Berkeley: University of California Press.

Gentemann, K. M., & Whitehead, T. L. (1983). The cultural broker concept in bicultural education. *Journal of Negro Education 52*(2), 118–129.

Guernica, A., & Kasperuk, I. (1982). *Reaching the Hispanic market effectively*. New York: McGraw-Hill.

Johnson, R. (1986–1987). What is cultural studies anyway? *Social Text, 16*, 38–80.

Honomichl, J. (1982, January 18). How to research U.S. Hispanic market. *Advertising Age*, p. 22.

Marcus, G. E., & Fischer, M. M. J. (1986). *Anthropology as cultural critique: An experimental moment in the human sciences*. Chicago: University of Chicago Press.

Meehan. E. (1984). Ratings and the institutional approach: A third answer to the commodity question. *Critical Studies in Mass Communication, 1*(2), 216–225.

Omi, M., & Winant, H. (1986). *Racial formation in the United States*. New York: Routledge & Kegan Paul.

Paine, R. (Ed.). (1971). *Patrons and brokers in the East Arctic* (Newfoundland Social and Economic Papers No. 2). Newfoundland: Institute of Social and Economic Research, Memorial University of Newfoundland.

Pitts, R. (Ed.). (1986). Towards an understanding of the Hispanic market [Special issue]. *Psychology and Marketing, 3*(4).

Pratt, M. L. (1986). Fieldwork in common places. In J. Clifford & G. E. Marcus, (Eds.). *Writing culture* (pp. 27–50). Berkeley: University of California Press.

Richer, S. (1988). Fieldwork and the commodification of culture: Why the natives are restless. *Canadian Review of Sociology and Anthropology, 25*(3), 406–420.

Rustin, D. (1972, October 2). The Spanish market. *Television/Radio Age*, p. 20.

Schlesinger, P. (1987). On national identity: Some conceptions and misconceptions criticized. *Social Science Information, 26*(2), 219–264.

Seymour-Smith, C. (1986). *Dictionary of Anthropology*. Boston: G. K. Hall & Co.

Spanish-speaking are $20 billion U.S. Market. (1973, November 21). *Advertising Age*, p. 56.

Sugg, J. (1982, February 15). Miami's Latin market spans two continents. *Advertising Age*, pp. M40–M41.

Weiner, R. (1978, October 23). Hispanic population's growth has big marketing implications. *Television/Radio Age*, pp. A3–A4, A8, A10–A13, A16.

Williams, R. (1976). *Keywords: A vocabulary of culture and society*. New York: Oxford University Press.

Yankelovitch, Skelly and White, Inc. (1981). *Spanish USA: A study of the Hispanic market in the United States*. Hartford, CT: Author.

III CROSS-CULTURAL ISSUES

7 National Boundaries in Magazine Advertising: Perspectives on Verbal and Nonverbal Communication

Fairfid M. Caudle
The College of Staten Island, City University of New York

International magazine advertising must overcome many obstacles to convey information across the boundaries posed by diverse languages and social patterns. This chapter explores both the nature of such obstacles as well as some of the strategies that have been devised to overcome them. It presents a qualitative and selective analysis of modes of communication utilized when brands originating in one country or nationality are advertised in publications, of other countries, that are designed for relatively affluent and literate markets. In the discussion that follows, a number of issues will be identified that arise when advertising across national borders. These include issues related to the use of language as well as to several nonverbal, visual modes of communication such as those provided by the depiction of national and cultural symbols and works of art. The goal of this chapter is to highlight aspects of communication that should be beneficial to consider when designing advertisements referring to or crossing national boundaries.

The Globalization Debate

Cultural characteristics and their role in shaping marketing strategy and advertising content have been the subject of considerable debate and research, and the following article citations represent only a small sampling of statements on this issue. One focus of this discussion was stated by Winram (1984) who, noting convergences in demography, culture, and media distribution, argued that common needs for products rather than differing national characteristics should carry greater weight. The existence of somewhat similar segments across countries has been proposed in support of strategies that are flexible and/or suggest partial standardization of approaches (Douglas & Dubois, 1977; Farley, 1986; Onkvisit & Shaw, 1987, Quelch & Hoff, 1986), and considerable standardization has been reported in actual practice (Ryans & Ratz, 1987).

In contrast, it has been argued that, although such segments may be useful in market planning, they are not necessarily comparable in terms of symbolic cultural cues thought to be critical to advertising effectiveness (Harris, 1984). Arguments for specific attention to cultural differences have been proposed (e.g., Hornik & Rubinow, 1981) and suggestions have been advanced as to methodology with which to approach such issues (e.g., Plummer, 1986).

Finally, numerous studies have made cross-cultural comparisons concerning consumer characteristics (e.g., Elbashier & Nicholls, 1983; Green & Langeard, 1975) and advertising content (e.g., Hornik, 1980; Johnstone, Kaynak, & Sparkman, 1987; Kaynak & Mitchell, 1981; Mueller, 1987). Such studies have, in general, served to highlight cultural differences.

What is Culture?

Because the globalization debate has concerned the importance of culture in marketing and advertising, it is appropriate to define *culture*. However, this is no easy matter. In this regard, several authors have cited Kroeber and Kluckoln (1952), who identified 164 definitions of culture and who added a 165th because none of the definitions were satisfactory (Douglas & Dubois, 1977; Elbashier & Nicholls, 1983).

A broad definition of culture was noted by Levine (1973), who viewed culture as:

> An organized body of rules concerning the ways in which individuals in a population should communicate with one another, think about themselves and their environments, and behave toward one another and toward objects in their environments. The rules are not universally or constantly obeyed, but they are recognized by all and they ordinarily operate to limit the range of variation in patterns of communication, belief, value, and social behavior in that population. (p. 4)

In a similar vein, von Raffler-Engel (1988) noted that:

> Culture is not as much what people do and how they express themselves, as their knowledge of the potential behaviors and cognitive maps of their in-group. It is the familiarity with certain forms of behavior and ways of thinking that makes people feel that they belong to the same culture. (p. 98)

With regard to the cultural setting of market behavior, Douglas and Dubois (1977) cited several broad and overlapping aspects: A common set of values, forms of social organization that influence roles and status positions as well as the conventions, rituals, and practices that guide behavior, and a communication system that includes not only language but nonverbal components as well.

Common to these delineations of culture are a shared communication system and common ways of thinking and behaving. As Elbashier and Nicholls (1983) noted: "Culture is *shared* by a group of people and thereby defines the boundaries of that group" (p. 71). Such boundaries, noted by Hornik (1980) and others, are the focus of this chapter. The discussion that follows considers how advertisements might function either to signify existing boundaries or to overcome them and to communicate across them, when a brand is advertised beyond the country in which it originated.

VERBAL COMMUNICATION ACROSS NATIONAL BOUNDARIES

The existence of a common language, one could argue, contributes heavily to the sense of nationality. It is certainly the case that a language can create a boundary separating those who are conversant in it from those who are not. In addition, language in printed form requires literacy and verbal fluency in order to be comprehended. Even when a language is shared, it is nevertheless the case that regional dialects, accents, idiomatic expressions, and slang terms can function both to limit communication and interaction and to delineate cultural subgroups. Suffice it to say that linguistic boundaries pose formidable obstacles when products originating in one nationality are advertised in publications of other countries, and it is instructive to consider examples of advertisements that have confronted this barrier.

Language in International Magazine Advertising

In publications having content predominantly in a language that differs from that of the nationality where the brands they advertise originated, several communicative strategies can be identified that have utilized language in contrasting ways. As the following examples illustrate, language serves not only its expected function as information is communicated through written advertising copy; language is also employed in a symbolic manner to identify a brand's country of origin.

Retention of Different Language in Copy.   One approach has been to ignore the language barrier entirely. For example, an advertisement for HongkongBank in a French magazine provided a discussion of the advantages of international electronic banking completely in English. However, it is of interest to note that this verbal copy occupied only about 20% of a two-page advertisement. The remaining area was filled with a pictorial montage combining images of an executive, a container ship, and computer screens displaying a logo and a menu on trade financing. Thus, the verbal copy was accompanied by pictorial information concerning the ease of communication and the scope of available transactions. In this example, the considerable verbal component of the advertisement was still given far less prominence than the visual material.

Parallel Texts.   Provision of parallel texts in the languages of both the country where the product originated and the country in which it is advertised provide another approach. For example, an advertisement for "*PAKETA*, The Original Russian Watch," that appeared in an American magazine, consisted of two segments. The first segment confronts the reader with text wholly in Russian. The text appears alongside a clenched fist and bare wrist on a red background, reminiscent of a wartime poster from an earlier era. The second segment, on a separate page, provides the fully translated text. In this segment, the wrist, formerly bare, now wears the wristwatch, whereas the clenched fist has been transformed into a victory sign. Considering the advertisement as a whole, the red background, the images of the hand, and the unexpected encounter with copy in Russian serve both to involve the reader and to evoke associations of the originating country. One might speculate that the initial encounter with printed Russian, arguably an unusual event in an American magazine, might prompt the reader to examine more closely the subsequent copy in English. In this instance the Russian copy, rather than serving a purely linguistic purpose, functions both to emphasize a national boundary and to reinforce the idea that the brand is imported.

Original Language Captions for Pictorial Advertisements.   In contrast with advertisements that provide extensive copy in the original language are those that, although the original language is retained in them, are predominantly pictorial and have minimal copy. For example, an advertisement for Marc O'Polo clothing appeared in a German magazine. Beneath a black and white photograph of a man and woman walking on a beach, the advertisement contained a single line of copy in English, "Deauville in the month of April," and, in smaller print, the phrase, "Only nature's materials." The advertisement conveys associations of casual comfort and romance through its visual content. In contrast with the HongkongBank example noted earlier, which dealt with abstract and technical information, the clothing advertisement did not require extensive verbal copy to portray essential characteristics of the brand.

It is of interest that the impact of the advertisements in the preceding examples has been achieved largely through visual means rather than through the verbal copy included. However, even in those instances in which the content of an advertisement is largely visual, it is nevertheless of interest to consider the functions that may be served by language, when brands originating in one nationality are advertised in publications of other countries.

Common Pictorial Content with Copy Variations. When a brand is advertised in a number of languages, one obvious solution is to present a predominantly nonverbal, pictorial advertisement with minimal copy that can be varied for each country. This approach has been utilized to advertise Samsara perfume and cosmetics in magazines in France, Germany, and the United States, among other countries. The verbal copy of the Samsara advertisement, at most a few words, is in the language of the magazine in which the advertisement appears. In general, this copy might be translated roughly as presenting the product as the embodiment or center of femininity.

The impact of the Samsara advertisement flows less from its minimal copy than from a number of nonverbal characteristics. Warm red tones fill nearly every surface, including those of the product, as well as the model's clothing, jewelry, and lipstick. This red color provides an expansion of the color of the cosmetic containers and thus constitutes a memory prompt. The draped folds of the model's dress, echoed in the strands of her necklace, communicate softness, richness, and opulence. The perfume is held in a central position in front of the woman's torso, as if it is of great value. The product is nestled in one palm and shielded by the other in a pose of nurturing protectiveness. The bright gold cap of the container might suggest to some a similarity to a candle flame that is being sheltered by the hand above it. Thus, the position in which the product is held and the pose of the model's hands serve to reinforce the verbal copy suggesting that the product is the embodiment of femininity.

Incorporation of Foreign Characters and Phrases

Written Characters as National Symbols. Written characters that do not serve a purely linguistic function in the context of an advertisement may nevertheless be utilized as national symbols. The reader who does not understand the specific linguistic meaning of such a symbol may nevertheless recognize its country of origin. An advertisement for Sumotomo Bank utilized such a symbol to provide the focal point of an advertisement. An oversized Japanese character for "Tomo," the second half of the bank's name, dominated a full-page advertisement. The brief copy in English translated this character as "friendship" and thus served both to identify the national origin of the company and to provide a focus for the communication of positive attributes about it.

Linguistic Fragments. It is sometimes the case that "catch words," borrowed from other languages, supplement the predominant language of the advertisement. For example, an Italian advertisement for easy-care lacey feminine white lingerie borrowed the English phrase "No problem," and a German advertisement for Völkswagen displayed the automobile against a background of blue jeans and included the headline "Forever young," followed by German copy. Similarly, the Italian drink Campari was advertised in a German magazine with German copy supplemented with English phrases such as "Campari on the rocks." In these examples, the information in the advertisements was largely visual. When languages other than that of the magazine were used, they appeared in brief phrases that were in different physical locations within the advertisement rather than being continuous with whatever copy the advertisement contained. Such fragments may enable a readership distributed among a number of languages to find some verbal point of context and recognition, even if it is only a phrase.

Linguistic Mosaics. It is also of interest to note that foreign words and phrases may be incorporated into the syntactic structure of verbal copy. A series of advertisements for Colt automobiles (built by the Japanese firm of Mitsubishi Motors Corporation and sold by the American company, Chrysler-Plymouth and Dodge) each contained a headline that substituted Japanese characters for English words. Among the captions were: "Introducing a giant _____ forward in wagon value;" "How to find the best wagon without spinning your _____ ; "Holy _____ . A free automatic transmission and $500 cash back!;" and "Colt is now a horse of a different _____ ," among others. Japanese characters replaced the English words in the American idiomatic expressions "giant leap forward," "spinning your wheels," "holy cow," and "horse of a different color."

In each of these Colt advertisements, the copy was in English, but the brand name, Colt, was also rendered in Japanese (by characters that might be translated as "excellent"), together with the exhortation that "It's all the Japanese you need to know." In these examples, the Japanese characters serve several functions. They stand out from the copy, in the sense of figure against background, and provide an attentional mechanism. And they encourage the reader to respond actively to the copy by mentally filling in the word, which in each instance is part of an idiomatic expression in American English. This usage of American idiomatic expressions supports the contention of Onkvisit and Shaw (1987) to the effect that Japanese firms design advertisements tailored to the U.S. market rather than repeating campaigns from non-U.S. markets. Finally, the Japanese characters identify the national origin of the brand and thus function as visual symbols of another nationality rather than serving a true linguistic function. Although these examples incorporate Japanese characters into American advertisements, it is of interest to note that the inclusion of American and European words into Japanese copy is also popular (Mueller, 1987).

Another example may be found in advertisements for a brand of vodka originating in the United States, GEORGI, in which the letter R has been reversed so that it becomes Я, a letter in the Cyrillic alphabet. This alteration of a single character results in GEOЯGI. The contrast between the shapes of foreign letters or characters and those of the country in which the advertisement appears both attracts the reader's eye and may evoke associations of that nationality. Because many persons already associate vodka with Russia, imparting this association to a domestic brand may increase the brand's attractiveness to consumers. Thus, whereas the Sumotomo example illustrated how foreign characters may serve to identify the national origin of a company or brand, the example of GEOЯGI illustrates how characters from foreign alphabets can impart qualities of "foreign-ness" to domestic brands.

The preceding examples suggest that, when advertisements cross national boundaries, the customary use of language to communicate information in verbal copy may at times give way to communication that is predominantly nonverbal and that instead utilizes language in novel linguistic formats. However, although advertising copy may be augmented with nonverbal forms of communication, the preservation of a brand name poses additional problems when advertisements communicate beyond the nationality where the brand originated.

Language and Brand Name Issues

Thus far, in considering verbal communication across national boundaries, examples have been noted to illustrate a variety of formats for the presentation of verbal *copy* in advertisements for brands that originate in one nationality but are advertised in others.

In considering approaches to language in advertisements that cross national boundaries, a number of issues arise in relation to *brand names*, with regard both to meaning and to linguistic characteristics.

The Problem of Meaning. Several characteristics of brand names have been identified by vanden Bergh, Adler, and Oliver (1987). In their analysis, these authors found the most frequently used linguistic device to be "semantic appositeness," which was defined as a fit of name with object. An example of semantic appositeness can be seen in the brand Bufferin, formed through combining the word "aspirin" with the word "buffer," which might be defined as "a protector." Thus, the brand Bufferin communicates the idea of "aspirin that protects."

Robertson (1989) suggested a number of characteristics of desirable brand names, including attributes such as simplicity, distinctiveness, meaningfulness, mental association with the product class either through meaning or sound, eliciting a mental image, emotion, and the use of linguistic characteristics such as repetitive sounds.

Both vanden Bergh et al. (1987) and Robertson (1989) noted the value of incorporating into a brand name the attribute of *meaning appropriate to the brand*, a characteristic that poses special problems when brand names cross national boundaries. With regard to meaningful versus nonword brand names, vanden Bergh et al. (1987) cited Boyd (1985), who suggested that multinational marketers may employ nonsense combinations of letters and numbers in brand names in order to minimize cross-cultural problems. And Robertson (1989) noted that, when nonwords are employed as brand names, attention should be given to national linguistic rules in developing international names.

Problems of brand name are compounded when the original brand is composed of terms having concrete meanings (e.g., the brands Pour Homme and Far West). The potential advantages of a concrete name, with its possibilities for portrayal in advertising imagery, must be weighed against the ready identifiability that may result when a brand name moves unchanged from one language to another.

And, finally, consider the problems that result when a brand that has acquired worldwide recognition is introduced into a new market. Among the notable successes has been the introduction of Coca-Cola into mainland China. A quasi-phonetic rendering of the brand name in Chinese resulted in "Ke Kou Ke Le," for which the Chinese characters stood for "can-mouth-can-happiness." Thus, a literal translation of Coca-Cola in Chinese might be rendered as "can drink, can be happy." However, one could argue that the achievement of such a serendipitous combination of positive meaning with phonetic similarity to the original brand name occurs much more rarely than those who create advertisements would prefer. One example of the perils of retaining a brand name was noted by Kaynak and Mitchell (1981), who, citing Martyn (1964), referred to the problems that ensued when Colgate-Palmolive introduced Cue toothpaste into French-speaking countries without knowing that "cue" was considered a pornographic word in the French language.

Linguistic Characteristics of Abstract Brand Names.   Issues that arise when concrete versus abstract brand names are considered for international brand names are illustrated by the brand Samsara, noted earlier. Samsara is an abstract name that incorporates a number of positive linguistic characteristics indicated by vanden Bergh et al. (1987), such as repetitive consonants. In addition, it is readily pronounceable and it does not need to be translated. One might go further and note that, because it ends in the vowel *a*, it might be viewed as a feminine name, at least in the languages that include both feminine and masculine word endings. Furthermore, the soft vowel ending of Samsara might suggest qualities reminiscent of femininity (in contrast with the hard consonant ending of the brand Bik, one of the examples noted by vanden Bergh et al., 1987). For all of these reasons, one might predict that the brand Samsara can readily move beyond national and linguistic barriers.

Contrasting Alphabets and Characters.   Several brand names noted earlier illustrate issues that arise when brand names are written in languages that utilize different alphabets or written characters. One approach is the provision of parallel versions of a brand name, as in the brand Colt and its Japanese character version, which, rather than having the same meaning as the American word colt, might be translated as "excellent" in Japanese.

However, although Japanese characters are easily distinguished from the letters and words of the Western alphabet, this is not the case for some other foreign alphabets, such as the Cyrillic alphabet. For example, the Russian brand of watch, Paketa, is composed of characters that superficially resemble those in the familiar Western alphabet but that in fact are letters from the Cyrillic alphabet. To one familiar with this alphabet the brand is pronounced "Raketa," a point not noted in the advertisement. Equivalent versions of written and vocal pronunciations of brands must be determined when campaigns are not limited to magazines but also include radio and/or television commercials.

Pronounceability.   Although the preceding example is one in which correct pronunciation of the brand name was not emphasized, a series of advertisements for Wyborowa, a Polish brand of vodka, has made the difficulty of pronunciation into a humorous focal point. Advertisements in the United States for this brand have had as their theme the difficulties encountered in attempting to pronounce the brand name. Each advertisement in the series provides a phonetic pronunciation guide ("vee-ba-rova") and expands on the theme, "If you can't say it, you can't have it," with allusions to the varied ways in which consumers meet this pronunciation challenge. One example portrays an elegantly dressed woman with a bored expression who "couldn't say it if her trust fund depended on it" whereas, in another, a smugly smiling man "thinks he's saying it right." A burly man, dressed as a special officer, whose crossed arms and taciturn, unsmiling expression communicate stubborn resistance, is portrayed as someone who "can say it, but won't."

In addition to the focus on brand name and the difficulty of its foreign pronunciation, the Wyborowa advertisements provide further comparisons with examples noted earlier. In contrast with Samsara advertisements, which utilize in different countries the same image with roughly equivalent, translated, and very brief copy, the Wyborowa advertisements vary the visual content and the equally brief copy in order to direct the advertisements to an American audience through pointed references to recognizable stereotypes.

When advertisements cross linguistic boundaries, the examples cited here are among many that suggest that communication through words largely gives way to nonverbal communication, unless the copy is translated or rewritten in the language of the country where the advertisement appears. When verbal copy is employed, it is often very brief and may incorporate novel linguistic formats. The difficulties related to brand names, noted earlier, underscore the importance of creating names that can move freely across linguistic boundaries.

Finally, words or characters from a foreign language, in addition to the linguistic communication of meaning, can serve as symbols of another culture. The role of national and cultural symbols in advertising are considered in the following section, within the context of visual, nonverbal modes of communication across national boundaries.

NONVERBAL COMMUNICATION ACROSS NATIONAL BOUNDARIES

In view of the communicative barriers posed by the use of written language in advertisements that cross national boundaries, it is not surprising that nonverbal communication assumes greater importance. One question of interest, then, concerns the forms that such nonverbal communication may take. Recall that the advertisement for Samsara, although it presented very brief copy in various languages, nonetheless relied primarily on nonverbal, visual communication to portray an image of elegant femininity appropriate to an affluent market segment that is found in a number of nationalities, rather than in one particular country. The national origin of this brand was in no way emphasized in the advertisement, which, one could argue, is directed toward what Onkvisit and Shaw (1987) described as "horizontally homogenous" market segments in which particular market segments of one country are similar to equivalent segments in another country. In contrast, consider now how some advertisements that cross national boundaries do so by presenting brands in ways that emphasize the context of the nationality or culture in which the brand originated.

Defining Boundaries Through National and Cultural Symbols

How is national identity communicated in advertising? One visual means of establishing the origin of a product is to incorporate a national or cultural symbol or artifact into the advertisement. In general, such symbols need to satisfy the criteria of identifiability, distinctiveness, and conciseness. Note that, when national or cultural boundaries are communicated through such symbols, similar strategies may be employed in advertisements with broadly differing objectives. National and cultural symbols appear in advertisements for travel to foreign countries, and, as noted earlier, in advertisements for domestic products for which an aura of foreign-ness is desired. In addition, where there are competing brands from different nationalities within a broad product category, national symbols are used to identify the country of origin and to impart its distinctive attributes to the brand. The following examples illustrate a few of the diverse forms that such national and cultural symbols assume.

Monuments and Landmarks. A number of specific monuments, buildings, or architectural styles have become virtually synonomous with particular nationalities, regions, or cities and appear in advertisements as national and cultural symbols. Among the examples that come to mind are the Eiffel Tower of Paris, India's Taj Mahal, the Pyramids of Egypt, Moscow's St. Basil's Cathedral, Sydney's Opera House, London's Big Ben and Tower Bridge, Pisa's Leaning Tower, and New York City's Empire State Building and Chrysler Building. These and numerous other buildings and monuments adorn print advertisements that range from full-color two-page magazine advertisements to the tiniest notices found in the crowded pages of a newspaper's travel section. Such symbols may be used to associate a particular nationality with a brand, or, when combined into a collage, they may collectively indicate a brand's broad appeal. In one example, Johnny Walker Red scotch utilized such a collage to provide a concrete illustration of its assertion that "All over the world people have one thing in common. They start the evening with Red." The collage included a number of silhouettes against the red sky of sunset (an additional association with the brand name), including the Eiffel Tower, Big Ben, and the Empire State Building, among others.

One question of interest concerns why these monuments and landmark symbols appear so frequently in advertisements. If we consider what each of them has in common with the others, it becomes apparent that a shared characteristic is a contour that is highly discriminable and that can be easily identified, even when minimum visual information is provided, as in a silhouette. The inclusion of such a monument in an advertisement immediately establishes the identity of a particular locale.

In some instances an advertisement need only allude to such a monument rather than depicting it in its entirety in order to utilize it as a communicative tool. For example, an advertisement for Ragú Pasta Sauce in a British magazine utilizes an image of a leaning "tower" composed of three jars stacked on top of each other to illustrate the idea that the three sauces each "lean toward the Italian." Other than a pun alluding to "a Pisa cake," no direct mention is made of the Leaning Tower of Pisa. Thoughts of this well-known monument, together with accompanying associations of Italian taste, are evoked by this image and thus enhance the perception of Italian characteristics in this nonItalian brand.

Geographic Features. Geographic features have been among the national and regional symbols that meet the criteria of identifiability, distinctiveness, and conciseness, and they have been utilized in advertising to identify national origin, to distinguish among brands, and to impart desirable associations to them. For example, the geographic feature of the Swiss alps, with readily recognized snow-covered peaks, appeared in an advertisement for Switzerland Cheese that invited the reader to "Enjoy a piece of Switzerland" by incorporating a tantalizing view of these mountaintops into the distinctively shaped blade of a cheese knife about to cut the cheese. That such a geographic feature need only be suggested rather than actually portrayed was demonstrated in an advertisement for the Swiss brand of chocolate Toblerone, which incorporated an associative link with the Swiss alps through presenting a close-up view of the pointed mounds and steep slopes of chocolate that form an individual bar, shown without its wrapping. The brief copy noted that "The Alps aren't the only great slopes of Switzerland."

In addition to topographic features, the depiction in advertising of animals and plants characteristic of particular countries or areas suggests or evokes associations of those regions. Among examples that have been utilized to suggest or to reinforce particular regions or nationalities are the koala, the panda, and the buffalo, among animals, and the maple leaf, the cactus, the palm tree, and the orchid, among plants.

Cultural Artifacts. Objects created for use within a particular cultural or national setting have also been used to suggest or to reinforce the visual portrayal of national or cultural identity. Consider drinking containers as one example. Ringnes Export, a Norwegian brand of beer, has been portrayed in a clear crystalline glass designed in the shape of an animal's horn as if to resemble a Viking's drinking vessel, just as the beer stein is prominent in advertisements for German beer.

Modes of transportation have also been used to identify a region or nationality. Among the vehicles that have appeared in advertisements are the gondola, aerial cable car, stage coach, junk, and the taxi, including the stately black London variety or the once plentiful Checker cab of the United States.

Musical instruments, cooking utensils, dishes, and furniture are among the many forms of cultural artifacts that have been used to identify products as originating in one nationality or region. Occasionally, artifacts associated with an ancient culture provide an advertising context. Kamora Coffee Liqueur has reproduced images of Mayan artifacts such as statuettes, tribal masks, and pieces of pottery. Such images both suggest the Mexican origin of the brand and serve to classify the liqueur as similar to the Mayan pieces unearthed in archeological excavations in that it too is "the hidden treasure of Mexico."

Ceremonial Costumes and National Dress.   Among the cultural artifacts that are depicted in advertising, ceremonial costumes and items of national or regional dress appear frequently.

One reason may be that some items, such as headgear, possess distinctive contours, which, similar to those of buildings and monuments, may be readily identified with minimal visual information. For example, the distinctive shape of Napoleon's hat has often appeared in advertisements for Courvoisier Cognac to reinforce the idea that it is "the brandy of Napoleon," whereas the Australian bush hat has also been featured in a wide array of advertisements. Other distinctive articles of headgear that have been used to designate nationality in advertisements have included the English bowler hat and the feathered helmets of London's Buckingham Palace guards, the French beret, the American cowboy hat, the Indian turban, the horned helmet of the Scandinavian Vikings, the Mexican sombrero, and the beribboned hat of the Venetian gondolier.

In addition to headgear, costumes associated with particular nationalities or geographical regions are utilized to communicate the national origin of a brand. For example, the logo of the St. Pauli Brewery of Bremen, Germany, consists of the St. Pauli Girl, dressed in a dirndl, with its close-fitting bodice, full skirt, and apron. In an advertisement for the Japanese brand, Suntory Draft Beer, a Japanese woman is portrayed dressed in a silk kimono embroidered with figures of dragons and displaying the long slit sleeves characteristic of this form of national dress. She is posed in profile and so that the reader sees much of the expanse of the robe covering her back. Against a background of the sun setting over water, she holds out a glass of beer, which is referred to as "a taste of another culture" and as "the beer that will make you turn your back on other imports," an idea that is concretely supported by her pose.

Other distinctive forms of dress that have been used to identify nationality or region have included the Scottish kilt, the Indian sari, the ruffled dress of a Spanish flamenco dancer, and the Hawaiian hula skirt, among others. However, it should be noted that the use of such images may have unintended results. In one such instance, Dole pineapple products, through imagery portraying women in hula skirts in Hawaiian surroundings, inadvertently created the impression that pineapple products, and pineapple juice in particular, did not provide nutrition equivalent to that of orange or tomato juice and were not commonly consumed for breakfast (Dichter, 1985).

Mythical Characters and Personalities. Characters that have become identified with a particular nationality or that embody characteristics valued within a culture appear as national and cultural symbols in advertising. Some characters, such as the dragon or the leprechaun, have been taken from myths, stories, or fables associated with particular nationalities. Others have been drawn from various genres, such as fiction or the performing arts of theater, opera, and film, which have been placed within particular national settings.

A series of advertisements for Gordon's Gin has portrayed a number of symbols associated with England. In one example the advertisement noted that England is "known for its stately homes" but illustrated this with the readily recognizable contour of Sherlock Holmes' profile, thus making a play on words. Other advertisements in this series have featured several symbols that fall into categories noted earlier, including Stonehenge, a London taxi, Buckingham palace guards, and someone with hair in the distinctive punk style.

The Italian wine Bolla has featured Harlequin, a clown prominent in Italian comedy and pantomime, cavorting with giant-sized implements associated with wine. In one advertisement, Harlequin has been shown balanced on the edge of a wineglass, whereas, in another, he has been portrayed clinging to a gigantic corkscrew. Advertisements in this series have presented images that combine a cultural symbol with implements associated with the product.

The use of a mythical character as a national symbol in the Bolla advertisements might be viewed as somewhat comparable to an advertisement for a chain of Japanese restaurants in the United States. In this humorous advertisement, the Japanese steakhouse chain, Benihana, celebrated the 25th anniversary of its creation by the restaurateur Rocky Aoki with a clever image that combines references both to this Japanese Rocky as well as to the mythical American hero immortalized in the series of Rocky films that portray high achievement and the overcoming of great odds. The advertisement portrays a muscular Japanese boxer, with the name "Benihana" on his trunks and wearing boxing gloves held high in the air. However, the boxing gloves hold a chef's knife and fork, and the boxer wears a chef's hat. Directly underneath appears the caption, "Rocky XXV The Anniversary," a reference both to the long series of Rocky films that have appeared and also to the "American classic" that the Benihana restaurant chain has become 25 years after the first restaurant was opened.

Brands as Cultural Symbols. A Swissair advertisement invited the reader to "Let us fly you to Americana," illustrated with an array of artifacts that—in addition to a cowboy boot, baseball glove and ball, Checker cab, and hot dog—presented "Americana" with labels carrying such brands as Coca-Cola, Wrigley's, Campbell, and Heinz. One could argue that the portrayal of culture in advertisements has come full circle, with the advertising images and the products represented by them now viewed as cultural artifacts.

The examples of national and cultural symbols noted earlier communicate meaning in part through an associative process. That is, to the extent that the depicted symbol evokes associations related to its national origin, some proportion of those meanings will be transferred to the brand that has been contiguously paired with it in the advertisement. A taxonomic analysis of such associative advertisements can be found elsewhere (Caudle, 1988a).

Nonverbal Communication Through Advertising Art

Works of art presented in advertisements provide nonverbal communication routes across national boundaries, and they have been utilized in a variety of ways. In addition to communicating by means of an associative process, referred to earlier in relation to national and cultural symbols, advertising art may communicate through other nonverbal means to be considered in the discussion that follows.

Recognized Works of Art. Some works of art, and the artists who created them, have become so widely recognized and so closely associated with their countries of origin that they have assumed a status approximating that of a national symbol. When advertisements pair widely recognized works of art with products originating in the same country, one objective is to achieve for the product some of the recognition that already exists for the work of art. Thus, an advertisement in an American publication that equated Perugina Chocolates and Michaelangelo's *David* as "great Italian tastemakers" has, at the same time, identified the national origin of the brand and has also gained recognition and status for the brand by associating it with the high standing already achieved by this particular work of art. A somewhat similar approach was utilized in the Kamora Coffee Liqueur advertisement noted earlier, which equated the brand with Mayan works of art as part of "the hidden treasure of Mexico."

Works of art reproduced in advertisements need not be so well known to communicate effectively. For example, an advertisement for Belle Ami Eau De Toilette Pour Homme, a French brand of cologne, reproduced a drawing by the Austrian artist Gustav Klimt in an advertisement that appeared in an Italian magazine. The advertisement contained brief copy in French and Italian. However, it was hardly necessary to understand the French words ("Il se parfume. Elle s'abandonne," which might be translated as "He perfumes himself. She abandons herself.") because Klimt's drawing of a nude asleep on her back, one arm raised over her head, provided an erotic image suggestive of the potential impact of Bel Ami upon a woman.

Commissioned Works of Art. In addition to associating products with works of art by recognized artists, advertising art has been utilized to communicate across national boundaries by presenting original works of art that have been commissioned for the advertisement. For example, an advertisement for a Swedish brand of mineral water, Ramlösa, reproduced an original water color to establish a number of associative connections. The painting depicted sky, mountains, and lake in icy blue, crystalline tones that echoed those of the product, shown beneath it. The picture's caption, "Swedish Water Colour," thus had a triple meaning and referred to the painting, the pure waters that it portrayed, representative of Sweden, and the bottled water of the brand.

An original still life commissioned by a Spanish wine company, Codorniu, presents not only an elegant work of art entitled "Codorniu with artichoke and broken walnut shell" but also incorporates the product into the image, which is reminiscent of still life compositions by such classic artists as Cézanne. Furthermore, the advertisement provides instructions for ordering a larger reproduction of the painting, insuring that those who chose to order and to frame the print would obtain a lasting reminder of the brand.

Advertisements promoting shoes from Italy, sponsored by the Italian Trade Commission of New York, presented a series in which each advertisement was a still life construction that included objects selected from various segments of the arts. In one example, an Italian shoe formed part of a construction that included a violin, a musical manuscript, a tuning fork, and a model of an operatic stage set. In another example, the construction displayed a shoe amidst a number of objects associated with building and architecture, including a model of the distinctive dome of the Duomo of Florence, rulers, drafting and writing implements, and old architectural plans. These examples illustrate how products may be incorporated into original works of art that are constructed from objects that relate to some aspect of a national culture.

The incorporation into advertisements of commissioned works of art or recognized works of art represent only two of a number of advertising formats that utilize art as a communicative medium, and a more complete discussion of the forms and styles of advertising art can be found elsewhere (Caudle, 1989a; 1989b). While considering the role of advertising art in communicating across national boundaries, it is also of interest to consider the processes through which advertisements that embody such art may achieve their impact. Earlier examples have discussed the use of art works in advertising for their associative value; the following discussion adds to this repertory of cognitive mechanisms examples of communication in advertising art through concretization, on the one hand, and the closely related use of visual metaphor and symbolism, on the other.

Concretization. As the term is used here, concretization refers to the transformation of a thought or concept into a concrete, visual image. As shown earlier, concretization was utilized in the Ragú Pasta Sauce advertisement as the idea of "leaning toward Italian" was transformed into the concrete representation of three jars of sauce forming a leaning tower similar to Italy's Tower of Pisa.

An advertisement in a French magazine for Diapositives Kodak Ektachrome (film for photographic slides) communicated both the function of the film and the beautiful results that can be obtained through its use by means of a two-page, full color advertisement that portrayed a sunset image of a wooden pier extending into a peaceful lake surrounded by trees. The function of the slide in capturing this image was visually portrayed through placement of a giant slide frame at the end of the pier that "framed" someone against a background formed by a segment of this scene. The exaggerated size of the slide frame was emphasized through the portrayal of children sitting upon its top and leaning against it. The result was an evocative image that provided a concrete portrayal of the product's function.

Similarly, a French organization dedicated to raising funds for the preservation of the city of Venice utilized a powerful image that concretely represented the future fate of Venice if action is not taken to counteract the rate at which it is sinking. The advertisement portrays a Renaissance-style portrait of a man (in actuality, a reference to Giovanni Bellini's early sixteenth century portrait of the Doge of Venice). We might view this portrait as a symbol of the city of Venice and its artistic treasures. However, this advertisement goes beyond the simple portrayal of a symbol; the man in the portrait is wearing 20th-century scuba diving equipment and seems about to be submerged beneath the surface of the water. Although the headline exhorts the reader in French to "Save Venice," this caption is virtually unnecessary in order to understand the meaning of this image, at least to an art lover. The fusion of incongruous elements from different eras into a single image provides much of the evocative power of this advertisement. Such fusion of elements was the communicative focus of the Benihana advertisement described earlier and is found in other forms of advertising symbolism as well.

Visual Metaphor and Symbolism.   A metaphor might be defined as a figure of speech in which one thing is likened to some other, different object by referring to it as if it were that object. A visual metaphor is created through portraying this implied comparison through a concretized image rather than in words, and the preceding example provides a visual metaphor of the sinking of Venice. Thus, although the Renaissance portrait is indeed a symbol of the city of Venice, it provides a symbol in the denotative sense. That is, the referent of the symbol, or what it represents, is readily apparent.

However, consider a broader use of symbols. Just as symbolic images are integral to the visual arts, so are they an important mode of communication in advertising images. Some symbols may evoke associations and emotional responses for reasons that are not immediately apparent to the viewer, and they may achieve their impact in part through the condensation of multiple meanings into a single image that may be interpreted simultaneously on a number of levels.

Although a full discussion of such symbolism is beyond the scope of this chapter, consider as one readily interpretable example an advertisement for the French liqueur Grand Marnier that appeared in a German magazine. The advertisement depicts an elegantly dressed woman seated on the left side of a restaurant table. On the table rest flowers, candles, and a bottle of Grand Marnier between two delicately shaped glasses into which the liqueur has been poured. Across from the woman is her dining companion, wearing an elegant tuxedo. However, atop the spotless white collar of his evening suit appears the head of a leopard, to which the reader's eye is drawn. This powerful image, formed of the fused elements of elegant, sophisticated male and wild cat, vividly communicates such readily apparent meanings as power and sleekness. On an unconscious level the image may suggest animal nature and sexuality. The advertisement as a whole suggests visually that the liqueur may enhance the enjoyment of the woman and her partner. To be sure, there is copy, in German, in which the woman remarks: "If you wish to suggest an adventure, then be prepared for a dangerous love affair."

However, this copy is overshadowed by the strong and provocative visual imagery.

Although the Benihana, "Save Venice," and Grand Marnier advertisements each present visual metaphors created by fusing together dissimilar elements, one could argue that the Grand Marnier advertisement embodies a richer form of symbolism in that it may evoke a wider spectrum of associations and emotions. It should be kept in mind that this advertisement is directed toward a sophisticated, affluent market that perhaps falls into the category described by Quelch and Hoff (1986) as "ego-driven consumers who can be appealed to through myths and fantasies shared across cultures" (p. 60). Hornik (1980), among others, noted that cultural background influences how a message is perceived, and it is likely that the symbolism of the leopard would be viewed quite differently in a culture in which such animals were found in places other than zoos. However, as another author noted: "Advertisers know how to adjust their products to the countries to which they are geared. They are the best semioticians by far" (von Raffler-Engel, 1988, p. 82).

Concretization and symbolism provide nonverbal modes of communication of potential value when advertisements cross national boundaries. Additional examples of these forms of representation, together with a fuller discussion of their hypothetical role in evoking viewer response, can be found elsewhere (Caudle, 1989a, 1989b), as can a discussion, within a psychoanalytic framework, of parallels between symbols in the visual arts and in advertising images (Caudle, 1990b). It should be kept in mind that the preceding examples have reflected the Western artistic tradition. Those who would advertise to cultures with differing artistic traditions, such as Arab countries, would likely find it of value to explore the visual and decorative arts of those cultures for imagery to utilize as the basis of advertising (Elbashier & Nicholls, 1983). Finally, Douglas and Dubois (1977) underscored the importance of considering cultural conventions of pictorial interpretation that may influence the perception of advertising imagery.

Facial Expression, Gesture, and Physical Appearance

This chapter has thus far considered nonverbal advertising strategies that have been deliberately designed either to emphasize or to communicate across national boundaries. There remain, however, additional aspects of nonverbal communication that concern the portrayal of the face and body. Some categories of these forms of communication were described with regard to television advertising (Haley, Richardson, & Baldwin, 1984). Although magazine advertisements are limited to static visual images rather than including the sound and movement found in television commercials, one could argue that both the portrayal of facial expressions and gestures, as well as the details of physical appearance, constitute channels of nonverbal communication that may influence the perception of a magazine advertisement. As has been noted: "Much of the difficulty in intercultural communication is . . . a matter of understanding . . . nonverbal signals that are generally coded so automatically within a culture that we are unconscious of them" (Cole & Bruner, 1971; cited in Hornik & Rubinow, 1981, pp. 9–10), The face and body play an important role in the transmission of such cues. Although it is beyond the scope of this chapter to fully explore these forms of nonverbal communication, they are included here to provide a more complete spectrum of potential communication channels across national boundaries.

Facial Expression.   The burgeoning literature on facial expression has revealed three general aspects of emotional facial expressions and their perception that may have relevance to nonverbal communication in cross-national advertisements. Two of these aspects of emotional facial expressions were noted by Ekman and Oster (1979) in their review of research on facial expressions of emotion. First, certain facial expressions are labelled similarly by observers, regardless of culture. However, a second point of interest to the present discussion is that the facial expression of genuine emotion may be altered according to socially learned, culture-specific display rules. Finally, a third aspect of the perception of emotional facial expressions of interest is that genuine and spontaneous expressions of emotion may be perceived and responded to differently than nongenuine, intentional expressions (Buck, 1984; Ekman, 1985). At present, little is known concerning the impact of emotional facial expressions in advertisements, particularly those that cross national boundaries. The identification through cross-cultural research of cultural differences in the public display of emotions, as in, for example, the observations reported by Morsbach (1988b), suggest that the accurate portrayal of emotional facial expressions may be of importance in cross-cultural advertising. Further discussion of emotional facial expressions in relation to advertising can be found elsewhere (Caudle, 1990a).

Gesture and Body Position.   In addition to the discovery of culture-specific rules for emotional facial expressions, cultural differences in gestural movements and positions of the body have also been documented. A valuable taxonomic analysis of nonverbal behavior was provided by Knapp (1978), and the collection of articles edited by Poyatos (1988), together with the extensive references cited in individual chapters, provides a useful foundation for the consideration of the role of gesture and body position in advertisements. The potential for misinterpretation of gestures has been discussed by von Raffler-Engel (1988) within the general context of covert factors in cross-cultural communication, and the role of gestures in perpetuating cultural stereotypes in advertising was noted in a discussion of bowing in Japan (Morsbach, 1988a). This author pointed out that the importance of bowing has been documented both in Japan since 600 A.D. and in the West throughout the Middle Ages until recently. The author then described an example of how the gesture of bowing was utilized in an advertisement:

> These days, Japanese tend to think of bowing as being something "uniquely Japanese." This is shown in a large poster I photographed in a London tube station. It shows a Japanese salesman bowing while pointing at a Volkswagen car, saying, "Volkswagen is the Number 1 imported car in Japan." Bowing is used in this advertisement, as well as in others (e.g., by Japan Air Lines), to emphasize something uniquely Japanese. Of course, such bowing is *not* unique, since it is found in many other non-Western countries as well; but it seems that in advertising at any rate, the Japanese want Westerners to think of it as a specifically Japanese trait. Since many of these advertisements are created by Westerners, it may be a case of Westerners furthering stereotypes to get the message over for their (Japanese) client. (Morsbach, 1988a, pp. 189–190)

Physical Appearance. The cues provided by physical appearance provide still another route of communication across cultural boundaries. Although physical appearance might be broadly considered as including physiognomy and build, it also includes clothing and adornments such as cosmetics, jewelry, and hairstyle.

Earlier in this chapter, the use of clothing and headgear to identify a brand's national origin is discussed. However, a far broader analysis of the communicative importance of clothing has been made by Vicary (1988; see also the extensive reference list included for this author). In a discussion of clothing as nonverbal communication, Vicary emphasized the role of clothing and adornment in the communication of group membership, age, gender, and social status:

> To enhance body movements, posture displays, gestures, and facial expressions, the Naked Animal has added a variety of thousands of cultural material artefacts to the body—clothes, adornment, tools, and equipment—which further modify appearance. Thus, clothing on moving bodies becomes signs and symbols of a communication system as complex, and precise, as most verbal language. (Vicary, 1988, pp. 292–293)

The analysis provided earlier of a Samsara advertisement describes how the details of clothing and jewelry worn by the model connote elegance and high status. Among the anecdotal examples that might be cited to demonstrate the influence of adornment on response to an advertisement is one provided by Farley (1986), who described how a drawing of a Ghanian family, intended as the focal point of a campaign for a hygiene product being introduced into Ghana, was viewed by Ghanian women as signifying that the product was intended for foreigners rather than native Ghanians. This was due to the inadvertent portrayal of foreign hairstyles for the women included in the family drawing.

With regard to the potential impact of facial expression, gesture, and physical appearance in communicating across national boundaries, a broad evaluation of the sources cited earlier (Knapp, 1978; Poyatos, 1988) seems to suggest that small details, particularly if they are contrary to the norm in a particular culture, might affect viewer response in significant ways. The suggestion was made by Haley et al. (1984) that nonverbal cues are more likely to detract from the effectiveness of an advertisement rather than to enhance its success. As a means of eliminating incorrect details, several authors have suggested that members of the cultural group to whom materials will be directed should be involved in the creation of the materials (Hornik & Rubinow, 1981; Plummer, 1986). However, even when this is done, copy testing may yet reveal that small details have been misrepresented and that they have a negative impact on the effectiveness of the advertisement (Farley, 1986). It appears that much remains to be learned concerning the impact in cross-national advertising of the nonverbal cues provided by the face and body.

FINAL THOUGHTS

This survey of modes of verbal and nonverbal communication in magazine advertisements is intended as a contribution to the ongoing debate concerning the globalization of advertising, through identifying ways in which advertisements define, and communicate beyond, national boundaries. Although advertising strategies that have been included represent only a fraction of those that have been employed, they have been selected to illustrate issues that arise when advertising across national borders. It is hoped that discussion of nonverbal communication through advertising art will be useful in suggesting creative approaches to advertising communication across the barriers of language and culture.

ACKNOWLEDGMENTS

The section of this chapter on national and cultural symbols draws upon material originally included in Caudle (1988b).

The author gratefully acknowledges the assistance of Ilse York and Maki Kurokawa, who translated portions of advertisements, and of George Jochnowitz, of the College of Staten Island, who suggested the example of Coca-Cola rendered in Chinese.

REFERENCES

Boyd, C. W. (1985). Point of view: Alpha-numeric brand names. *Journal of Advertising Research, 25*(5), 48-52.

Buck, R. (1984). *The communication of emotion.* New York: Guilford Press.

Caudle, F. M. (1988a). Associative strategies in magazine advertising: An illustrated taxonomy. In L. F. Alwitt (Ed.), *1987 Proceedings of the Division of Consumer Psychology, American Psychological Association* (pp. 84-91). Washington, DC: American Psychological Association, Division of Consumer Psychology.

Caudle, F. M. (1988b). National and cultural symbols in magazine advertisements. Paper presented at Ninth International Congress of the International Association for Cross-Cultural Psychology, Newcastle, New South Wales, Australia.

Caudle, F. M. (1989a). Advertising art: Cognitive mechanisms and research issues. In P. Cafferata & A. Tybout (Eds.), *Cognitive and affective responses to advertising* (pp. 161-217). Lexington, MA: D. C. Heath/Lexington Books.

Caudle, F. M. (1989b). Association, imitation, and synthesis as communication strategies in advertising art. In R. C. King & J. K. Collins (Eds.), *Social applications and issues in psychology* (pp. 191-199). North Holland: Elsevier Science Publishers.

Caudle, F. M. (1990a). Communication and arousal of emotion: Some implications of facial expression research for magazine advertisements. In S. J. Agres, J. A. Edell, & T. M. Dubitsky (Eds.), *Emotion in advertising: Theoretical and practical explorations* (pp. 127-159). Westport, CT: Greenwood Press/Quorum Books.

Caudle, F. M. (1990b). If Freud could see us now: Psychoanalytic perspectives on advertising. In M. Gardner (Ed.), *1989 Proceedings of the Society for Consumer Psychology, American Psychological Association* (pp. 100-106). Washington, DC: American Psychological Association, Society for Consumer Psychology.

Cole, M., & Bruner, J. S. (1971). Cultural differences and inferences about psychological processes. *Americal Psychologist, 26*, 867-876.

Dichter, E. (1985). What's in an image. *Journal of Consumer Marketing, 2*(1), 75-81.

Douglas, S., & Dubois, B. (1977). Looking at the cultural environment for international marketing opportunities. *Columbia Journal of World Business*, Winter, 102-109.

Ekman, P. (1985). *Telling lies: Clues to deceit in the marketplace, politics, and marriage.* New York: W. W. Norton.

Ekman, P., & Oster, H. (1979). Facial expressions of emotion. *Annual Review of Psychology, 30*, 527-554.

Elbashier, A. M., & Nicholls, J. R. (1983). Export marketing in the Middle East: The importance of cultural differences. *European Journal of Marketing, 17*(1), 68-81.

Farley, J. U. (1986). Are there truly international products—and prime prospects for them? *Journal of Advertising Research, 26*(5), 17-20.

Green, R. T., & Langeard, E. (1975, July). A cross-national comparison of consumer habits and innovator characteristics. *Journal of Marketing, 39*, 34-41.

Haley, R. I., Richardson, J., & Baldwin, B. M. (1984). The effects of nonverbal communications in television advertising. *Journal of Advertising Research, 24*(4), 11-18.

Harris, G. (1984). The globalization of advertising. *International Journal of Advertising, 3*, 223-234.

Hornik, J. (1980). Comparative evaluation of international vs. national advertising strategies. *Columbia Journal of World Business*, Spring, 36–45.

Hornik, J., & Rubinow, S. C. (1981). Expert-respondents' synthesis for international advertising research. *Journal of Advertising Research, 21*(3), 9–17.

Johnstone, H., Kaynak, E., & Sparkman, R. M., Jr. (1987). A cross-cultural/cross-national study of the information content of television advertisements. *International Journal of Advertising, 6,* 223–236.

Kaynak, E., & Mitchell, L. A. (1981). Analysis of marketing strategies used in diverse cultures. *Journal of Advertising Research, 21*(3), 25–32.

Knapp, M. L. (1978). *Nonverbal communication in human interaction* (2nd ed.). New York: Holt, Rinehart & Winston.

Kroeber, A. L., & Kluckholn, C. (1952). Culture: A critical review of concepts and definitions. *Papers of the Peabody Museum of American Archeology and Ethnology* (Vol. 47[1]). Boston: Harvard University Press

Levine, R. A. (1973). *Culture, behavior, and personality.* Chicago: Aldine Publishing Company.

Martyn, H. (1964). *International business, principles and problems.* New York: Collier-Macmillan.

Morsbach, H. (1988a). Nonverbal communication and hierarchical relationships: The case of bowing in Japan. In F. Poyatos (Ed.), *Cross-cultural perspectives in nonverbal communication* (pp. 189–199). Toronto: C. J. Hogrefe.

Morsbach, H. (1988b). The importance of silence and stillness in Japanese nonverbal communication: A cross-cultural approach. In F. Poyatos (Ed.), *Cross-cultural perspectives in nonverbal communication* (pp. 201–215). Toronto: C. J. Hogrefe.

Mueller, B. (1987). Reflections of culture: An analysis of Japanese and American advertising appeals. *Journal of Advertising Research, 27*(3), 51–59.

Onkvisit, S., & Shaw, J. J. (1987). Standardized international advertising: A review and critical evaluation of the theoretical and empirical evidence. *Columbia Journal of World Business*, Fall, 43–55.

Plummer, J. T. (1986). The role of copy research in multinational advertising. *Journal of Advertising Research, 26*(5), 11–15.

Poyatos, F. (Ed.). (1988). *Cross-cultural perspectives in nonverbal communication.* Toronto: C. J. Hogrefe.

Quelch, J. A., & Hoff, E. J. (1986). Customizing global marketing. *Harvard Business Review*, May–June, 59–68.

Robertson, K. (1989). Strategically desirable brand name characteristics. *Journal of Consumer Marketing, 6*(4), 61–71.

Ryans, J. K., & Ratz, D. G. (1987). Advertising standardization: A re-examination. *International Journal of Advertising, 6,* 145–158.

vanden Bergh, B., Adler, K., & Oliver, L. (1987). Linguistic distinction among top brand names. *Journal of Advertising Research, 4,* 39–44.

Vicary, G. Q. (1988). The signs of clothing. In F. Poyatos (Ed.), *Cross-cultural perspectives in nonverbal communication* (pp. 291–314). Toronto: C. J. Hogrefe.

von Raffler-Engel, W. (1988). The impact of covert factors in cross-cultural communication. In F. Poyatos (Ed.), *Cross-cultural perspectives in nonverbal communication* (pp. 71–104). Toronto: C. J. Hogrefe.

Winram, S. (1984). The opportunity for world brands. *International Journal of Advertising, 3,* 17–26.

8 Hard Sell Versus Soft Sell: A Comparison of American and British Advertising

Sandra Bradley
Jacqueline Hitchon
University of Wisconsin — Madison

Esther Thorson
University of Missouri — Columbia

There is general agreement that American and British advertising differ, both print and broadcast, and that the difference reflects a difference in culture between the two nations (e.g., Carey, 1975; Dowling, 1980; Lannon, 1986). Advertising that is not tailored to the cultural norms and tastes of its intended audience will fail to communicate effectively (Aydin, Terpestra, & Yaprak, 1984; Chevalier, & Foliot, 1974; Lee, Faber, & O'Guinn, 1985). Despite general agreement on the broad conceptual issue, however, there is little empirical support for the view that American and British advertising differ in fundamental ways (Lyonski, 1985; Taylor, 1983). Strong evidence of dissimilarity can be found in Weinberger and Spotts' (1989) study of humor in British advertising, which reveals greater use of humor overall, and of pun and satire in particular. The problem with findings that relate to a single executional dimension, such as the use of humor, is that they do not allow us to grasp the underlying philosophical difference that results in dissimilarities at the microlevel.

Establishing the extent and nature of these differences has never been more important than at the present time. The 1980s saw a general trend toward globalization in the advertising industry. As agencies merged and, in the process, acquired subsidiaries overseas, clients likewise crossed the Atlantic with a view to global expansion. The result is that by 1990, 4 of the top U.S. agencies were British-owned, whereas 5 of the top 10 in Britain had American parents (Katz, 1990). Furthermore, in the second half of 1989, American companies were responsible for 28% of the $50 billion spent worldwide on acquiring companies in Europe (Fuerbringer, 1990). A likely result of these mergers and takeovers is a degree of standardization of advertising campaigns across the two nations. Hertz, for example, believed that it is reassuring for rental car customers to find the same selling points expounded in Norfolk, England as in Norfolk, Virginia (Fraser, 1990).

However, the way in which key selling propositions are communicated may need to be different in Britain than in America. In some instances, the selling proposition itself may need to vary to be consistent with the different assumptions that underlie British and American cultures (Carey, 1975; Farley, 1986). Unfortunately, advertisers have in the past shown a tendency to be culturally myopic (Hornik, 1980; Lee, 1968). Indeed, many advertising campaigns that have been successful in the U.S. have ultimately failed in other countries because advertisers do not fully understand the foreign cultures and their social norms (Hornik, 1980; Quelch & Hopp, 1986).

The concern must be, therefore, that existing differences in advertising styles will not be perceived by advertisers for lack of comprehensive, empirical research on the issue. Furthermore, those differences may well be swept away before a relationship to advertising effectiveness within a given cultural context can be fully investigated.

Based on this reasoning, the purpose of this chapter is to establish in what comprehensive respect American and British television advertising differ. For measurable differences to be meaningful (in the sense of perhaps being worthy of preservation), they need to be founded upon cultural values rather than simply be the result of advertising ignorance or incompetence.

Insight into an important source of cultural variance, and its impact on advertising style, is provided in the literature (Gilly, 1988; Hong, Muderrisoglu, & Zinkhan, 1987; Madden, Caballero, & Matsukubo, 1986). Root (1986) observed the slightly pessimistic, cynical attitude held by British viewers toward television in general. In the case of advertising, this cynicism is compounded by greater opportunity to avoid commercials altogether — only two out of four networks broadcast commercials, and ads are shown less frequently and at greater intervals than on the American networks. Advertisers in Britain have been forced to make their messages subtle and entertaining in order to gain the attention of an unwilling and skeptical audience not conditioned to the "sell society" common in the United States (Dowling, 1980; Lannon, 1986; Root, 1986). This kind of advertising has been described as more audience-oriented than product-oriented or, in advertising terminology, can perhaps be better expressed as more soft sell than hard sell.

The idea of soft sell dates back to 1918, when a copywriter for General Motors touted the idea that a soft sell copy style would better create the long-term relationship considered necessary between a car manufacturer and its customers. He believed the only way to penetrate the subconscious of the reader was through a slow accumulation of positive messages. Soft sells, according to Wells, Burnett, and Moriarity (1992), are those that use subtlety, intrigue, and ambiguity to sell products. Some critics have suggested that advertisers are merely selling moods and dreams rather than products. The soft sell approach includes greater use of humor and drama, and less of the fact-based model that Lannon believed to be dominant in American advertising.

Hard sell advertising can be equated with informational advertising, particularly the kind that uses strong arguments and demands for action. The most common hard sell approach, however, is the type that emphasizes tangible product features and benefits. Such messages can be described as "putting the product up front"; hard sell "tries to convince the consumer to buy because it's very good, better, the best" (McCollum/Spielman Topline, 1986).

The hard sell/soft sell dichotomy necessitated by cultural differences in attitudes to television, provides us with an overriding conceptual framework for the investigation of differences between American and British advertising. The following sections develop this idea in greater detail, list our hypotheses, describe the method for the content analysis used to test the hypotheses, present the results of the study, and conclude with a discussion of the findings and their implications.

LITERATURE REVIEW

Television Systems in America and Britain

The comparison of British and American commercials is particularly interesting because the two cultures are so closely related historically, linguistically, and politically. Focusing on the television systems in the two countries, however, reveals some important differences. Although both have a mixture of public and private channels, Britain still relies far more on public TV whereas America relies on privately owned channels (Clarke, & Bradford, 1992). Viewing in Britain is almost evenly divided between the two government-supported channels (BBC1 and BBC2), which show no commercials, and the two independent, advertising-supported channels (ITV and Channel 4). Cable is still in an embryonic stage (e.g., Lycett, 1989). In contrast, in the United States, the three broadcast networks (ABC, CBS, NBC) all show advertising and command more than 60% of the viewing audience (Katz, 1990). The vast majority of the remaining American viewers are exposed to commercials on cable channels as well.

In addition to having a more elusive audience, British advertisers face higher media placement costs, which usually comprise the largest portion of advertising costs overall. It is estimated that British advertisers pay up to 64% more for air time than do those in France, Japan, West Germany,

Italy, or America, with commercial rates rising an average of 15% each year (Harper, 1988). Moreover, although both British and American systems consider commercial time a commodity, with prices based on the market laws of supply and demand, the system in Britain is fully preemptible. That is, if one advertiser agrees to pay a certain amount for a spot on primetime but, the day before, another advertiser offers more for that same spot, the one offering more will be given the time slot. In the United States, advertisers usually buy time up to 1 year in advance, knowing exactly how much they have paid for the spot and when it will air.

Not only is it more expensive and difficult for companies to reach a British TV audience, but once contacted, the audience is also perceived as being more skeptical of messages received via television. In a multicountry study of attitudes toward the media in general, 69% of the American sample had confidence in the media, compared to only 38% in Britain (Parsiot, 1988). Recently, British ads have leaned toward the use of "seductive visual glamour" and the growing use of humor to retrieve a cynical audience wary of messages that blatantly push products at viewers (Root, 1986).

THE RELATIONSHIP BETWEEN CULTURE AND ADVERTISING

Many researchers have said that advertising shapes the way people live (e.g., Berger, 1972; Peterson, 1983), whereas others have argued that advertising merely echoes existing patterns (e.g., Peterson, 1975). But, if advertising merely reflects the values of the culture and society of which it is a part, it has become an important enough reflection of society that it must be regarded as a significant factor in reinforcing and strengthening the life it portrays (Pollay, 1983). In other words, a balanced conclusion seems to be that advertising both reflects and molds life (e.g., Kuhns, 1970; Williamson, 1978).

One of the ways in which advertising can influence reality is by presenting a distorted image of life in a particular culture (Holbrook, 1987). However, the particular distortions of advertising's *content* that may vary from America to Britain are not the subject of this chapter. Rather, our concern is with an overall difference in *manner of presentation*, or style. No comparison is made of content consisting of such things as the presence of stereotypes or frequencies of minority portrayals, for example. The question then becomes whether a certain manner of presentation has been culturally determined and is particularly effective in the cultural context of interest.

Given the range of variables that culture is believed to influence (e.g., value systems, attitudes, and perception processes [Rokeach, 1973]), it seems likely that advertising style would be within its scope. In fact, in the context of the communication process, the sender's cultural background has been shown to affect *message form*, just as the receiver's cultural background determines *message perception* (Elbashier, 1983).

HARD SELL VERSUS SOFT SELL

The general framework of hard sell versus soft sell is discussed here with reference to specific indicants of each approach.

Use of Humor and Other Emotional Approaches.   Humor is exemplary of the subtle approach Lannon (1986) believed characterizes British advertising. In a more recent study, Weinberger and Spotts (1989) supported Lannon's view by surveying executives in Britain and America and found that both groups thought humor was valuable in enhancing attention, name registration, and mood. However, the British executives were much more positive about the value of humorous ads for gaining attention, comprehension, persuasion, action, and source credibility; they were also less worried about the potential harmful effects of humor on recall and comprehension.

British commercials also differed from American commercials with respect to the types of humor used. The British made greater use of pun and satire than the Americans. These types of humor require greater deliberation for comprehension than straight farce, for example. It is likely, therefore, that American advertisers do not believe that their audiences will take the time to think through such subtle uses of humor, given the more heavily cluttered environment in which American commercials need to survive. It is worth noting, however, that although British advertisers take the risk of using nonobvious ploys, they also scored more highly than U.S. advertisers for integrating humor well with a particular product.

Finally, the use of humor in the two nations differs with respect to the segment of the population targeted. U.S. executives thought that humor was best suited to younger, better-educated, male, upscale, and professional audiences. The British group was generally less biased toward these subgroups and more positive toward the use of humor with a wider array of audiences. Nevertheless, the two groups agreed that humor is best used on younger audiences and least appropriate for older groups.

Despite no direct evidence to support the proposition that British ads will elicit emotions other than humor to a greater extent than American ads, it is a natural extension of the hard sell/soft sell reasoning. Although, the 1980s saw an increase in the use of emotion in advertising (Holbrook &

& O'Shaughnessy, 1984), especially in television commercials, U.S. advertising continues to contain highly rational content aimed at providing reasons for brand selection (Holbrook, 1987).

Information Content. Information is at the core of the term hard sell. Information cues can run the gamut from a direct address of the product's attributes to demonstrations of the product's effectiveness. American ads, on the whole, are considered to be the kind that tout product information and relay information much more directly than British ads seem to (Lannon, 1986).

Product Centrality. There is no existing methodology for measuring centrality of product in television commercials. After viewing a presample of British ads, it became apparent that products were treated very differently in British commercials than in American ads. Rather than being the focus or "star" of the commercial, products in the British ads were treated almost as secondary components in the ads' scenarios. The product in some British ads often was not introduced until the end of the ad and discussion of product attributes was often minimal. It was rare to see a British ad that lectured about the product or its attributes, or one that contained an urge to action. Instead, British advertisers evoked humor or drama to establish some sort of interest in the audience's mind and subsequently tagged the ad with the product or brand name.

Structure and Execution. Lectures and dramas are two broad execution types that exemplify direct and indirect methods of presentation (Deighton, Romer, & McQueen, 1989). Drama refers to an indirect address (Wells, 1988). In a pure drama, characters interact in the context of a plot, and the viewer is an eavesdropper on their interactions. Because soft sell is based on the idea of subtly getting a message across, we would expect drama to be used to a greater extent in British commercials. In a lecture, a narrator speaks directly to the viewer through the television screen, often while displaying the product. This type of presentation seems to match the idea of hard sell, and more instances of this method of presentation would be expected in American ads. Specific information-oriented (lecture) approaches include narration, demonstration, and product display. In assuming that American ads use more hard sell, we also assume that they use more of these information-oriented approaches.

HYPOTHESES

The general proposition derived in this chapter is that American ads rely more on hard sell techniques whereas British ads are often exemplified by a soft sell approach. The specific hypotheses (H) for each dependent variable are outlined here.

We expect the British ads to be more humorous overall and to use different types of humor than American ads, given Weinberger and Spotts' (1989) results.

H1a: British commercials use more humor than American commercials.

H1b: British commercials use a greater variety of humor types than American commercials.

Emotional Content.   Because soft sell is defined as "ads with indirect appeal that use mood, ambiguity, and suspense to create an intriguing message," (Wells, Burnett, & Moriarity, 1992), one would expect emotional appeals to be used more in British ads, whereas more rational appeals would be found in American ads.

H2: British ads show more emotional content than American ads.

Information Content.   An "informative" ad is defined as one that contains information cues (e.g., details of product characteristics, price, etc.) that a consumer might use in the purchase decision process.

H3: American ads use more information cues in their ads than British ads.

Product Centrality.   The factors that contribute to the concept of "product centrality" include the timing of product and brand name introduction, how often the product is shown and/or talked about, and whether ambiguity is a part of the ad's appeal.

H4: Products in American ads are given a more central role than in British ads.

Structure and Execution.   As discussed earlier, we expect British ads to use drama more than lecture, whereas American ads we expect to rely more on information-oriented appeals such as demonstrations, narrations, and product displays that typically accompany lecture-style presentations.

H5a: British ads rely more on dramas as a structural form whereas American ads rely more on lectures for conveying their messages.

H5b: American ads use more narration, demonstration, spokespeople, and product display as methods of presentation, than British ads.

RESEARCH METHODS

This study uses content analysis (Kassarjian, 1977) to establish whether ads from America and Britain vary on the dimensions noted earlier.

Selection of Commercials.   Three hours of primetime (7:00 to 10:00 PM) ads were sampled from several typical evenings (special programs excluded) from Channel 3 (the main commercial channel in Britain), and the same procedure was applied to each of the three American networks (ABC, NBC, CBS). The ad samples were then matched for product categories, yielding a final sample of 50 ads from each of the two countries.

Channel 3 is operated by the Independent Broadcasting Authority (IBA) in London, and is one of two channels containing advertising in Britain, the rest are owned by the government. On IBA, an average of 6 minutes of advertising is allowed per hour, and the ads may only be shown at the beginning and end of programs and during "natural breaks" in them. This way of presenting the ads in larger groups was one reason for assuming that the ads would need to be more unusual and creative in their presentation to withstand the competition from the clutter (IBA, 1987; Mattelart & Palmer, 1991).

The programming in both countries is basically similar, with the bulk of the programs representing either dramas or situation comedies. By gathering ads from these similar programs, we hoped to eliminate confounding due to target audience differences for other types of programming.

MEASURES

Humor.   Commercials were coded for type of humor and how humorous the ad was perceived to be by the coders. Type of humor was measured by giving coders a list of definitions (expanded from Kelly & Solomon, 1975) for nine types of humor that could be found in the ads and having them check the categories that applied. The nine categories were: cute, pun, understatement, joke, silliness, absurdity, satire, sarcasm, and irony.

Cute humor was added to Kelly and Solomon's original list because the list seemed to be lacking in representation of that type of humor and it was one that seemed to appear often in many of the ads in the sample.

Assessment of amount of humor in the ad was achieved by using a semantic differential scale ranging from 1 (not at all) to 7 (very much).

Emotional Content.   The initial pleasure-arousal scale for this study was derived from Mehrabian and Russell (1974). It was felt, however, that the scale was somewhat incomplete, and some adjectives were added to make the adjective list more comprehensive in its emotional scope.

A semantic differential scale of 1 (slightly) to 7 (very much) was used to measure items of pleasure and arousal. The coders were given a list of adjectives and asked to check any that applied to the ad that they were viewing. The list included these adjectives: stimulated, happy, irritated, excited, unhappy, bored, disgusted, contented, amused, surprised, confused, disappointed. The adjectives were then summed into two scales, one for pleasure and one for arousal.

Information.   Coders were given a list of 14 information cues, derived from Resnik and Stern (1977). They were asked to identify how many cues they saw in the ad. The list included:

1. Price or Value
2. Quality
3. Performance
4. Components or Contents
5. Availability
6. Special Offers
7. Taste
8. Packaging or Shape
9. Guarantees or Warrantees
10. Safety
11. Nutrition
12. Independent Research
13. Company-Sponsored Research
14. New Ideas

Product Centrality.   Coders were asked 11 questions that related to: (a) How central the product was to the ad's scenario, using a semantic differential scale of 1 (not at all) to 7 (very much), (b) time measures of when the brand name and/or product was first introduced (beginning, middle, or end of the ad), (c) when and how often the product is shown and/or talked about (Not at all − Little − Moderate − Great exposure), (d) how confusing or ambiguous the ad seemed to be (Confusing − Somewhat confusing − Not confusing).

Structure and Execution.   Coders were asked to first identify whether the ad was a lecture, drama, or combination of both, and then to identify what specific method of presentation the ad embodied (i.e., celebrity endorser, demonstration, narrator, etc.).

The coders were also asked to identify which specific strategy best described the one used in each ad.

TABLE 8.1
Kendall Coefficient of Concordance For Intercoder Reliability on Scale Items

Cases	W	Chisquare	d.f.	Sig.
3	.828	12.35	19	.0078

Note. A high level of significance means high agreement among the coders.
Cases (coders) = 3
Variables (ads coded together) = 20

CODERS

Three students were trained to code the ads. As a check, all three judges coded 10 of the same ads together to ensure agreement and understanding of the coding scheme. As an additional guarantee of agreement, 20 ads were coded separately by all three judges. Agreements across the three coders were calculated across each category of variables for these 20 ads.

Consistent with the procedures of Schneider and Schneider (1979), disagreement among the coders was settled via discussion and consensus. The rest of the ads were then allocated to one of the three coders and judged individually.

For the scale items, an intercoder reliability was achieved using Kendall's coefficient of concordance. This measure was used for items relating to centrality, humor scale, and emotion scales. A coder-by-ad matrix was created and a mean rank for each variable was calculated over all the cases, yielding a Kendall's W and corresponding chisquare statistic (see Table 8.1). For the dichotomous items, a coder-by-item matrix was created in accordance with Krippendorf's (1980) methodology. This measure was used for information content, humor types, methods of presentation and structures (see Table 8.2).

RESULTS

The distribution of products in each category, for both countries, is illustrated in Table 8.3. An analysis of variance was conducted on scale

TABLE 8.2
Percent Agreement Between Coders for Intercoder Reliability on Dichotomous Items

Coders = 3, Ads = 20, Alpha = .89

TABLE 8.3
Percent Distribution of Products Within Categories (U.S. &
U.K. Combined)

Products	Percentage
Food/Snacks	46.9
Personal & Beauty Care	7.1
Automobiles	8.2
Drugs & Medicine	2.0
Institutional	2.0
Alcoholic Beverages	6.1
Pet Food	4.1
Household Cleaning	16.3
Clothing	3.1
Finance	4.1

items whereas dichotomous items were analyzed using crosstabulations and chi-square statistics.

Humor.   The hypothesis (H1a) that British commercials use humor more than American commercials was supported by analysis of variance results for overall use of humor, with the British ads showing a significantly greater usage of humor (see Table 8.4).

Usage of various types of humor (H1b) was fairly similar between the two countries, with British ads using cute and ironic humor more, and not using pun or satire as much as expected (see Table 8.5).

Emotion.   The hypothesis that British ads contain more emotional content than American ads (H2) was not supported by the data. No significant differences were found in any of the pleasure or arousal categories.

Information.   The greatest difference between the two countries appears in the use of information, supporting the hypothesis that American ads contain more informational content than British ads (H2) (see Tables 8.6 and 8.7).

TABLE 8.4
Mean Humor Rating as a Function of Country

	U.S.	*U.K.*	*F*	*d.f.*	*p*
Mean humor rating	1.76	2.86	3.5	1	.004

TABLE 8.5
Percent Representation of Humor Types for Both Countries

	U.S.(%)	U.K.(%)	ChiSquare	d.f.	p
Cute	12.2	21.4	3.7	1	.054
Pun	3.1	5.1	0.5	1	.461
Understatement	–	–	–	–	–
Joke	3.1	4.1	0.2	1	.695
Silliness	8.2	5.1	0.8	1	.372
Absurdity	2.0	1.0	0.3	1	.558
Satire	0.0	1.0	1.0	1	.315
Sarcasm	1.0	2.0	0.3	1	.558
Irony	0.0	6.1	6.4	1	.011

TABLE 8.6
Number of Information Cues Per Ad for Each Country

	U.S.	U.K.	F	d.f.	p
Information content			12.1	1	.0008
Number of *information cues*					
0	5.1	17.3			
1	10.2	17.3			
2	23.5	8.2			
3	6.1	5.1			
4	4.1	2.0			
5	0.0	0.0			
6	1.0	0.0			

TABLE 8.7
Ads That Contained At Least One Information Cue

	U.S.(%)	U.K. (%)	ChiSq	d.f.	p
No information cues	5.1	17.3			
At least one information cue	44.9	32.7			
			8.44	1	.004

Centrality of Product. The hypothesis that products in American ads are given a more central role than in British ads (H4) was supported by the data in Table 8.8. The brand name and/or product is introduced in the beginning or middle of the ad approximately as frequently in both countries, but British ads differ significantly from American ads in that they more frequently wait until the end of the ad before mentioning the product being sold.

Both countries showed similar results regarding when the product is first seen and how much the spokesperson talks about the product, but are significantly different in how often the ads show the product. British ads

TABLE 8.8
Centrality of Product as a Function of Country

	U.S.(%)	U.K. (%)	ChiSq	d.f.	p
When product is first introduced			6.8	2	.033
Beginning	35.7	28.6			
Middle	14.3	15.3			
End	0.0	6.1			
First introduction of brand name			8.7	2	.013
Beginning	32.7	27.6			
Middle	17.3	14.3			
End	0.0	8.2			
First time product seen			6.7	3	.081
Not Applicable	3.1	1.0			
Beginning	29.9	25.8			
Middle	15.5	15.5			
End	1.0	8.2			
How much spokesperson talks about the product			3.1	3	.375
Not at all	2.0	7.1			
Little	18.4	17.3			
Moderate	17.3	15.3			
Great	12.2	10.2			
How often the product is shown			10.0	4	.041
Not at all	3.0	1.0			
Little	11.2	24.5			
Moderate	21.4	11.2			
Great	14.3	13.3			
How often the product is talked about			5.7	3	.126
Not at all	1.0	7.1			
Little	14.3	16.3			
Moderate	19.4	15.2			
Great	15.3	11.2			
When made clear what was being sold			5.6	2	.060
Beginning	33.7	27.6			
Middle	16.3	17.3			
End	0.0	5.1			

tend to show the product only a little to moderate amount, whereas American ads show the product a moderate to a great amount.

Structure/Execution. The hypothesis that British ads rely more on drama as a structural form whereas American ads rely more on lectures for conveying their messages (H5a) was supported. A significantly greater number of British ads were described as pure dramas, while American ads were either pure lectures or some form of drama that incorporated a lecture at the end as a voice over (see Table 8.9).

It was also found that American ads use more narration, demonstration, spokespeople, and product display as a method of presentation than British

TABLE 8.9
Percent Representation of Dramas, Lectures, and Hybrids as a Function of
Country

	U.S.(%)	U.K. (%)	ChiSq	d.f.	p
Dramas or lectures			12.5	4	.014
Pure lecture	7.2	4.1			
Pure drama	3.1	17.5			
Drama with lecture at end	10.3	7.2			
Drama with voiceover or lecture throughout	9.3	3.2			
Hybrid	19.6	16.3			

Note. The bulk of the hybrids were described as "a series of unconnected images," often with a lecture voiceover.

ads (H5b). These traditional hard sell methods were represented significantly more in the American ads (see Table 8.10).

DISCUSSION

The results support the basic tenet that British advertising can be broadly characterized as soft sell, whereas American advertising is better described as hard sell. Specifically, and as expected, the British ads were significantly more humorous than the American ads. Interestingly, cute and ironic humor was used more by the British in our sample, whereas Weinberger and Spotts' (1989) previous study shows greater use of satire and pun. This may be due to the differences in the samples of ads used.

The failure to find greater use of emotion overall in British ads is at first glance surprising. Two possible explanations come to mind. First, the specific samples of British and American ads used may have been atypical in this regard, although it is hard to pinpoint why an anomaly might have occurred given the selection criteria. Second, despite their preference for a soft sell approach, the British tend to despise sentimentality. The popular

TABLE 8.10
Percent Representation of Information-oriented Method of Presentation as a
Function of Country

	U.S.(%)	U.K. (%)	ChiSq	d.f.	p
Celebrity endorser	5.1	0.0	5.3	1	.022
Typical person endorser	10.2	5.1	2.0	1	.161
Spokesperson	5.1	4.1	0.1	1	.727
Narration	16.3	5.1	7.3	1	.007
Demonstration	18.4	6.1	7.9	1	.005
Product display	24.5	12.2	6.3	1	.012

use of warmth in U.S. advertising that focuses on familial demonstrations of affection (Aaker, Stayman, & Hagerty 1986) would probably be considered in poor taste in Britain.

To avoid pushing a sell, British ads often will not introduce the product until the middle or end of the ad, and often do not show or talk about the product a great deal. By contrast, the American ads were typically filled with brand name and product repetition. In addition, British ads used indirect address (dramas) in preference to direct address (lectures) whereas American ads contained more direct address and lecture/drama hybrids.

Studying British advertising has particularly interesting implications, especially at this time in the early 1990s when many British agencies are buying up American advertising agencies. It is very likely that the advertising that comes out of these newly purchased agencies will have a British influence. The results of this research can perhaps predict some of the directions advertising in America, as well as in Britain, will take.

This chapter contributes to research in international marketing, which currently is lacking. Most cross-cultural studies have focused on East/West comparisons (e.g., Hong, Muderrisoglu, & Zinkhan, 1987; Madden, Caballero, & Matsukubo, 1986; Yau, 1988); comparatively few have used European countries for comparison. The change in trade barriers in 1992 makes the European market a particularly interesting focus for cross-cultural research. The difficulty of advertising in this environment comes from the broad range of cultures represented in a small geographic location. European advertising will need to span a variety of cultural backgrounds and beliefs.

Understanding different cultures and how advertising varies crossculturally is a first step in developing more effective advertising campaigns. Although this study does not directly address the issue of whether soft sell is more effective in Britain and hard sell more effective in the United States, it provides a springboard for future research by identifying crucial differences. The relationship of effectiveness to these differences can then be studied.

REFERENCES

Aaker, D. A., Stayman, D. M., & Hagerty, M. R. (1986). Warmth in advertising: Measurement, impact and sequence effects. *Journal of Consumer Research, 12*, 365-381.

Aydin, N., Terpstra, V., & Yaprak, A. (1984). The American challenge in international advertising. *Journal of Advertising, 13*(4), 49-59.

Berger, P. D. (1972). Vertical cooperative advertising ventures. *Journal of Market Research, 9*(3), 309-312.

Carey, J. W. (1975). Communication and culture. *Communication Research, 2*(2), 173-191.

Chevalier, M., & Foliot, J. M. (1974). Which international strategy for advertising agencies. *European Business, 2*, 26-34.

Clarke, D. B., & Bradford, M. G. (1992). Competition between television companies for advertising revenue in the United Kingdom: The Independent Television regions prior to deregulation. *Environment and Planning A, 24,* 1627-1644.

Deighton, J., Romer, D., & McQueen, J. (1989). Using drama to persuade. *Journal of Consumer Research, 16*(4), 335-343.

Dowling, G. (1980). Information content in U.S. and Australian television advertising. *Journal of Marketing, 44,* 34-37.

Elbashier, A. M., & Nichols, J. R. (1983). Export marketing in the Middle East: The importance of cultural differences. *European Journal of Marketing, 17,* 89-94.

Farley, J. (1986). Are there truly international products and prime prospects for them? *Journal of Advertising Research, 3,* 17-20.

Fraser, I. (1990). The day of the empire-builder. *The Independent,* (Feb. 4), 31.

Fuerbringer, J. (1990, February 8). U.S. acquisitions surge in Europe. *New York Times,* p. C2.

Gilly, M. C. (1988). Sex roles in advertising: A comparison of television advertisements in Australia, Mexico, and the United States. *Journal of Marketing, 52,* 75-85.

Greenhouse, S. (1988, November 18). Building a global supermarket. *New York Times,* p. 34.

Harper, T. (1988, May 16). U.K. eyes new demand to ease prices. *Advertising Age,* p. 68.

Holbrook, M. B. (1987). Mirror, mirror, on the wall, what's unfair in the reflections of advertising? *Journal of Marketing, 51,* 95-103.

Holbrook, M. B., & O'Shaughnessy, J. (1984). The role of emotion in advertising. *Psychology and Marketing, 1*(2), 45-64.

Hong, J., Muderrisoglu, A., & Zinkhan, G. (1987). Cultural differences and advertising expression: A comparative content analysis of Japanese and U.S. magazine advertising. *Journal of Advertising, 16*(1), 55-62.

Hornik, J. (1980). Comparative evaluation of international and national advertising strategies. *Columbia Journal of World Business, 1,* 36-45.

IBA, (1987). *Television and radio 1987: Guide to independent broadcasting.* E. Croston (Ed.). London: Independent Broadcasting Authority.

Kassarjian, H., (1977). Content analysis in consumer research. *Journal of Consumer Research, 4,* 8-18.

Katz, H. (1990). You say tom-a-to and I say tom-ah-to: A study of British and American TV advertising. Paper presented at the ICA Annual Conference, Dublin.

Kelly, J. P., & Solomon P. J. (1975). Humor in television advertising. *Journal of Advertising, 4*(3), 31-35.

Krippendorff, K. (1980). *Content analysis: An introduction to its methodology.* Sage Publications, Inc.

Kuhns, W. (1970). *Waysteps to Eden: Ads and commercials,* New York: Herder and Herder.

Lannon, J. (1986). New techniques for understanding consumer reactions to advertising. *Journal of Advertising Research, 26*(4), RC 6-9.

Lee, W., Faber R., & O'Guinn, T. (1985). Advertising, persuasion, and cultural values. *Proceedings of the Conference on Cross-Cultural and Subcultural Influences on Consumer Behavior.* American Marketing Association.

Lycett, A. (1989, March 29). Cable comes in from the cold. *New York Times,* p. 40.

Lyonski, S. (1985). Role portrayals in British magazine advertisements. *European Journal of Marketing, 19*(7), 37-55.

Madden, C., Caballero, M., & Matsukubo, S. (1986). Analysis of information content in U.S. and Japanese magazine advertising. *Journal of Advertising, 15*(3), 38-44.

Mattelart, A., & Palmer, M. (1991). Advertising in Europe: Promises, pressures and pitfalls. *Media, Culture and Society, 13,* 535-556.

McCollum/Spielman Topline. (1986, August). The hard sell: How is it doing? Great Neck, NY: McCollum Spielman.

Mehrabian, A., & Russell, J. A. (1974). *An approach to environmental psychology.* Cambridge, MA: MIT Press.

Parsiot, L. (1988). Attitudes about the media: A five country comparison. *Public Opinion, 1*, 18-19.

Peterson, R. T. (1983, December 23). Marketers have a social obligation to screen out negative roles in ads. *Marketing News*, 2.

Peterson, T. (1975). *Magazines in the twentieth century*, (2nd ed.), Urbana, IL: University of Illinois Press.

Pollay, R. W. (1983). Measuring the cultural values manifest in advertising. *Current issues and research in advertising, 2*(1), 71-92.

Quelch, J. A., & Hopp, E. J. (1986). Customizing global marketing. *Harvard Business Review, 2*, 59-68.

Resnik, A., & Stern, B. (1977). An analysis of information content in television advertising. *Journal of Marketing, 1*, 50-53.

Rokeach, M. (1973). *The nature of human values*. New York, Free Press.

Root, J. (1986). *Open the box*. London: Comedia Publishing Group.

Schneider, K. C., & Schneider, S. (1979). Trends in sex roles in television commercials. *Journal of Marketing, 43*(2), 79-84.

Taylor, D. (1983). The information content of women's magazine advertising in the UK. *European Journal of Marketing, 17*(5), 49-59.

Weinberger, M., & Spotts, H. (1989). Humor in U.S. versus U.K. TV commercials: A comparison. *Journal of Advertising, 18*(2), 39-44.

Wells, W. D. (1988). Lectures and dramas. In P. Cafferata, & A. Tybout (Eds.), *Cognitive and Affective Responses to Advertising*. Lexington, MA: D. C. Heath.

Wells, W., Burnett, J., & Moriarity, S. (1992). *Advertising: Principles and practice*. Second edition. Englewood Cliffs, NJ: Prentice Hall.

Williamson, J. (1978). *Decoding advertisements: Ideology and meaning in advertising*. London: Marion Boyars.

Yau, O. (1988). Chinese cultural values: Their dimensions and marketing implications. *European Journal of Marketing, 22*(5), 57-69.

9 Advertising in the People's Republic of China

Paul R. Prabhaker
Illinois Institute of Technology

Paul Sauer
Canisius College

Western advertising agencies and multinational corporations that are planning on entering the People's Republic of China market need to be fully aware of the unique traits of the Chinese economy. Understood properly, these traits can turn into marketing opportunities. If misunderstood, these very same traits can turn into fatal obstacles to competing in the Chinese market.

Hence, before looking at all the mechanics of advertising a foreign product in China it is necessary to appreciate the uniqueness of the Chinese economy. A partial listing of the characteristics of the economy is as follows:

- China's trade/GNP ratio is one of the lowest in the world.
- However, imports have been increasing at a phenomenal rate, in the range of 20% to 50% per year. Import capacity, in terms of foreign exchange availability, is expected to stabilize at about 11% in the early part of the 1990's.
- Energy related exports amount to 25% of foreign exchange earnings.
- 47% of China's Gross Domestic Product is from industry. To put this in the proper perspective, the corresponding figure for other developing nations is below 33%.
- The Gini coefficient for China's is a very low 0.16. The average for all nations is 0.43. The Gini coefficient is a measure of the urban income inequality in a country.

- Abundant (almost unlimited) cheap labor coupled with low production costs.
- Over 35, 000 factories for export processing have been set up in the last 10 years. Most of them in the late 1980's.
- City dwellers in China earn three times more than people living in the countryside.

What implications do these facts have for marketers and advertisers? First, the market potential for both industrial and consumer products, is enormous. Equally important is the *homogeneity* of the vast market. This is a very rare characteristic of large markets that marketers of consumer packaged products would find very appealing. What may not be so obvious is the importance of market homogeneity for manufacturers of industrial products and intermediate goods. A large, homogenous population will necessarily imply a relatively large ancillary demand for industrial products. This is especially the case if the market were agri-industrial based, as is the case in China, rather than being driven by strong consumer spending.

Second, foreign exchange availability seems to be tied to the international energy market. If the current slump in oil prices is any indication, payment to Western firms for products and services in hard foreign currency will be severely limited. Corporations and entrepreneurs will have to devise innovative means of payment. This provides a clear opportunity for full service advertising agencies and marketing research firms to utilize their creativity and knowledge of new markets in helping consummate business deals. One payment procedure that is becoming increasingly popular is the payment-in-kind variety.

Third, Western firms can use the unusually high proportion of GNP through industry to market more intermediate products. As mentioned earlier, the demand for intermediate and industrial products is more immediate and has received a correspondingly higher governmental priority.

Finally, the Gini coefficient is a very clear indication that there are no income classes among the masses to speak of. Although there is an extremely small "elite class," typically the top members of the ruling party, a vast majority of the citizens have an almost identical standard of living. Hence, targeting of advertising messages is much less of a factor in China than it is in other more developed economies. Communication should be aimed at the masses in general. The copy themes themselves should reflect a sincere understanding and appreciation of the simple lifestyle of the vast majority, something that Japanes outdoor board advertisers fell short of.

The analysis just given is meant to provide some guidelines on how one should evaluate and understand the *aggregate market situation*. Once this is done, it is important to evaluate the different ways of introducing new products and services to the vast Chinese market through proper communication. Communicating with the marketing industry has to be a multidimensional strategy. Advertising is just one of those dimensions. Clearly, different business environments call for different communications strategies. It would therefore be extremely myopic to think of advertising as a communication tool that rarely fails, especially in international markets where the business environments are very different. In fact, as far as China is concerned, advertising was ranked below personal selling and trade shows in terms of effectiveness of communications (Ho & Chan, 1989). It is important to understand that the aggregate market analysis indicated here should complement the typical marketing and consumer research done by advertising professionals. By no means is the analysis indicated here a substitute for traditional consumer research. The rest of this chapter focuses on evaluating the current situation in China, with respect to advertising.

ADVERTISING

Advertising in China as an industry, has been growing at a very strong rate of 30% and upward (Agnew, 1987). Being in its infancy, the share of the advertising market derived through expenditure on advertising foreign products and services is only about $25 million. Advertising in China used to be done primarily through the print media, as the targeted audience consisted of professionals rather than average customers. But with over 800 advertising agencies in China (Curry, 1988), broadcast advertising is rapidly catching up. Currently, television reaches approximately 35% of China's population and can be accessed in about 30% of the total land mass (Schmuk, 1987). A goal of the present 5 year plan (1986–1990) is to build up capacity to reach 75% of China's population with television. However, there continues to be a wide disparity in television coverage between urban economic centers and the countryside. About 90% of the former can be reached by TV, whereas the corresponding figure for the latter is only about 20%.

Nowadays, the granting of greater decision-making power to end-users has complicated the picture. Foreign advertisements are officially welcome, regardless of how little they account for in the overall advertising revenue. Though market penetration via advertising remains difficult for most Western firms, major international advertising agencies are continuing to view China with cautious optimism. In any event, advertising in China is already a business worth much more than $200 million annually and it is growing. Recent estimates are difficult to obtain. However, $133 million was spent on advertising in 1983, $170 million in 1984, and $228 million in

1986. The Japanese lead the way in terms of total amount spent by foreign advertisers. It is estimated that American firms still total less than their Japanese counterparts in terms of advertising dollars spent in China.

A clear understanding of the ground rules that shape the advertising business in China is essential prior to any market penetration. Many advertising budget related decisions are made by *local work units*. These decisions are primarily made based on the chinese principle of *Guanxi*. Guanxi is the principle of building long-term, committed relationships between various parties. It must also be understood that the media in China are, even now, to a large extent, official arms of the government (Hughes, 1986). Western agencies should interpret this as meaning that the Chinese media are not significantly dependent on ad sales for revenue. In short, attempting to influence decisions on advertising budgets and timings based on short-term profitability rationales may not work especially if such approaches are short on Guanxi. To better understand the hierarchical structure of the advertising decision making process in China, consider the representation in Fig. 9.1.

The chart in Fig. 9.1 clearly illustrates the control of the Chinese Communist Party (CCP) in the decision making process within the adver-

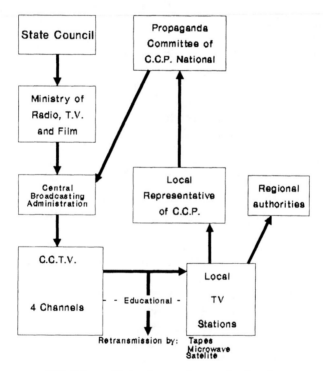

FIG. 9.1.   National network versus local stations.

tising industry. To paraphrase Nathan (1986), up to one half of all the professional staff in the various major media—television, radio, magazines, newspapers—are also members of the CCP.

MEDIA PLANNING

Media planning for the Chinese consumer and industrial markets is characterized by certain uniqe problems. On the one hand, a potential advertiser in the PRC is faced with the problem of having to choose from a staggering array of different kinds of media. For instance, there are several radio stations and national and regional television stations eager to sell air time to foreign corporations. There are literally hundreds of newspapers and magazines that have the ability to reach different types of audiences. Television continues to be the fastest growing medium, growing at almost 50% per year. Television and newspapers are the two dominant media in the PRC marketplace. Radio and magazines, although they are plentiful and can reach the common man, account for less than 5%, each, of the total advertising market.

Proper media planning would be complex under these conditions even in normal circumstances. However, in the Chinese market it turns out to be an extremely frustrating task due to the lack of any credible audience data. Agencies in the PRC are hampered by the lack of marketing research, audience ratings, readership profiles, and so on. (Curry, 1988). Marketing and advertising research is in its infancy, as currently practiced in China.

There are strong cultural barriers that make it difficult to conduct Western style marketing research in China. In addition to the traditional Chinese secretiveness (Fox, 1987), the citizens tend to be suspicious of foreigners collecting information. Events, such as the one that occurred in Tiananmen Square in the summer of 1989, only tend to inflame such suspicions. Telemarketing is not a viable survey tool in China and will not be for at least the next 10 years. Door-to-door approaches to gathering data seem to work fairly well. Free samples and product trials have proven successful too. In any case, regardless of the process of gathering information, the data interpretation has to be done very cautiously. This is because Western agencies are accustomed to reading Western markets, and the principles that apply here do not necessarily hold in China.

There are isolated instances of organizations conducting research prior to making media decisions. Hence, due to the lack of any substantive media data, companies find it easier to embark on mass corporate or "good-citizen" company awareness type advertising rather than attempting informative campaigns targeted toward specific market segments.

Television advertising in China gives true meaning to the phrase "mass advertising." Where else can an advertiser expect a guaranteed audience well in excess of 200 million? Where else can advertisers hope to find consumers as hungry for information through television advertisements? Although there is less than one television set for every 10 Chinese citizens, multiple or communal viewing is common. In rural areas it is not uncommon to find up to 500 people watching programs on one television set! For all these reasons and many more, television advertising in China holds immense potential.

There is only one national network, CCTV, but, according to Agnew (1987), over 100 television stations for advertisers to choose from. Rates for 30-second spots vary widely. Table 9.1 is a partial rate-list provided by a popular trade publication:

The process of actually buying air time on television is not very complicated, though it can be time consuming. Advertisers can chose from among four different alternatives in the buying process. First, they can choose to deal directly with the media. This is not likely to be the most efficient alternative for most Western media buyers in China, as price negotiations are highly limited and are affected only by personal "connections" (Guanxi). Second, one can opt to purchase air time through an off-shore media representative. This is a fairly popular option, as there are quite a few media representatives located in Honk Kong who are well versed in the technical and cultural intricacies of buying media time on the Chinese television. Third, it is possible to establish an official link with a Chinese advertising corporation and have them do the actual media buying. The drawback with this alternative is that there is very often a communication problem within such arrangements. One veteran advertiser claimed that, with the effort it takes to set up such an arrangement, one might as well deal with the media personnel directly. A fourth alternative would be to deal with a program supplier. This is a promising option, as the Chinese television industry is still in a very early part of the growth phase; they do not have too many programming alternatives to choose from. Thus, program suppliers will tend to have more clout with the media.

The program-cum-advertising package put together by CBS in 1983, for China is said to be a seminal event in media buying in China. Essentially,

TABLE 9.1
Prices for 30-second Spots on Chinese TV

Station	Cover (millions)	Cost Per 30 Seconds
CCTV (Channel 3)	300.0	$4000
CCTV (channel 8)	3.2	$1340
Guangdon TV (Canton)	50.0	$1413
Beijing TV	3.2	$ 702
Fujian TV	9.0	$ 396

Note: Adapted from Reaves, L. (1985).

CBS offered several hours of free programming to CCTV in China in return for the right to include several minutes worth of commercial time within the programming. The effort was strongly supported by major corporations such as Eastman Kodak, Proctor & Gamble, Boeing, and so on (Dunlap, 1985). Prices for 30-second spots were set competitively such that packages of 32 minutes of air time were sold to corporations for $300, 000.

If anything, the CBS package deal established the fact that the Chinese decision makers were receptive to barter deals involving free programming in return for free air time. This trend has been taken advantage of by other corporations such as Disney, RCA/Paramount Pictures, Twentieth Century Fox, and so on, who negotiated barter deals of their own.

A word of caution about advertising on television in China. The organizational link between CCTV network and its local affiliates is somewhat of a mystery. There have been cases of local television stations choosing to preempt television commercials aired by CCTV, in the very last minute, without notice (Schmuck, 1987). What makes such situations difficult to deal with is that CCTV is not notified of such preemptions by the local stations, sometimes not even after the fact, resulting in the network being unaware of such happenings. In all fairness, it must be said that CCTV has now significantly increased its control over the local stations.

The print media in China is unlike its broadcast counterpart. As mentioned earlier, the weakness in Chinese television, from a commercial standpoint, is the inability to reach specific audiences. However, the print medium is made up of several hundred trade publications, some general magazines and newspapers. In fact there are over five hundred newspapers and four thousand magazines available for commercial advertising of foreign products. Thus, here we have numerous media vehicles capable of delivering precise audiences. A drawback, however, is the lack of a true "mass" vehicle. The China Daily is the only major international and independent daily newspaper in English. A sampling of price quotes for some popular magazines and journals is provided below in Table 9.2.

TABLE 9.2
Rates for advertising space in Chinese magazines

Magazine	Circulation (1000's)	Cost of Four-Color Full-Page
Technical & Industrial Radio	1300	$3710
Tourism World	350	$2085
Guangzhou – Arts & Culture	250	$1590
Tour	800	$1485
Mobile Technique	200	$1413
Internaitonal Aviation	75	$1060

Note: Adapted from Reaves, L. (1985).

According to Reaves (1985) there are some restrictions regarding the position of advertisements in the magazines and also with regard to the use of full-color advertisements.

Payments for advertisements are based on a two-tier price structure. Local firms pay lower rates and may pay in local currency. Foreign firms pay higher rates and should pay in hard (foreign) currency. This is one more instance of the Chinese decision makers being very aware of the attractiveness of the huge Chinese market potential to Western firms, and accordingly charging an *entry fee* into their market.

CREATIVITY

Conventional wisdom, in regard to advertising new foreign products and services in a market that is still in its infancy, is to utilize simple informational ads without using approaches that may be deemed as too sophisticated. "Slice-of-life" approaches and "product use information" advertisements would be considered appropriate. In China, a Western agency may not have much of a choice when it comes to decision making on the creative side of advertisements, as the level of technical expertise and equipment available is very limited (Boudot, 1988). This coupled with the fact that the Chinese government is extremely wary of "capitalist tools" such as advertising would suggest that very basic, fundamental advertising is what is called for.

A recent analysis of television commercials shown on CCTV indicated that "using the product in its normal environment" was the most popular type of advertising (Stewart & Campbell, 1988). There were very few "mood" or "image" type of advertisements. Another empirical study examined several newspaper ads in China and performed content analyses on them (Tse et al., 1989). The results overwhelmingly indicate that Chinese print advertisements concentrated on utilitarian appeals. These advertisements did not stress hedonic values, nor did they point to American lifestyle as a goal for consumers.

Along with the tremendous increase in the volume of advertising there seem to be ever increasing cases of unethical (foreign) advertising. This has resulted in the Chinese government becoming very leery of possible deceptive advertising and bait-and-switch advertising styles (Semenik, 1986). The major concern, however, is the role of foreign advertising in encouraging excessive interest in material possessions. This has given rise to a constant evolution of ever-changing advertising regulations and enforcement procedures.

As the Chinese would say, creative decisions on advertising really come down to a better understanding of their concerns and problems, their goals and aspirations.

LEGAL AND SOCIETAL RESTRICTIONS

Advertising in China is primarily in its infancy by Western standards. Most consumers tend to accept, literally, the messages that reach them through various forms of advertising. Hence, the masses react very well to basic, informative advertisements that provide product performance information in a simple descriptive format. However, for such advertising to be effective, it is very important that firms build up among the masses a favorable predisposition toward their corporation and their product line. In other words, it is suggested that foreign firms anticipate and plan their entry into the Chinese market several years in advance. This will provide them with the time needed to build a corporate image, which in turn will make product introduction much easier.

The Western corporations that have been successful in China, such as Kodak, Pepsi, Proctor & Gamble, and so on, have carefully planned their marketing activities. Typically, they have had several corporate image type campaigns running for several months prior to actual product attribute type campaigns. One simple way to build a suitable corporate image is by sponsoring appropriate television programs. Given the Chinese penchant for Western programming, this strategy should not be difficult to implement. Once this is done, however, the product advertising should be practical and simple without trying to be too clever.

The decision makers in China seem convinced that advertising, as an institution, can help pave the way toward bigger and better societal benefits. However, the rapid proliferation of advertising in the Chinese market has not been totally costless. First, there is some concern that foreign advertisements may influence the existing political, moral, and social systems. The Chinese government, in fact, has taken several steps to outlaw this problem. Many of these recent rulings have clear implications for the operations of foreign advertising agencies. For instance:

- All local advertising agencies now have to register with the bureau of industry and commerce.
- Advertising of tobacco and liquor products have been banned except in a few select locations.
- Restrictions on the actual copy (wording) of the advertisements has been spelled out in a governmental document.

Second, there is a strong concern that the advertising industry, by inundating the Chinese masses with a constant barrage of advanced lifestyle type advertisements, would create unduly high expectations and new wants. However, the problem surfaces when the people are unable to satisfy these new wants as the products being advertised are sometimes way beyond the reach of an average citizen. A classic example of this is when some Japanese multinational corporations advertised their automobiles and electronic appliances via huge billboards. For most Chinese consumers, constant exposure to such advertisements apparently resulted in frustration, as many of those products are far too expensive. As a result, the Chinese government came down with a total ban on billboard advertising in the main sector of Beijing.

The tragedy in Tiananmen Square during the summer of 1989 is a glaring example of the consequences of pushing for social change much too rapidly, without considering the historical and cultural environment within which such a change has to take place. Although the manner in which the Chinese government chose to handle the situation is unquestionably deplorable, there is plenty of blame to go around. Foreign firms, drawn inexorably by visions of a billion-consumer market, are partly to blame for the rate at which Chinese citizens were introduced to outside lifestyles. The part played by advertising, acting as a catalyst in the whole process, was by no means insignificant.

Third, the still primitive regulations and enforcement procedures serve as no deterrent for advertisements in China to freely make undocumented claims (Stewart & Campbell, 1988). For instance advertisements for wine and other alcoholic drinks are sometimes centered around "their health-giving properties". there is also evidence of increasing advertising malpractices (Ho & Sin, 1988) in the form of *deceptive advertising* and *trademark violations*. All this finally led to the establishment of the *China Consumer Council*. Part of the role of this council is to serve as a watchdog on the advertising industry.

DISCUSSION

Some of the issues mentioned earlier need to be highlighted as critical issues confronting foreign advertising in China. First is the concern of the Chinese decision makers that increased awareness of the outside world's standard of living would cause the expectations of the masses to rise too rapidly. In the long run, it is feared, this could lead to social and economic turmoil. Foreign advertising is very often identified as the culprit responsible for this increased awareness. Foreign advertisers should therefore consider it a high priority to develop a sympathetic understanding of the broader problems that they may, in effect, exarcberate.

Second, it is important to realize that as long as China's foreign exchange is very carefully controlled and the Chinese remain very cautious about spending large sums on "intangibles" such as advertising, the country is unlikely to become the source of significant agency billings in the near future unless the agencies come up with more imaginative schemes. Some recent contracts build on the Chinese inclination for offering payment-in-kind to overseas partners in place of precious foreign exchange upfront. Very simply, this means that Western advertisers will need to become more involved in the overall business dealings if they are serious about cultivating the Chinese market. One example of this is the barter agreement, wherein programs are exchanged for air time, as transacted by CBS and subsequently followed by several other corporations.

Third, advertisers are required to obtain certification from an array of regulatory agencies. Public health agencies must pass foodstuffs and medicines, quality control inspection agencies must testify to quality grade claims, weighing and measuring instruments must be certified, and trademarks must be registered. These add to the procedural difficulty of advertising in China. Again, these type of obstacles point to the need for a better understanding of the human and social side of "target" audiences in China.

Fourth, the problems related to the allocation of advertising expenses in China is not different from problems unique to the budgeting process in centralized economies in general. This means that the actual allocation may frequently be unknown until several months have elapsed. Once the budget has been allocated, there tends to be a rush to use up foreign exchange in the second half of the budget year. This results in many campaigns becoming one-shot deals with no sustained impact. The implication here is that media planning and scheduling decisions in the PRC are fraught with a high degree of uncertainty and should be flexible.

Fifth, it is critical to understand that, to the PRC, advertising, as an institution, symbolizes a very high form of capitalism. Some Chinese managers, when asked for their reaction to advertising, indicate overkill. They feel that there are too many commercials on television and on radio (Semenik, 1986). They also believe that foreign advertising tends to make consumers buy things that they do not need. What they would like to see is advertising used to promote values and satisfaction with the current standard of living. In essence, they would like to see the cost of social and economic change being spread out over a longer period of time. Western advertising agencies need to be sensitive to this concern and need to play the role of solid community citizens.

Finally, it is necessary to accept that, in terms of doing business in China, it is easier and more profitable to advertise and market intermediate and industrial products than consumer packaged products. The priorities set up by the Chinese government are very clear. Goods and services that will help the country develop its infrastructure will be given preference. Such preferential treatment could be in the form of lower tarriffs, lower advertising rates, and so on. Products that do not fall in such preferred categories may have a more difficult time. Problems such as payment difficulty due to inadequate foreign exchange, cases of the Chinese not meeting their contractual obligations, and sudden imposition of hefty taxes, are not unexpected. This is not to say that the consumer market is not a viable one. Rather, the message here is that when dealing in a consumer packaged good in China, such as Pepsi, one needs to have a clear perspective of what the Chinese economy is gaining by that transaction, not the Chinese consumer. More jobs? Foreign investment? Availability of precious foreign exchange?

CONCLUSION

The research in this chapter is an approach to synthesizing the numerous factors that characterize and affect the advertising of foreign products and services in China. As discussed here, there are several obstacles to be overcome. Overall, however, the challenge that advertising in China poses is well worth it, as the rewards are enormous.

REFERENCES

Agnew, J. (1987, January 30). China now implementing capitalist tool. *Marketing News, 21*(3), 10.

Boudot, E. (1988, June). Chinese puzzles for foreign advertisers. *Asian Business, 23*(6), 82-85.

Curry, L. (1988, November 9). International profiles: China. *Advertising Age, 59*(48), 110.

Dunlap, W. (1985, September). Want to reach 600 million television fans? *Marketing and Media Decisions, 20,* 73-78.

Fox, M. (1987, November 2). Marketing/advertising research: In China "Guanxi" is everything. *Advertising Age, 58*(47), S12, S14.

Ho, S., & Chan, C. (1989). Advertising in China — problems and prospects. *International Journal of Advertising, 8*(1), 79-87.

Ho, S., & Sin, Y. (1988). Consumer protection in China: The current state of the art. *European Journal of Marketing, 22*(1), 41-46.

Reaves, L. (1985, September 16). China: A new frontier for advertisers. *Advertising Age, 56,* 74.

Schmuck, C. (1987, Fall). Broadcasts for a billion: The growth of commercial television in China. *Columbia Journal of World Business, 22,*(3), 27-34.

Semenik, R. (1986). Chinese managers' attitudes towards advertising in China. *Journal of Advertising, 15*(4), 56-62.

Stewart, S., & Campbell, N. (1988). Advertising in China and Hong Kong: A preliminary attempt at some comparisons of style. *International Journal of Advertising, 7,*(2), 149-154.

Tse, D. K., & Belk, R. (1989, March). Becoming a consumer society: A longitudinal and cross cultural content analysis of print ads from Hong Kong, the People's Republic of China and Taiwan. *Journal of Consumer Research, 15,*(4), 457-472.

10 The Difficulty of Standardizing International Advertising: Some Propositions and Evidence from Japanese, Korean, and U.S. Television Advertising

Charles R. Taylor
Villanova University

Gordon E. Miracle
Michigan State University

Kyu Yeol Chang
Pepperdine University

This chapter reports the results of a content analysis of over 3000 Japanese, Korean, and U.S. television commercials for several objectively measured variables. Cultural explanations for possible differences in these variables are proposed. If differences in advertisements can be shown to be culturally related, there may be important implications for international firms and advertising agencies. The long-standing international advertising controversy over standardization versus specialization still rages today. Investigation of whether there are differences in objectively measured content could lend further insight into this controversy.

Many prior studies and discussions have used the terms *standardization* and *specialization* (or localization) without clearly stating what is being standardized or specialized. In this chapter, we propose a classification scheme to guide researchers and managers in making these definitions. Major categories in this framework are advertising objectives, message strategies, media strategies, and budgeting. The diversity of these categories makes it apparent that complete standardization across two or more cultures is, indeed, rarely appropriate. Important differences in business practices often complicate matters, as evidenced by the varying proportions of commercials of different lengths in the three countries investigated here. Tradition, government influence, and other factors may lead to a common, entrenched practice in a given country. Further complicating the ability to standardize is the possible impact of cultural differences. Three cultural differences between the two Asian countries and the U.S. are proposed as possible reasons for differences in the variables analyzed here. Because the subject of advertising standardization or specialization is so complex, this study is limited to advertising message strategies used in television commercials and one aspect of media strategy.

To carry out this research, samples of television commercials were taped off-the-air in Japan, the Republic of Korea and the United States. A content analysis was performed on commercials from a board range of nationally advertised product categories. Reported here is the analysis of the following "timing and counting" variables:

1. Commercial length.
2. Time until brand name is identified.
3. Time until company name is identified.
4. Time until the product or package is shown.
5. Time the product or package appears on screen.
6. Time company name or logo is on screen.
7. Time brand name is on screen.
8. Number of times company name or logo appears on screen.
9. Number of times brand name is on screen.
10. Number of times company name is mentioned.
11. Number of times brand name is mentioned.

An important feature of these variables is that they can be measured objectively in each culture.

The research questions were:

1. What differences are there in the relative frequency of commercials of different lengths in Japan, Korea and the United States? What are the reasons for such differences?
2. Are there differences in the advertising strategies used in the three countries, as evidenced by the differences in the means of the timing and counting variables? If such differences exist, can they be attributed at least in part to cultural variation? Or, are the differences in advertising at least consonant with what the literature leads us to hypothesize?
3. What are the implications of the findings for advertising managers and for those who create television commercials?

DEFINING STANDARDIZATION

Before discussing prior literature on standardization of advertising, it is necessary to clearly define the term. Several prior studies have used the term without describing which elements of international advertising they are applying it to. A framework that is useful for the purpose of clearly specifying which aspects of advertising are being standardized is shown in Fig. 10.1 (Miracle, 1968, 1990). Figure 10.1 shows four primary dimensions of advertising between nations that may or may not be standardized: objectives, message strategies, media strategies, and budgets. Because all of these dimensions, or even subsets of them, can be standardized, research directed at investigating the degree of standardization that is (or is not) feasible should clearly specify which dimensions are being dealt with. It should also be aimed at specifying conditions under which the several aspects of advertising can or should be standardized.

This study investigates questions relative to several components of advertising message strategies and one aspect of advertising media strategy. The timing and counting variables represent elements of message strategy. It may be the case that the mean values for several of these variables differ between the three countries analyzed. For example, it may be much more common to show the company name often in Japan and South Korea than it is in the United States. If this is the case, and if such differences in message strategy are linked to cultural factors, one might infer that it would be difficult to standardize this element of message strategy in the United States and the two Asian countries.

Commercial length is an element of media strategy. It may be that due to customary business practices, government regulations, or culturally based factors that commercials of a certain length are more common in one culture than another. If so, one could infer that there is some difficulty associated with standardizing this element of media strategy across cultures.

Advertising Objectives
    Clear communication tasks (many possibilities, e.g., hierarchy)
    Defined target audience (e.g., purchasers, users)
    Specified periods of time

Advertising Message Strategies
    (e.g., themes; appeals; positive vs. negative; much or little information; image vs. product, company or brand; comparisons or not; a spokesperson or voice over; color mix)

Advertising Media Strategies
    (e.g., which media vehicles; size of ads or length of commercials; flighting; pulsing)

Advertising Budgets
    (e.g., heavy, light or medium weight; by product; by market area; by selected media; for selected creative or message approaches; match or not match competitors; contracyclical or not)

FIG. 10.1. Illustrative examples of dimensions of advertising that may or may not be standardized between nations. *Note.* Additionally, one may consider standardizing the methods or process by which the above decisions are made.

LITERATURE REVIEW

Standardization versus Specialization

The degree to which advertising in international markets can be standardized has long been controversial. The literature surrounding the debate has been well summarized elsewhere, (e.g., Walters, 1986), so what is presented here is designed only to give the reader an overview of the general arguments that have been presented on each side of the debate, and what types of evidence have been provided. It is not intended to be comprehensive.

Several writers have argued that advertisers are well advised to standardize. Although proponents of some form of standardization probably existed much further back, Elinder (1961) is often credited with being among the first to bring the issue to the attention of modern day marketers. Elinder believed that the time had come in Europe when similarities in aspects of consumer behavior outweighed "national traits". He reasoned that standardization of advertising for the European market was feasible for this reason and also because of the increasing availability of international media and the greater mobility of European consumers.

Fatt (1967) was another proponent of standardization. He argued that there are universal appeals that can be effective in advertising. Fatt believed that improvements in international communications and transportation made standardization increasingly possible. Additionally, when the opportunity to standardize did arise, he suggested that it should be exploited, because truly creative and effective promotional campaigns are a scarce commodity.

Buzzell (1968) argued that there are several benefits of standardization. Although he admitted that there are some limitations based on local differences, he felt that standardization was often possible and desirable. The specific benefits he pointed to were cost savings, consistency of dealing with customers, exploitation of ideas with universal appeal, and improved planning and control.

Levitt (1983) proclaimed that the dawn of the global village was upon us. Citing technology, communications, and transport, he maintained that the globalization of markets would lead marketers to use standardized strategies, especially brands and products.

Peebles (1989) also advocated standardized strategies, primarily due to the need to create and maintain world brand images. He also asserted that many opponents of standardized advertising rely on examples where it has not worked in the past to infer that it can never work. Peebles admitted that the cost advantages of standardization, if present at all, had probably been overstated by past standardization advocates. The need for consistent images in an increasingly global market, however, was presented as a factor that should make managers strive to find standardized advertising approaches rather than simply assuming that they cannot be useful based on examples where it has been misapplied.

It can be seen from the arguments given that the proponents of standardized advertising have relied mainly on logical and theoretical arguments rather than empirical evidence. The same can also be said for those who believe that all advertising must be customized for local markets. Some researchers who have taken a middle ground in the debate and have focused on factors that make standardized advertising more (or less) feasible in a given situation have performed empirical research. As Walters (1986) pointed out, these studies have relied almost exclusively on surveys of managers. We return to this point after discussing the primary arguments of those favoring customization in the vast majority of cases.

Weissman (1967) emphasized differences of those living in different nations. He argued that these deep rooted dissimilarities required different marketing programs. Especially with regard to consumer goods, Weissman emphasized that the differences in consumers among those of different nationalities outweighed the similarities.

Ricks, Arpan, and Fu (1974) cited several examples where standardized advertising failed badly. They stressed the need to know the culture(s) being operated in, saying that differences in customs, attitudes, and needs must always be taken into account. Thus an approach in which individuals from multiple cultures (at least representatives from headquarters and the host country) plan advertising strategy abroad was advocated.

Hornik (1980) compared U.S. advertising campaigns with locally tailored Israeli advertisements for the same product. Generally, it was found that localized themes are preferred except in the small number of instances in which the ad was geared toward an international appeal, a worldwide corporate image, or a common international connotation.

Harris (1984) argued strongly in favor of local adaptation. He refuted four major arguments in favor of standardization: cost savings, increased similarity of markets in demand characteristics, advantages of world brand images, and exploitation of marketing skills, concluding that the range of products for which standardization can be applied is very limited.

Many researchers have sought more neutral ground with regard to the standardization issue and have focused either on current practice and what can be learned from it or have attempted to identify contingencies that suggest when standardization is more/less appropriate. Several authors, including Miracle (1968), Dunn (1976), Peebles, Ryans, and Vernon (1977), have suggested that, when investigating an international market, process standardization is advisable. Thus, advertising managers must take a variety of features of a country's environment into account when making international advertising decisions. Similarly, several authors have suggested that a variety of contingencies must be considered in determining the degree to which advertising can be standardized (e.g., Quelch & Hoff, 1986; Kreutzer, 1988; Jain, 1989). The level of compatibility of such environmental variables between countries determines the extent to which advertising can be standardized.

Although much of the work involving process standardization has not been empirical in nature, there have been some studies that have surveyed managers. Sorenson and Weichmann (1975), for instance, surveyed 37 consumer packaged goods managers of large MNC subsidiaries in Europe, and concluded that although the benefits of standardizing marketing may be circumstantial, it is advisable to engage in process standardization.

Boddewyn, Soehl, and Picard (1986) surveyed European Economic Community firms, finding that although substantial barriers to standardized advertising existed, it was practiced by many managers. Specific variables linked to standardization success were the nature of the product (consumer vs. industrial), the extent of national differences (tastes, regulations, etc.), the level of competition, and economic conditions.

Hite and Fraser (1988) replicated the Boddewyn et al. (1986) study, using a sample of successful multinational U.S. firms. They found that only 9% of the firms standardized for all foreign markets, with the majority relying on a mix of standardization and adaptation. They, too, developed a list of factors that managers felt were important determinants of the success or failure of standardization programs.

Although research surveying managers may be useful in determining current business practices, it is inherently limited. Research testing the impact of specific variables related to standardization is needed. This study attempts to take a step in that direction by suggesting specific cultural differences between East and West that may be related to differences in the objective content of advertising in the countries included in the study. Because the research is descriptive, and not experimental, in nature, it, too, is limited. It does, however, suggest some very specific hypotheses relating cultural differences to objectively measurable advertising content that could be used in future experimental studies. The specific cultural differences hypothesized to play a role in determining the advertising content of the three countries are now discussed.

Cultural Differences

Context. Different languages may exhibit contextual variations. Hall (1976) described the difference between high and low context cultures in the following way:

A high context (HC) communication or message is one in which most of the information is already in the person, while very little is in the coded, explicit, transmitted part of the message. A low context (LC) communication is just the opposite; i.e., the mass of the information is vested in the explicit code. Twins who have grown up together can and do communicate more economically (HC) than do two lawyers in a courtroom during a trial (LC), a mathematician programming a computer, two politicians drafting a regulation, two administrators writing a regulation.

Hall (1976) and Hall and Hall (1987) observed that the United States is characterized by a low context culture, whereas Japan has a relatively high context culture. Other writers have noticed the high context nature of the Korean culture. Yum (1987), for instance, attributed the high context nature of Korean culture to Confucian influences. Yum also cited a traditional deemphasis of oral (vs. written) communication and the high value placed on reading nonverbal cues as being characteristic of the Korean culture. Kang (1988) and Gudykunst, Yoon, and Nishida (1987) also pointed out the high context nature of the Korean culture, finding indirectness and nonobviousness in communication to be preferred over the directness and obviousness that are more valued in the West.

Additionally, the Japanese written language uses Chinese characters (Kanji) rather than an alphabet. Koreans now use a more nearly phonetic system (Hangul) that is comparable to an alphabet. However, Koreans have long used Chinese characters (Hanja), and their use persists among Korean intellectuals even today. Each character is a symbol that often carries more meaning than a letter or a few letters of an alphabet, and often as much as several words or a sentence. In addition, the meaning is communicated in a more visual way, as a picture or image. Meaning that is transmitted and received visually can be grasped more quickly, and Japanese and Koreans may be able to "read" more rapidly than Americans. Thus, in a high context culture (which is comparatively more visually oriented) it is expected that the length of commercials will tend to be shorter than in a low context culture (which is oriented comparatively more toward verbal messages.

Wells (1986) stressed the need for global advertisers to pay attention to contextual variation. High context cultures are relational, intuitive, and contemplative as opposed to low context cultures, which are analytical and action oriented. We would expect communication styles to differ in high and low context cultures. In particular, it is expected that advertisements in relatively high context cultures would be more likely to place more emphasis on mood, and less on the brand/company/product, and vice versa. These different communication styles should show up in the mean values of the timing and counting variables, because Japan and Korea are high context cultures and the U.S. is a low context culture. Commercials in a high context culture that stress mood would probably be more likely to build a mood in the first part of the commercial and to identify the brand or show the product later in the commercial. It is less likely that the brand name, company name, or product will be shown early and/or often in advertising in such cultures. Conversely, commercials in a low context culture would probably show the brand, company, or product earlier and repeat the brand or company name and show the product relatively more often.

Confrontation

Madden, Caballero, and Matsukubo (1986) cited the need to know key cultural differences when advertising products in foreign markets. One characteristic of Japanese culture that they consider to be important is the avoidance of confrontation. Assertive, bold, aggressive forms of advertising are rarely found in Japan. Thus, a direct approach in which the seller urges consumers to act immediately would be less likely to be used in Japan than in the United States, where assertive, direct statements and confrontation seem to be more frequent.

Students of Korean culture also notice a tendency to avoid confrontation in communication. Yum (1987), for instance, characterized the Korean communication style as being "accommodation oriented" as opposed to confrontation oriented. He noted:

> The Korean language . . . is abundant with implicitness and indirectness. This aspect is a consequence of the Confucian legacy of putting the highest value on human relationships. Indirect communication helps to avoid embarrassment and rejection by the other person, leaving the relationship intact.

Paik (1968) and others noted that the traditional face consciousness of Koreans makes confrontations in social interaction generally unpleasant. Such observations reveal the relative similarity of the Japanese and Korean cultures on this dimension.

Stewart and Furse (1986) found the presence of a brand-differentiating message to be the single most important advertising executional factor in the United States when judged on measures of persuasiveness. Therefore, it is expected that U.S. commercials will take a relatively confrontational approach, characterized by more direct references to the brand and product as a means of differentiating the brand from others. In contrast, because confrontation is discouraged in Japan and Korea whereas harmony is sought, it is expected that commercials in the two countries will contain relatively fewer direct brand references to the brand and product as a means of differentiating the brand from others. Thus, it is expected that the mean length of time until a brand, product, or package is shown on screen will be longer in Japan and Korea than in the United States. It is also expected that the amount of time and the number of times the brand name or logo or the product/package is mentioned or shown will be lower in Japan and Korea than in the United States.

It should be noted that frequent appearance or mention of the company name may or may not be an important part of a confrontational approach. The company name may never be mentioned in a confrontational advertisement if the goal is to focus attention on the brand name, a frequent U.S. approach when consumers tend to buy primarily on the basis of brand name or loyalty. On the other hand, if consumers tend to buy on the basis of the seller's reputation, firms may prefer to flash the company name often and mention it frequently as part of a confrontational approach. To influence consumer purchases of such products, it may be important to leave a strong impression of the company name in the consumer's mind. Thus, no general effect of the use of a confrontational approach on the frequency of mention or appearance of the company name can be inferred.

Individualism versus Collectivism

A third proposed cultural factor relates to the ideas of dependence and independence. Individualism implies independence and collectivism implies dependence or interdependence. In the United States, individualistic and independent behaviors are valued relatively highly, whereas dependence often has a negative connotation. Miracle (1987) pointed out that in Japan, individualism is viewed relatively negatively and dependency is viewed positively. Hoare and Pares (1988) indicated that Koreans also value dependency highly, as evidenced by their willingness to rely relatively more on extended families for various forms of emotional, social, and economic support, compared with the United States. Paik (1968), Kim (1984, 1985) also noted that the individual has not been the unit of social life in traditional Korean society. Instead, a spirit of mutual assistance and cooperation among groups prevails, manifesting itself (among other ways) in cooperation among rural and urban dwellers in harvesting rice or dealing with droughts. The Korean people are typically willing to "pitch in" for the good of their country.

Miracle (1987) compared the logic between Western and Japanese advertising. He noted that advertising executives who have experience in both Japan and the United States often feel that, in Western advertising, the logic is basically to tell the audience:

- how your product is different.
- why your product is best, clearly stating information about its benefits.
- consumers will then want to buy, because they have a clear reason or justification for the purchase.

- if they are satisfied, consumers will like and trust the company and the product and they will make repeat purchases.

Discussions with such experienced executives (Miracle, 1987) also suggested that the logic behind Japanese advertising is essentially the opposite. The sequence tends to be:

- make friends with the audience.
- prove that you understand their feelings.
- show that you are nice.
- consumers will then want to buy because they feel familiar with you and trust you.
- after the purchase consumers will find out if the product is good and what the benefits are.

It important to note that the first three steps in the Japanese sequence often take place before any mention of the brand or advertiser is made. Thus, it seems as if the commercials are designed so that Japanese consumers can feel comfortable with and depend on the advertiser in making the purchase decision; this occurs to a greater extent in Japan than in the United States. Therefore, we would expect that the first mention or appearance on screen of a brand, company name, or product take place later in a typical Japanese commercial than in a typical U.S. commercial. Given that Koreans share a high value on dependency, similar results are expected from the Korean data.

Hofstede (1980, 1983), in his work on cultural differences in work-related values, noted the collectivistic nature of the Japanese and Korean cultures in comparison to the United States (Gudykunst et al., 1987). Hofstede found the United States to rate among the highest of the 50 countries he studied, whereas Japan and Korea rank considerably lower. He noted that, in collectivistic cultures, there is a preference for "a tightly knit social structure in which individuals can expect other in-group persons to look after them." Thus, Hofstede's data would support the notion that it is important for Japanese and South Korean advertisers to make an effort to give the audience a feeling that they can be relied upon.

An advertiser who is attempting to create or reinforce a belief that the company's products can be relied upon may feel that it is necessary to make sure that the viewer knows what company is presenting the message. Hence, there may be some pressure toward mentioning or showing the company name earlier and more often in a Japanese or South Korean commercial than in an American one. Differences from U.S. commercials may, however, be offset by the use of a confrontational approach in the United States, in which the company name is a component.

HYPOTHESES

Keeping in mind that the primary purpose of this chapter is to investigate whether culturally based differences make standardization difficult, all hypotheses are stated in a nondirectional manner. Nevertheless, specific deviations in mean values that differ from what the literature might lead one to expect are commented on.

The first hypothesis is that the relative frequency of commercials of different lengths is different in Japan, Korea and the USA. Thus:

H1: The relative frequency of commercials of 15, 20, and 30 seconds is significantly different for Japanese, US and Korean commercials.

The remaining ten hypotheses propose that the mean values of the timing and counting variables for Japanese, Korean, US commercials vary significantly. The rationale for these hypotheses is based upon the cultural dimensions discussed in the literature review. Thus:

H2: The mean number of seconds before the brand name is identified is significantly different in commercials in Japan, Korea, and the United States.

H3: The mean number of seconds before the company name is identified is significantly different in commercials in Japan, Korea, and the United States.

H4: The mean number of seconds before the product or package is identified is significantly different in commercials in Japan, Korea, and the United States.

H5: The mean number of seconds that the product or package is on screen is significantly different in commercials in Japan, Korea, and the United States.

H6: The mean number of seconds that the company name or logo is on screen is significantly different in commercials in Japan, Korea, and the United States.

H7: The mean number of seconds that the brand name is on screen is significantly different in commercials in Japan, Korea, and the United States.

H8: The mean number of times that the company name or logo is on screen is significantly different in commercials in Japan, Korea, and the United States.

H9:   The mean number of times that the brand name is on screen is significantly different in commercials in Japan, Korea, and the United States.

H10:   The mean number of times that the company name is mentioned is significantly different in commercials in Japan, Korea, and the United States.

H11:   The mean number of times the brand name is mentioned is significantly different in commercials in Japan, Korea, and the United States.

RESEARCH METHODS

Sample

Television commercials were taped off-the-air in Japan, Korea, and the United States in the fall of 1988 and winter of 1989. In order to obtain a representative and proportionate sample across all major nationally advertised product categories, taping was done over a period of several weeks, including all major listening times, and avoiding unusual times or days such as holidays. For this analysis 1253 Japanese, 1228 American, and 867 Korean commercials were available. For the purposes of testing the hypotheses, commercials of all lengths were included in the calculation of the mean values of the timing and counting variables. To test for the possibility of an effect of commercial length on the results, 15- and 30-second commercials were also categorized and analyzed separately. Commercials of other lengths, including 20 seconds (which is the most common length in Korea) were not analyzed separately because of their infrequent occurrence in two of the three countries.

The sample represented a broad range of products and services advertised nationally (see Fig. 10.2). This generally excluded local advertising, political advocacy, government, and generic demand advertisements.

Coding Instrument and Coding Process

The timing and counting variables were taken in part from the work of Stewart and Furse (1986) and were part of a larger coding instrument to study information cues and executional techniques. An initial pilot study was run, and appropriate modifications to the coding instrument and other parts of the research process were made. To measure the timing and counting variables, native speakers of the language of each commercial were used. Because the timing and counting variables were measured

a) Food, beverages
b) Alcoholic beverages
c) Tobacco products
d) Over-the-counter drugs
e) Automobiles and bicycles
f) Lawn and garden equipment
g) Automobile supplies and parts
h) Cosmetics, personal care
i) Detergent, cleaner, air freshener
j) Household and gardening supplies
k) Clothing and shoes
l) Textiles and fabrics
m) Furniture, floor and wall coverings
n) Ceramics, glassware
o) Household electric appliances
p) Electronics and Equipment
q) Home Entertainment supplies
r) Cameras/ camera related
s) Photographic supplies
t) Computers, computer hardware
u) Computer supplies
v) Clocks, watches
w) Communication, telecommunication equipt.
x) Toys, games
y) Sporting goods
z) Pets, Pet food and supplies
aa) Publications
bb) Stationary and home office supplies
cc) Musical instruments
dd) Building materials
ee) Other products
ff) Hotels, Motels
gg) Restaurants, bars
hh) Movies, theaters
ii) Department stores
jj) Supermarkets
kk) Other retailers
ll) Banking, finance
mm) Transportation services
nn) Telecommunications services
oo) Schools, education
pp) Hospitals, medical services
qq) Other services

FIG. 10.2.   Product/service categorization scheme used in study.

separately and were the last to be recorded in the study, coders who had demonstrated proficiency in earlier coding were chosen, trained (in their native language), and viewed each commercial a sufficient number of times to make the required measurements to the nearest second with a stopwatch.

Analysis and Treatment of Data

Because commercials of different lengths were included in the calculation of the means for each test variable, it was necessary to divide each measure by the commercial's whole length. In this way, "proportional" measures that served to normalize the means for commercials of various lengths were obtained. If, for example, the proportional mean for the "time until the brand name is identified" variable was.388, it would indicate that the brand name was identified after 38.8% of that commercial's whole length (see first variable in Table 10.2). In the case of those timing and counting variables that measure how long some event occurs during the commercial (e.g., time the product or package appears on screen), the proportional mean indicates the overall percentage of the commercial during which the event occurs. Thus, if the proportional mean for the time the product or package was on screen is.547, this indicates that the product or package was on screen for 54.7% of the commercial's whole length.

To answer the first research question, χ^2 tests were performed to test for differences in the relative frequencies of 15-, 20-, and 30-second commercials. Commercials of other lengths were not included as a separate category, because they accounted for less than 10% of the sample in all three countries (1.1% in Japan, 5.1% in Korea, and 7.7% in the United States). To answer the second research question (which asked if there are significant differences in the means of the timing and counting variables), analysis of variance (ANOVA's) tests were used. All tests were run utilizing the SPSS/PC+ statistical package. In all cases, the.05 level of significance was used as the standard by which the hypothesis tests were judged. With regard to the ANOVA tests for differences in group means, it should be remembered that in a test on three groups (as is used here), even if two means are very similar and the other is substantially different, the F-tests will produce statistically significant results if the sample is reasonably large (Blalock, 1979). This is viewed as being appropriate for the purposes of this chapter, because if the mean in even one country differs from that of the other two, the implication is that the element of advertising strategy being investigated should not be standardized across all three countries.

Before turning to a presentation of the results, a few points regarding the calculation of mean values must be made. First, the reported means for variables in which there is time until some event occurs is recorded (e.g., time until brand name is identified) do not include commercials in which the event does not occur. For example, if the brand name is not identified in an advertisement, that commercial would be omitted from the calculation of the mean time until the brand name is identified. This is important to realize, because there are a large number of U.S. commercials in which the company name is never identified (about 56%). But identifying the company name is common in Japan and Korea — 94% and 90% of the commercials, respectively, make this identification. These differences are considered in interpreting the results.

Another consideration in calculating means was how to treat outlying values when the variable dealt with how often an event occurred (e.g., how often the company name was shown on screen). In a few commercials (less than 1% in each country) the event occurred a very large number of times. Therefore, instances in which the event occurred more than 20 times were simply recorded as "numerous" and are not included in the calculation of means. It was felt that the inclusion of such commercials might distort the mean value for a country. For example, if a commercial such as one of the "Bud Bowl" advertisements, in which the brand name is shown over 100 times, was included in the calculation of the number of times the brand appears on screen in the United States, an inflated mean would be reported.

Finally, it should be pointed out that this methodology does not allow for rigorous testing of the influence of culture on advertising strategy. However, it does indicate whether television advertising characteristics are associated or in harmony with each domestic culture. In addition, it may show how culture can be used as a guide to managerial practice.

RESULTS

Table 10.1 shows the results of the χ^2 test for differences in the relative frequency of commercials of 15, 20, and 30 seconds in the three countries. As can be seen, the results are significant. Indeed, each country has a different commercial length as its most common one — 15 seconds in Japan, 20 seconds in Korea, and 30 seconds in the USA, suggesting a fundamental difference in the standard practices of each nation.

Table 10.2 shows the proportional means of each country for each of the remaining timing and counting variables across all commercial lengths. As can be seen, the F-tests indicate that there are significant differences in all cases. It should be observed, however, that some of the differences in the

TABLE 10.1
Relative Frequency of 15-, 20-, and 30-Second Commercials by Country

	Japan		U.S.		Korea	
	N	%	N	%	N	%
15 seconds	814	65.7	366	32.3	275	33.4
20 seconds	1	0.1	11	0.9	322	39.1
30 seconds	424	34.2	757	66.8	226	27.5

$\chi^2 = 1264.97$, 4 D. F., $p < .000$.

TABLE 10.2
Adjusted Means of Timing and Counting Variables For All Commercials

Variable	Japan	U.S.	Korea	F	p-value
Time until brand id./ commercial length	.388	.261	.250	97.0	.000
Time until company id./ commercial length	.428	.322	.659	179.5	.000
Time until pdt. or pckg. shown/comm. length	.286	.263	.256	4.2	.015
Time pdt. or pckg. is on screen/comm. length	.547	.449	.428	61.1	.000
Time company name or logo is on screen/comm. length	.233	.295	.128	152.7	.000
Time brand name or logo is on screen/comm. length	.274	.330	.231	66.4	.000
# times comp. name or logo is on screen/comm. length	.127	.061	.078	155.0	.000
# times brand name or logo is on screen/comm. length	.176	.133	.163	36.8	.000
# times comp. name is mentioned/comm. length	.054	.039	.058	32.7	.000
# times brand name is mentioned/comm. length	.088	.102	.153	218.5	.000

Note. Sample size: Japan = 1253, U.S. = 1228, Korea = 867. Reported are proportional means, sample sizes (*n*), and *p*-levels.

raw level of the means are much more striking than others. It can be seen, for instance, that the average number of times the company name is mentioned in Japanese advertisements is close to twice that of U.S. advertisements. On the other hand, the differences for both the time until the product or package is shown and the number of seconds that the product or package is on screen are not especially striking, in spite of the finding of statistical significance. For the most part, however, these findings seem to indicate fairly substantial differences in the timing and counting variables. Most of the findings are also consistent with the direction predicted by the proposed cultural explanations. Notable exceptions include the relatively small differences in the two variables related to the product or package and the Korean results for hypotheses related to brand name. Because these exceptions could be related to the shorter mean commercial lengths in Japan and Korea, it is important to explore the results of tests in which commercial length was constant.

Table 10.3 shows the means of each timing and counting variable for 15-second commercials in each country. Nine of the ten F-tests produced a statistically significant result. In the lone exception, the mean amount of time until the product or package is shown is remarkably similar in each of the three countries. Again, all of the findings relating to company name are consistent with the cultural explanations. With regard to brand name, the Japan/United States differences are consistent with the hypothesized direction as is the mean amount of time the brand name appears on screen. The brand name in Korea, however, is identified slightly earlier in the commercial and is also shown and mentioned slightly more often.

In Table 10.4, which shows the means for 30-second commercials, 8 of the 10 hypothesis tests indicate statistically significant results. The exceptions are the time until the product or package is shown, and the number of times that the company name is mentioned. This latter finding may be explained by the inclusion of many commercials in the U.S. sample in which the company name was not mentioned (over half of the commercials) as well as the possible conflicting effects of dependency and context on this variable. Again, the results of the Korean means are mixed with regard to the direction of the differences, although the finding that the brand name is on screen for less than one half of the amount of time in a 30-second Korean commercial than it is in the United States is striking, and consistent with the literature review. It should be stressed at this point that the questionable consistency of the South Korean "brand" findings in no way undermines the overall finding of a substantial difference in the means of at least two countries making it difficult to standardize advertising in all three countries,

TABLE 10.3
Means of Timing and Counting Variables For 15-Second Commercials

Variable	Japan	U.S.	Korea	F	p-value
Time until brand name is identified	5.71	4.17	4.02	28.4	.000
Time until company name/logo is ident.	6.33	5.88	11.17	87.7	.000
Time until pdt. or pckg. is shown	4.19	4.22	4.36	0.2	.829
Time pdt. or pckg. is on screen	8.71	7.40	6.68	31.4	.000
Time company name or logo is on screen	3.87	4.66	2.03	63.0	.000
Time brand name or logo is on screen	4.59	5.61	3.78	33.0	.000
# of times comp. name or logo is on screen	2.29	0.80	1.29	118.1	.000
# of times brand name or logo is on screen	3.27	2.53	2.87	14.8	.000
# of times comp. name is mentioned	0.92	0.51	0.85	26.8	.000
# of times brand name is mentioned	1.58	1.96	2.70	96.3	.000

Note. Sample size: Japan = 814, U.S. = 366, Korea = 275. Reported are means, sample sizes (n), and p-levels.

TABLE 10.4
Means of Timing and Counting Variables For 30-Second Commercials

Variable	Japan	U.S.	Korea	F	p-value
Time until brand name is identified	12.09	7.61	7.59	44.2	.000
Time until company name/logo is ident.	13.17	9.12	17.25	42.8	.000
Time until pdt. or pckg. is shown	8.76	7.76	7.59	2.7	.069
Time pdt. or pckg. is on screen	14.37	12.97	12.04	6.3	.002
Time company name or logo is on screen	5.61	8.81	3.42	63.4	.000
Time brand name or logo is on screen	6.24	9.33	4.54	43.8	.000
# of times comp. name or logo is on screen	2.42	1.98	1.72	7.0	.001
# of times brand name or logo is on screen	2.94	3.56	2.37	7.4	.001
# of times comp. name is mentioned	1.26	1.27	1.37	0.5	.595
# of times brand name is mentioned	1.75	2.76	3.67	90.6	.000

Note. Sample size: Japan = 424, U.S. = 757, ROK = 226. Reported are means, sample sizes (*n*), and *p*-levels.

because the Japanese means are strikingly different across both commercial lengths and for the entire sample.

Managerial Implications

The findings generally support the notion that it is difficult to standardize across the three countries' commercial lengths (media strategy) and elements of message strategies, related to the timing and counting variables. Clearly, due to cultural variables, entrenched business practices, government regulation, or some other force, average commercial lengths in the three countries vary substantially. Additionally, the majority of the timing and counting variables have substantially different and managerially relevant differences in means. For instance, the mean time until the company name is identified in Korean 30-second commercials is over 8 seconds longer than for U.S. commercials of the same length. This finding should be of interest to anyone wishing to advertise in both countries. It would seem that generally, it would be a mistake to attempt to standardize advertising on these variables across the three countries.

A possible exception to the statement just made is the variables relating to the product or package. Across the entire sample and the individual commercial lengths tested, the values of the means may be too small to infer managerial significance. This suggests that it may in fact be possible to standardize this element of message across these three cultures. Although the hypothesized directions of differences for the timing and counting variables based on cultural characteristics generally held up well, it would appear that some other factor may be related to the use of the brand name in Korean advertising. The general finding of the brand name being shown for a shorter period of time in Korea than in the United States is supportive of the role of context in Korean advertising, but the apparent willingness to mention or show the brand name relatively early and often suggests that some other factor, perhaps relating to stage of economic development, may be at work.

Suggestions for Future Research

Although the results of this study seem to indicate that cultural characteristics warrant further investigation, it is clear that experiments are needed in which other factors that can be controlled are tested. Although some insight has been given on a few "East versus West" cultural dimensions, many more countries and cultures need to be analyzed. Additionally, many of the other possible dimensions of standardization of international advertising (see Fig. 10.1) need to be investigated.

There is a general need for more cross-cultural research on advertising. Both qualitative and quantitative studies are needed so that hypotheses with a sound theoretical basis can be tested. Hypotheses should be derived from both the experience of practitioners and from the scientific and scholarly literature.

CONCLUSION

This chapter analyzes the feasibility of standardizing a few elements of advertising message strategy and advertising media strategy across Japan, Korea, and the United States. Results seem to indicate that complete standardization across all three cultures would not be advisable. Additionally, the variables examined represent a small subset of those dimensions on which international advertising can be standardized. This suggests that the notion of complete standardization across many cultures is not feasible. It is clear, however, that much more research is needed to determine which elements of international advertising may or may not be possible to standardize.

ACKNOWLEDGMENTS

The authors gratefully acknowledge the support for this research provided by the Hoso Bunka Foundation (Tokyo), The Korea Broadcast Advertising Corporation (Seoul), ASI Market Research, Inc. (Tokyo), the Yoshida Hideo Memorial Foundation (Tokyo), and Youngshin Academy (Seoul).

REFERENCES

Blalock, H. M. (1979). *Social statistics*. New York: McGraw Hill.

Boddewyn, J. J., Soehl, R., & Picard, J. (1986). Standardization of international marketing: Is Ted Levitt in fact right? *Business Horizons, 29*, 69–75.

Buzzell, R. D. (1968). Can you standardize multinational marketing? *Harvard Business Review, 46*, 102–113.

Dunn, S. W. (1976). Effect of national identity on multinational promotion in Europe. *Journal of Marketing, 40*, 50–57.

Elinder, E. (1961). How international can international advertising be? *International Advertiser*, 12–16.

Fatt, A. C. (1967). The danger of "local" international advertising. *Journal of Marketing, 31*, 60–62.

Gudykunst, W. B., Yoon, Y. C., & Nishada, Y. C. (1987). The influence of individualism-collectivism on perceptions of communication in ingroup and outgroup relationships. *Communication Monographs, 54*, 295–306.

Hall, E. T. (1976). *Beyond Culture*. Garden City, NY: Anchor Press/Doubleday.

Hall, E. T., & Hall, M. R. (1987). *Hidden differences: Doing business with the Japanese*. Garden City, NY: Anchor Press/Doubleday.

Harris, G. (1984). The globalization of advertising. *International Journal of Advertising, 3*, 223–234.

Hite, R. E., & Fraser, C. (1988). International advertising strategies of multinational corporations. *Journal of Advertising Research, 28*, 9–17.

Hoare, J., & Pares, S. (1988). *Korea: An Introduction*. New York: Kegan Paul International.

Hofstede, G. (1980). *Culture's consequences: International differences in work-related values*. Beverly Hills: Sage.

Hofstede, G. (1983). Dimensions of national cultures in fifty countries and three regions. In J. Deregowski, S. Dziurawiec, & R. Annis (Eds.), *Explorations in cross-cultural psychology* (pp. 365–397). Lisse, Netherlands: Swets and Zeitlinger.

Hornik, J. (1980). Comparative evaluation of international vs. national advertising strategies. *Columbia Journal of World Business, 15*, 36–45.

Jain, S. (1989). Standardization of international marketing strategy: Some research hypotheses. *Journal of Marketing, 53*, 70–79.

Kang, S. P. (1988). Korean culture, the Seoul olympics, and world order. *Korea and World Affairs*, 347–362.

Kim, K. D. (1984). *Man and society in Korea's economic growth*. Seoul: Seoul National University Press.

Kim, H. E. (1985). *Korea: Beyond the hills*. Seoul: Samhwa Publishing Co.

Kreutzer, R. T. (1988). Marketing mix standardization: An integrated approach in global marketing. *European Journal of Marketing, 11*, 19–30.

Levitt, Theodore. (1983). The Globalization of Markets. *Harvard Business Review, 61*, 92–102.

Madden, C. S., Caballero, M. J., & Matsukubo, S. (1986). Analysis of information content in U.S. and Japanese magazine advertising. *Journal of Advertising, 17,* 38–45.

Miracle, G. E. (1968). International advertising principles and strategies. *MSU Business Topics, 9,* 29–36.

Miracle, G. E. (1987). Feel-do-learn: An alternative sequence underlying Japanese consumer response to television commercials. In F. Feasley (Ed.), *Proceedings of the 1987 Conference of the American Academy of Advertising* (pp. R73–R78). Columbia: University of South Carolina.

Miracle G. E. (1990). The advertising environment, advertising law, and the standardization of international advertising: The case of Japan and the USA. In P. A. Stout (Ed.), *Proceedings of the National Conference of the American Academy of Advertising* (pp. RC61–RC66) Austin: University of Texas.

Paik, H. K. (1968). The Korean social structure and its implications for education. *The Korea Journal, 8,* 7–17.

Peebles, D. M. (1989). Don't write off global advertising: A commentary. *International Marketing Review, 9,* 73–78.

Quelch, J. A. & Hoff, E. J. (1986). Customizing global marketing. *Harvard Business Review, 64,* 59–68.

Ricks, D. A., Arpan, J., & Fu, M. Y. (1974). Pitfalls in advertising overseas. *Journal of Advertising Research, 14,* 47–50.

Sorenson, R. Z., & Wiechmann, U. E. (1975). How multinationals view marketing standardization. *Harvard Business Review, 55,* 38–167.

Stewart, D. W., & Furse, D. H. (1986). *Effective television advertising: A study of 1000 commercials.* Lexington, MA: D. C. Heath.

Walters, P. G. P. (1986). International marketing policy: A discussion of the standardization construct and its relevance for corporate policy. *Journal of International Business Studies, 17,* 55–69.

Weissman, G. (1967). International expansion. In L. J. Adler (Ed.), *Plotting marketing strategy, a new orientation* (p. 197). New York: Simon & Schuster.

Wells, W., (1986 February 13). Global advertisers should pay heed to contextual variations. *Marketing News,* p. 18.

Yum, J. O. (1987). Korean philosophy and communication. In D. L. Kincaid (Ed.), *Communication theory From Eastern and Western perspectives* (pp. 71–86). New York: Academic Press.

11

"Are They Saying the Same Thing"? An Exploratory Study of Japanese and American Automobile Advertising

Stephen J. Gould
Baruch College

Yuko Minowa
Rutgers University

Previous studies comparing Japanese and American advertising have tended to find differences more of degree than of kind in terms of appeals and information provided (Hong, Muderrisoglu, & Zinkan, 1987; Mueller, 1987). Perhaps we should expect such results if we take a structuralist view of these nations' modern capitalistic economies. Thus, as inevitably occurs when any cross-cultural marketing question is posed, we confront Levitt's (1983) global, standardized marketing hypothesis. In terms of structuralist signifying dualities, Japan and the United States are both high tech as opposed to low tech, and modern as opposed to primitive.

Yet, to frame a perspective on their advertising, based solely on their modernistic similarities, would be to miss the differences in values and psychology that compose their societies (cf. Belk & Bryce, 1986; Belk & Pollay, 1985; Kumagai, 1988). Can we say that Levitt is right with respect to Japan and the United States? If not, then what is correct with respect to these two nations? For instance, Onkivisit and Shaw (1987) noted the ongoing controversy surrounding the validity and applicability of standardized advertising across countries and industries. This chapter explores this issue by considering the advertising for a product that has long been the hallmark of modern consumption, the automobile. In doing so, we perform content analysis on a number of ads for autos, matched for socioeconomic characteristics, and then, in conjunction with this analysis, draw some conclusions and implications.

CONCEPTUAL FRAMEWORK

Product Used in this Study

We chose to study the automobile because it has a variety of appeals of interest, both rational and emotional. Note that there is a fundamental difference in the nature of the demand for the automobile. Thus, the demand across the countries may be seen not only in terms of cultural factors, but also in terms of structural marketplace factors that often may be as important as cultural factors in determining communication messages and consumer behavior. In Japan, where fewer people own cars than in the United States, structurally, there is an excellent public transportation system and a relatively small amount of habitable area. Thus, the demand for cars is more on the basis of luxury than in the United States, where the car is more of a necessity and there is more wide open space.

Appeals Considered

The following appeals or aspects of appeals are considered in this study, based on past research and potential relevance to both theoretical and practical understanding: (a) soft versus hard sell, (b) individualism versus group consensus, and (c) status appeals.

Hard Sell Versus Soft Sell

Based on previous research (Mueller, 1987), we expect that Japanese car ads will display more soft sell and less hard sell appeals than their American counterparts. This can be attributed to the Japanese reliance on intuition and emotion as opposed to logical thought (Shibatani, 1980). Another reason may lie in the Japanese tendency toward understatement and indirectness, which leaves communication open to interpretation. This has been seen in sharp contrast to the American directness (Kishii, 1987). Haiku, which produces an effect by what is not said, exemplifies the Japanese approach to apparently preferring indirectness and softer image-oriented messages in ads.

H1: Japanese automobile ads will employ more soft-sell appeals than matched or comparable American ads.

H2: Japanese automobile ads will employ less hard-sell appeals than matched or comparable American ads.

Individualism Versus Group Consensus

It has been suggested that the Japanese engage more in group consensus behavior than Westerners (Weisz, Rothbaum, & Blackburn, 1984). However, Flanagan (1979) found that post-war Japan, in its modernization process, has experienced a shift in its value priorities toward more self-indulgence, secularism, permissiveness, independence, and self-assertiveness. Such strong value shifts may explain why Mueller (1987) found that individualism was emphasized in Japanese ads more than in American ads. We can attribute this to the fact that Americans may take for granted their individualism whereas the Japanese are a people in transition, culturally, as they apparently move toward more individualism. The advertising, in effect, is acting as a cheerleader encouraging more individualism. Therefore we expect to see more individualism in Japanese ads.

> H3: Japanese automobile ads will display a higher degree of individual/independent appeal than will comparable American ads.

Status

Both countries should display status in their car advertising, although we can perhaps expect more in Japanese ads, based on Mueller (1987).

> H4: Japanese automobile ads will use status appeals more than comparable American ads.

THE STUDY

A content analysis (Kassarjian, 1977) was employed to analyze 10 car print ads, 5 Japanese and 5 American, as described in the following section.

Sample of Ads

The ads were selected on a quota judgemental basis (Dillon, Madden & Firtle, 1987) from both men's and women's magazines This process was used to select 10 print advertisements from magazines of both nations. From Japan, three men's monthly periodicals—which aim to appeal to young as well as middle-age, middle class segments—were chosen. In addition, three women's monthly magazines—which aim at young, urban college students and also at office workers—were selected. Women's magazines targeted to women over 35 were excluded because only a small number drive their own car. U.S. magazines were selected on a matching

TABLE 11.1
Japanese and U.S. Magazines Selected for This Study

	Japanese magazines	American magazines
Men's and General Interest	Bungei Shunju	Fortune
	BIG Tomorrow	Esquire
	Playboy (Japanese edition)	Time
Women's	JJ	Self
	Can Cam	Savvy
	With	Working Woman

basis. Thus, although in the United States there are general magazines with large circulations, which consistently contain many automobile ads and which are targeted to both genders (e.g., *Time*, *Newsweek*), no equivalent across-gender magazine was found for Japan. Hence, in addition to *Time*, magazines that were more gender oriented were also selected for the United States. The magazines selected are shown in Table 11.1 and the characteristics of the Japanese magazines are shown in Table 11.2. It should be noted that *Fortune*, a professional magazine, was selected to compare with *Bungei Shunju*, a general middle-class magazine for men. The ads chosen are shown in Table 11.3.

Appeals

The descriptors used to assess the appeals were as follows:

Soft-Sell Appeal. A soft-sell appeal is one that is indirect and may employ such devices as mood, ambiguity, and suspense to create an intriguing message. Emotion is emphasized over rationality.

TABLE 11.2
Characteristics of the Japanese Magazines Used in the Study

Men's

1. *Bungei Shunju*: Most widely read middle class general magazine, appealing to both modern tastes and traditional sentiments. Circulation: 564,523.
2. *Big Tomorrow*: Provides practical information for men in today's modern society. Circulation: 680,000.
3. Playboy (Japanese Edition): Similar to U.S. *Playboy*. Circulation: 600,000.

Women's

4. *JJ*: Fashion and beauty magazine. 70% of readers are co-eds and office clerks. Circulation: 650,000.
5. *Can Cam*: Fashion and leisure magazine targeted to university co-eds and office clerks. Circulation: 550,000.
6. *With*: Lifestyle magazine for women 23 to 28. Circulation: 700,000.

Note. Adapted from Dentsu (1988).

TABLE 11.3
Print Advertisements Selected for
This Study

Japanese ads
Nissan March
Nissan Bluebird
Honda Prelude
Mitsubishi Galant
Peugeot 505
American ads
GM Chevrolet
Ford Scorpio
Mitsubishi Sigma
Honda Prelude
Toyota Supra

Hard-Sell Appeal. Such appeals are relatively straightforward and employ strong arguments and pushy demands for action. Such appeals are also direct and often emphasize product benefits.

Individualism/Independence Appeal. Individualism/independence appeals place an emphasis on the individual's being distinct and unlike others. Dependency is deemphasized (Mueller, 1987).

Status Appeal. Status appeals suggest that the use of the advertised product will improve some inherent quality of the user in others' eyes. This category also includes foreign status appeal — use of foreign words, phrases, models, and foreign celebrity endorsements (Mueller, 1987).

Analytical Procedure

Initially, 14 students were selected to evaluate the ads. We selected a varying sample of judges because there was the possibility of judges differing based on ethnic-cultural factors. Five of the students were Americans who were majoring in marketing and who had had no major exposure to Japanese culture. Four others were native Japanese students who were competent in reading English but had lived in the United States for less than 6 months. Two more were American students who had lived in Japan and were fluent in Japanese. The remaining three were Japanese students who had lived in the United States more than 4 years and had acquired a fair knowledge of U.S. culture. The ads were translated into English.

There were differences among the judges for appeal rating. A pretest was conducted to see how the analysis would proceed with the different cultural and language orientations of the raters. Differences and unacceptable interrater reliabilities were found with different combinations of raters. Although some of the problem might lie in the protocol used, nonetheless these results indicated to us some validity problems that have not been all that well-addressed concerning cross-cultural content analyses. For the final study, we included three raters whose ratings had the least deviations in average from the mean, that is, one Japanese, one American, and one bilingual/bicultural Japanese (language difference might make the ratings not fully comparable). The mean interrater reliabilities, as measured here by Pearson correlation coefficients and shown in Table 11.4 (cf. Hong, Muderrisoglu, & Zinkan, 1987), were all over .8, which is the minimal acceptable level supported by Kassarjian (1977) for content analyses in consumer research (correlations were used as a measure of agreement or tendency of agreement because the measures were on a continuous scale of 1 to 5).

RESULTS

The hypotheses, regarding the appeals, were tested through the use of analysis of variance (ANOVA). Table 11.5 shows the mean ratings for the three judges used.

Soft-Sell Appeals. The first hypothesis predicted that Japanese advertisements should employ more soft-sell appeals than American ads. A 2 (country) × 2 (sex) ANOVA was run. The results indicate that there were significant effects for both country, confirming the first hypothesis, $F(1, 8) = 112.03, p < .005$, and gender, $F(1, 8) = 89.69, p < .005$. These results were also borne out in t-tests run between countries and within both genders ($p < .01$ for both genders).

Hard-Sell Appeals. The second hypothesis stated that Japanese advertisements would employ less hard-sell appeals than U.S. advertisements.

TABLE 11.4
Inter-rater Reliability

Appeal	Bilingual and Japanese rater	Bilingual and American rater	Japanese and American rater	Mean reliability
Soft sell	.938	.939	.798	.892
Hard sell	.919	.943	.867	.909
Individual/independence	1.000	.753	.753	.836
Status	.917	.834	.682	.811

Note. Table entries are Pearson correlation coefficients and represent percentage of agreement (where .90 = 90% agreement).

TABLE 11.5
Means of the Judges Ratings for the Appeals

Appeal	Japanese Ads	American Ads
Soft sell		
Overall	3.72	2.14
Male Magazine	3.00	1.44
Female Magazine	4.44	2.83
Hard sell		
Overall	2.78	4.53
Male Magazine	4.00	4.89
Female Magazine	1.56	4.17
Individualism/independence		
Overall	3.64	3.25
Male Magazine	3.17	3.33
Female Magazine	4.11	3.17
Status appeal		
Overall	2.84	2.86
Male Magazine	3.67	2.89
Female Magazine	2.00	2.83

Note. The possible range of ratings is from 1 to 5, with a 5 indicating that the appeal was strongly present and a 1 indicating that it was not present at all.

Again, a 2 (country) × 2 (sex) ANOVA was run. There were significant main effects for both country, $F(1, 8) = 51.55$, $p < .005$, and gender, $F(1, 8) = 42.19$, $p < .005$, as well as a significant interaction between the two factors, $F(1, 8) = 12.48$, $p < .01$. Thus, the country effect provides support for the hypothesis. Further analysis of the interaction revealed that there was a major difference in the proportion of hard-sell ads across the genders between the Japanese and Americans. For the Japanese, hard-sell ads appear to be more acceptable to men than women by a far greater margin than for Americans, although hard-sell ads were seen to be more appealing for men in both countries.

Individualism/Independence Appeals.   The third hypothesis stated that Japanese ads should display a greater degree of individualism/ independence appeals than U.S. ads. This hypothesis was supported in the 2 (country) × 2 (gender) ANOVA, $F(1, 8) = 8.91$, $p < .025$ and $F(1, 8) = 8.91$, $p < .025$, for country and gender, respectively. In addition, there was a significant interaction, $F(1, 8) = 18.18$, $p < .01$. In this case, the male appeal was less than the female appeal in Japan, whereas the reverse was true in the United States.

Status Appeal.   The fourth hypothesis stated that status appeals Should occur more in Japanese automobile advertisements than in American ads.

However, a 2 (country) × 2 (gender) ANOVA failed to support the country hypothesis ($p > .05$). However, there were both significant gender, $F(1, 8) = 7.10$, $p < .01$, and interaction, $F(1, 8) = 13.92$, $p < .01$, effects. Although for both nations status appeals were higher for men, the effect was most pronounced for the Japanese, where a simple t-test revealed that males were significantly more likely to be exposed to a status appeal than were females.

DISCUSSION AND IMPLICATIONS

The present research signals caution when interpreting Japanese vis-a-vis American advertising. The results only partially confirm past research and in other ways contradict it. Several possible explanations and/or limiting factors may be cited. First, it is possible that content analysis techniques themselves are not standardized enough, especially in their execution, and therefore are problematic in producing replicable or reproducible results. Second, we were only able to use a small number of ads and it is possible that they were not really representative. However, although we acknowledge this possibility, we doubt it because although we analyzed only a relatively small number, we nonetheless had examined a far broader range of ads in other research and felt that, on that basis, the ads used were representative.

Another problem concerns raters' or judges' cultural biases. As a side experiment in this study, we attempted to use Japanese and American judges who possessed varying degrees of (non) biliguality and experience with the two cultures. Although we used the most reliable raters in the end, the results were quite variable when we used less reliable judges. Thus, not only is the selection of raters a possible problem here, but we suggest that it might be a problem in other studies as well and should not be overlooked. In fact, further research into perfecting the content analysis methodology in rater terms would be useful. This methodological problem also is symtomatic of the larger problem, that is, whether standardization can work – if trained raters from different countries have difficulties in developing common perspectives on ads, how much more difficult this might be for the typical advertising audience.

Fourth, particular products may be seen as being a part of a cultural constellation all their own so that projections from one category to another may not be valid, that is, our results here may not generalize beyond those for the automobile. A fifth problem concerns time considerations. Societies in transition are just that, and our results, of course, stem from a time subsequent to previously reported studies. All these problems should serve as cautions to both advertising researchers and creative advertisers who are trying to analyze or develop cross-cultural advertising.

In spite of these limitations, we can draw several provisional conclusions. First, our results support the conclusions of Mueller (1987) regarding hard-and soft-sell advertising differences in the two countries – Japanese ads tend to be more soft sell and American ads tend to be more hard sell. A good example of a Japanese soft-sell ad that we considered was one for the Prelude Image in the Japanese women's magazine *With*. It's poetic body copy is typical of many Japanese ads in which the product almost blends in as part of the socio-environmental background rather than being the focused object of desire. The car's benefits are mentioned in the copy not as overt selling points, but rather as almost oblique slivers of the poetic gestalt (e.g., "Runs, turns, and stops more sublimely than anything else." The actual visualized car is set in the ad as a part of the physical background and while the eye goes to it, it does so from a distance rather than as a direct frontal assault – the ad is soft sell in the picture as much as it is in the words. Such an effect might be compared to Zen-like qualities of *wabi*, the elegance of simplicity, and *sabi*, the elegance of quietness. Thus, a total or close reading of the ad, whether from a semiotic, literary critical, or other related point of view, should be able to decipher and even deconstruct the ad not merely in *etic* Western eyes, but also in Japanese *emic* eyes, without which, understanding will be as meaningful or as useful as a pouch of gold dust scattered to the wind. The wabi (the elegance of simplicity) and sabi (the elegance of quietness) of the ad as reflected in the words that follow will be missed:

It is a beautiful, content time
Continuum of a moment lasting forever
Sweet memory, Prelude Image
Runs, turns, and stops more sublimely than anything else.
Trailing of limpid fascination spurs artistic feeling
Pleasant sensation of being watched
Pleasant sensation of looking back
Honda Prelude, someone is watching.

Second, the limitation regarding products studied in comparative content analyses may be seen as an asset, especially as advertisers are often interested in a particular product category in any case. Thus, research should be carefully framed in specific categories rather than have broad cross-category or "categoryless" (i.e., lumping all product categories together) analyses.

Third, in spite of Levitt's (1983) views on global marketing and standardized advertising, our results reveal that it would be premature, assuming that we ever see such prospects come to pass, to generally expose the Japanese and Americans to the same advertising. Not only did the two countries differ in at least some of the aspects we consider here, but they also differ in many other aspects not considered. For example, the Japanese tend to favor the use of Caucasian or Caucasian-like models in their ads whereas Americans do not move the other way in using Japanese or other Asian models.

As another example, when the Japanese invoke certain historical or social images, such as the 11th-century mythological hero, Ushiwakamaru, who is depicted in a television commercial for Regain, a vitamin restoration beverage for men, they are engaging in complex symbolic communication that has meaning only for the Japanese. It is interesting that this same commercial also reflects a cultural tension between East and West. The individual requiring the power of Regain needs it to restore his energy lost in facing a group of Western businessmen who seem to be ganging up on him. Ushiwakamaru may be seen as representing the ultimate restoration of "Japaneseness" to the situation and saving the Japanese businessman from losing his own roots, the source of his own strength. Ironically, the product is called Regain, an English term, so that the restoration of power might be viewed as much in terms of taking power from the Westerners as from one's Japanese roots, themselves. Thus a major theme in much Japanese advertising involves the tension between West and East, as well as to a smaller and perhaps more subtle degree the tension between traditional and modern. These aspects should be read not only in terms of denotative meanings that often are enough to differentiate the advertising of two cultures, but also in terms of the rich connotative constellations of significations that generally are either imperceptible or meaningless to members of one culture with respect to another.

Our overall conclusion at this point is that the texture and richness of the Japanese and American cultures do not presage standardization so much as an interplay of cultural competition, imitation, positioning, and interaction that each culture translates into its own terms (cf. Sherry & Camargo, 1987 for a discussion of syncretism, cultural evolution, and the mediation of old and new accelerated by cultural contact). Our conclusion also agrees somewhat with that of Tse, Belk, and Zhou (1989) who found consumption differences among the "three Chinas," that is, the People's Republic of China, Taiwan, and Hong Kong. However, they emphasized convergence of consumption values and although we agree that such an effect may be occurring, we want to caution against an overemphasis on it.

The play of values, development, and structural marketplace differences (Olshavsky, Moore, & Lin 1988) across many countries may produce complex patterns of convergence and divergence, especially within product categories and within-country market segments. For example, Tansey,

Hyman, and Zinkan (1990) found both convergence and divergence of cultural themes in their study of Brazilian and U.S. auto advertising. Moreover, they suggested that in terms of various lifestyle/demographic factors, such as literacy and income, Brazilian business people are more like U.S. business people than they are like the average Brazilian worker. Such patterns and factors will play a role in determining and shaping the nature of advertising messages, making overly simplified formulas for designing them potentially harmful to the advertiser. Ultimately, the test for making standardization/adaptation decisions lies in the psychological meaning that consumers find in the advertising presented to them (Friedmann, 1986).

Thus, on a continually evolving basis, we expect that world advertising will follow the pattern of U.S. domestic advertising in which many ads are standardized across regions but in which local advertising and regional differences are sometimes emphasized. However, the ratio of localized to globalized advertising will vary, although it is likely to be quite a bit higher than that ratio is for U.S. domestic advertising for nationally distributed products. In particular, the Japanese seem quite bent on an ambivalent relationship with the West, which is reflected in their advertising, at once embracing the use of Western products, models, ambience, and music, and yet at the same time, reaching for traditional appeals or themes that reaffirm their own identity and also confirm their increasing power on the world stage.

REFERENCES

Belk, R. W., & Bryce, W. W., (1986). Materialism and individual determinism in U.S. and Japanese television advertising. In R. J. Lutz (Ed.), *Advances in Consumer Research* (Vol. 13, pp. 568-572). Provo, UT: Association for Consumer Research.

Belk, R., & Pollay, R. C. (1985). "Americanization in print advertising: An historical comparison of Japanese and U.S. advertising since 1945. In C. T. Tan & J. N. Sheth (Eds.), *Historical Perspective in Consumer Research: National and International Perspectives* (pp. 302-306) Singapore: Association for Consumer Research.

Dentsu (1988). Japan marketing/advertising yearbook. Tokyo: Dentsu, Inc.

Dillon, W. R., Madden, T. J., & Firtle, N. H. (1987). *Marketing research in a marketing environment*. St. Louis: Times Mirror/Mosby College Publishing.

Flanagan, S. C. (1979). Value change and partisan change in Japan. *Comparative Politics, 11,* 253-278.

Friedmann, R. (1986). Psychological meaning of products: A simplification of the standardization vs. adaptation debate. *Columbia Journal of World Business, 21,* 97-104.

Hong, J., Muderrisoglu, A., & Zinkan, G. M. (1987). Cultural differences and advertising expression: A comparative content analysis of Japanese and U.S. magazine advertising. *Journal of Advertising, 16*(1), 55-62, 68.

Kassarjian, H. H. (1977). Content analysis in consumer research. *Journal of Consumer Research, 4,* 8-18.

Kishii, T., Sato, H. (Ed.). (1987). Message vs. mood—A look at some of the differences between Japanese and Western television commercials. *DENTSU Japan Marketing/Advertising Yearbook* (pp. 51–57). Tokyo: Dentsu, Inc.

Kumagai, H. A. (1988). Ki: The "fervor of vitality" and the subjective self. *Symbolic Interaction, 11,* 175–190.

Levitt, T. (1983, May/June). The globalization of markets. *Harvard Business Review,* pp. 92–102.

Mueller, B. (1987). Reflections of culture: An analysis of Japanese and American advertising appeals. *Journal of Advertising Research, 27,* 51–59.

Olshavsky, R. W., Moore, D. J., & Lin, J. (1988). An information processing interpretation of cross-national consumer characteristics. *Journal of Global Marketing, 1,* 25–39.

Onkivisit, S., & Shaw, J. J. (1987). Standardized international advertising. *Columbia Journal of World Business, 22,* 43–55.

Sherry, J. F., Jr., & Camargo, E. G. (1987). May your life: English language labelling and the semiotics of Japanese promotion. *Journal of Consumer Research, 14,* 174–188.

Shibatani, A. (1980). It may turn out that the language we learn alters the physical operation of our brains. *Science '80, 8,* 22–27.

Tansey, R., Hyman, M. R., & Zinkan, G. M. (1990). Cultural themes in Brazilian and U.S. auto ads: A cross-cultural comparison. *Journal of Advertising, 19*(2), 30–39.

Tse, D., Belk, R. W., & Zhou, N. (1989). Becoming a consumer society: A longitudinal and cross-cultural content analysis of print ads from Hong Kong, the People's Republic of China, and Taiwan. *Journal of Consumer Research, 15,* 457–472.

Weisz, J. R., Rothbaum, F., & Blackburn, T. C. (1984). Standing out and standing in: The psychology of control in America and Japan. *American Psychologist, 39,* 955–969.

IV METHODS AND PARADIGMS

12

Developing A Text-Theoretic Methodology for Analyzing Subcultural Market Segments: A Pilot Study

Robert J. Corey
West Virginia University

Jerome D. Williams
The Pennsylvania State University

Marketers typically look for segmentation bases, such as culture, race, ethnicity, gender, and so on, that allow consumers to be placed in homogeneous categories so that specific advertising programs can be targeted to them. Because language is the device most often used to convert private thoughts into public expressions, it has the potential to play a crucial role in the development of our understanding of any market segment. Some psychologists believe that no other activity gives the same sort of insight into another person as does language. In fact, some early psychologists believed that higher mental processes could not be analyzed experimentally; they felt that the only way to understand complex psychological processes was by analysis of cultural products, which put the study of language in a central role (Miller, 1990).

Analyzing the use of language by different market segments builds on interpretivist methods employed by other researchers who have recently examined the use of language by consumers and advertisers; For example, word associations to capture the psychological meaning of products (Friedmann, 1989), linguistic characteristics to create brand names (Vanden Bergh, Adler, & Oliver, 1987), and symbolic anthropology and semiotics to understand the meanings of products (Durgee, 1986).

However, these interpretivist methodologies are not without controversy, particularly as they relate to the familiar consumer research debate between the proponents of positivism and interpretivism (Hudson & Ozanne, 1988). Researchers in the latter domain would reject the positivist notion that consumer segments could be studied like the physical world in a controlled experiment. They would argue that each segment must be examined from the perspective of the consumers involved. Numerous compelling arguments maintain that there is indeed added value to be realized by viewing marketing activity in terms of symbolic acts to be read and interpreted (e.g., Hirschman, 1986; Leigh & McGraw, 1989; Miles & Huberman, 1984; Prus, 1989). This more recent research view, detailed in the study of postpositivist philosophy of science, holds that marketplace exchange takes place in a socially constructed reality (e.g., Hirschman, 1986; Prus, 1989).

Without denigrating positivist methodology, in this chapter we accept the proposition that socially constructed reality can be meaningfully viewed as language relative, that is, a function of the choice of words used to present perspective, identify and label objects and ideas, and invite cooperation and identification with others. Thus, socially constructed reality, grounded in the empirical certainty of words, is available for analysis and interpretation in the form of qualitative data (text). Text is an artifact of language use. With appropriate interpretation the language of exchange relationships can provide a rich, detailed, and factually based answer to the question, "What is really going on here?" (Durgee, 1986).

In this chapter we develop a text-theoretic framework embracing elements of both quantitative and qualitative methodology to explore language characteristics as a basis for analyzing market segments. Although this approach could be extended to a global marketing context, we illustrate its use through a pilot study investigating ethnic language differences between African American and White consumers. Specifically, we provide an interpretive account of how these two market segments manage language to create meaning and present social reality. For advertisers, understanding segment "reality" can provide insight into what motivates market choice behavior and hence lead to greater marketing efficiency in the use of appropriate language in advertising and communication strategy.

The remainder of this chapter is divided into five sections. Because analytical methods incorporating rhetorical theory are relatively new to the marketing discipline (Bush & Boller, 1991), the first two sections provide background, first on the role of language as a basis of examining ethnic differences, and then on the theory of textualism. The third section outlines the pilot study, with particular emphasis on the procedure, and the fourth section details the results. The final section offers some concluding observations.

CULTURE, LANGUAGE, AND ETHNIC DIFFERENCES

No single definition of culture is likely to do justice to its complexity. One that is suitable for our purposes is that of Hofstede (1980). He defined culture as the collective programming of the mind. This seems appropriate because it links culture with cognitive processing. As noted by Peter and Olson (1987), culture is one of the most basic influences on an individual's cognitions and behaviors, because all facets of life are carried out against a backdrop of shared values and artifacts of society in which the person lives. Implicit in the link between culture and cognition is the role of language. Although various types of research have focused on language, there has been no agreement as to the relationship between language and culture and the relationship between language and cognition. Regarding culture, some view language as a part of culture, whereas others view language as impacting culture.

Regarding cognition, one view is that language shapes cognitive processing. Therefore the way we perceive reality would be a function of language, that is, the Whorfian hypothesis (Whorf, 1941). On the other hand, others view the language in which we express ourselves as an external reflection of the cognitive process. In the latter view, language provides the lens through which we can peer into an individual's mind to see what cognitive processing is taking place, that is, how the individual is structuring the world. It is this latter view that most clearly supports the methodology underlying the present exploratory study.

More specifically, Gregg (1984) drawing on anthropological, neurological, psycholinguistic, psychological, and literary theories has argued at length that cognitive principles are operationalized in culture, language, and other forms of symbolic activity. According to Gregg:

> All that we experience, all that we "know," all of the meaning we create and respond to is made possible by our innate capacity to symbolize. It is all symbolic behavior. Our neurophysiological processing is always and inevitably geared to structure our experiencing symbolically, and basic but complex principles of mind–brain activity guide and shape all of the symbolizing we engage in. (p. 131)

The implication of this perspective is that we can gain a better understanding of an individual's internal cognitive process by examining his or her language. To expand on this notion, within this section we will first develop a consumer behavior framework incorporating language as a segmentation variable and discuss implications, and then elaborate on the two basic assumptions for the pilot study: the existence of cognitive processing differences and the existence of language differences between African American and White consumers.

Language in a Consumer Behavior Framework and Implications

Borrowing from Peter and Olson (1987) and incorporating Gregg's (1984) perspective on language as symbolic action, we have developed a consumer behavior framework that incorporates language based on the view of language as consistent with basic principles of cognitive processing. As shown in Fig. 12.1, there are four major components of the framework: socio-cultural environment, marketing strategy environment, cognition/symbolic action, and consumer response behavior. The sociocultural environment includes the complex of physical and social stimuli in the external world of consumers, including culture, subculture, social class, reference groups, and family values and expectations expressed and conveyed through language and other forms of symbolic action. Language as a reflection of cognition is seen to operate within the symbolically structured sociocultural environment.

Although, from the consumer's viewpoint, the marketing strategy environment is just another part of the overall environment, it is treated separately in the framework due to its importance to the marketer. As is the case with culture and the other elements of the sociocultural environment, marketing strategy is formulated in a manner consistent with principles of cognition and made manifest through symbolic/physical action. Thus, language as a reflection of cognition also operates within this environment. Advertising strategy is a part of this component of the model.

Typically the study of language investigates the elements of form (e.g., verbal vs. nonverbal, phonology, morphology, syntax), content (e.g., lexicon, slang, semantics), and use (e.g., pragmatics, rhetoric, bargaining). As with all symbolizing activity, these elements of language reflect principles of cognition that serve to structure or pattern experience and guide and influence behavior. Thus, the cognition/symbolic action operating within the sociocultural and marketing strategy environments is reflected in language and/or overt physical acts that symbolically invite various consumer response behaviors. As Gregg (1984) pointed out:

Symbolic actions [language, etc.] guide perceptions and thus behaviors. Intentions, purpose, and choice making are involved at all stages of symbolic

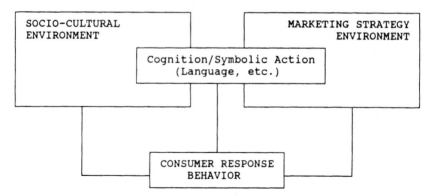

FIG. 12.1.   Consumer behavior framework incorporating language.

processing. Symbolic processing always induces partisanship in perception . . . At sophisticated levels of processing we always identify ourselves with sets of interest, goals, and explanations, eschewing alternatives. And we behave according to the partiality of our perceptions. (p. 135)

The implications for advertisers is that once a segmentation basis, such as ethnicity, gender, and so on, is established, they can gain additional marketing information about these segments by examining language differences. Accepting the assumption that language mirrors differences in the cognition/symbolic action of various consumer segments, then it should be possible to examine each segment's language to get at those processes. Understanding cognitive/symbolic processes may reveal a great deal about what motivates different consumer segments to engage in certain types of consumer behavior.

Once marketers have gained an understanding of a consumer segment's cognition through language, this information can be used in developing and implementing more effective marketing and advertising strategies. This puts the burden on advertisers to communicate effectively with consumers by using the appropriate messages, or language, which matches each segment's processing mode and symbolic reality. For example, Morland (1958) noted differences in word usage between lower and upper class members. Thus, an advertiser might select a radio or television announcer for commercials who projects a social class image through language and other forms of symbolic action consistent with the target audience. Knowledge of segment differences based on social class has enabled marketers to use appropriate language in segmenting the market (Schiffman & Kanuk, 1987).

Cognitive Processing Differences Between African American and White Consumers

For the methodology employed in the pilot study to be useful, there should be differences in cognition/symbolic action between the segments, that is, African American and White consumers. One concept that is helpful in explaining the effects of ethnicity on cognition is cultural script theory. A cultural script is a pattern of cognitive processing and social interaction that is characteristic of a particular social group (Triandis, Marin, Lisansky, & Betancourt, 1984).

For African Americans, the complex historic and sociocultural experience of growing up as members of a unique subcultural group has had an impact in shaping a different cultural script of identifiable lifestyles, attitudes, personality, and behavior compared to Whites (Wilcox, 1971). Ethnic and social psychologists have suggested that the African American cultural script is largely represented by concepts such as interpersonal interaction, affiliation, group orientation, peer influence and acceptance, and feeling orientation (Boykin, 1983; Nobles, 1980). Nobles (1976) presented a theoretical model of African American psychology that incorporates these elements.

This cultural script manifests itself in the way African Americans compared to Whites will cognitively process and behaviorally respond to environmental influences. For example, emphasis on affiliation, group orientation, and peer influence in the African American cultural script has been suggested as an explanation of why African Americans tend to respond more to referent social power compared to expert social power. Cosmas and Sheth (1980) found African Americans to be more responsive to opinion leaders ranking high on the dimension of peer influence and charisma compared to opinion leaders with a high degree of expertise. In educational settings, African American students tend to characterize the ideal teacher in terms of interpersonal prowess as opposed to technical proficiency (Hedegard & Brown, 1969). Relatedly, Slavin (1983) pointed to the greater importance of peer groups as a reason why African American students tend to learn significantly better in cooperative, group situations compared to White students, who learn better in individual, competitive situations.

It seems reasonable to conclude that cultural script also will have an effect on the processing of information and resulting behavior in an advertising context, because advertising reflects cultural values (Caudle, 1982). For example, African Americans tend to respond more to celebrity advertising compared to Whites (Hume, 1983). It has been suggested that this is because celebrity advertising is more consonant with referent social power, which tends to be more representative of the African American cultural script (Williams & Qualls, 1989).

Language Differences Between African American and White Consumers

As with cognitive differences, for the methodology employed in the pilot study to be useful, there should be differences in the use of language between the segments. White (1984) indicated that characteristics associated with concepts in Nobles' (1976) model of African American psychology are prominent themes in African American language. This should not be surprising given the fact that language is the most widely assessed cultural practice associated with ethnic identity. Many researchers consider language as the single most important component of ethnic identity (Giles, Taylor, Lambert, & Albert, 1976,; Leclezio, Louw-Potgieter, & Souchon, 1986; Taylor, Bassilli, & Aboud, 1973). In fact, previous research suggests that ethnic group members identify more closely with those who share their language than with those who share their cultural background (Giles, Taylor, & Bourhis, 1973).

There is substantial evidence to support the premise that the form, content, and use of language by African Americans and Whites is significantly different. For example, Haskins and Butts (1973) discussed how African Americans and Whites categorize experiences differently, and how the vocabulary of their languages forms a catalogue of categories that they use in perceiving, thinking, and communicating. Hecht, Ribeau, and Alberts (1989) considered the differences in the approach to conversation interaction between African Americans and Whites. Kochman (1982) asserted that African American and White subcultural differences contribute to communication breakdowns due to differing speech and subcultural conventions. As noted by Peterson (1979), Hall and Feedle (1975) even argue that African American patterns of thought and expression cannot be rendered in standard English.

TEXTUALISM

Textualism, the theory that "all problems, topics, and distinctions [in social action] are language-relative — the result of having chosen to use certain vocabulary, to play a certain language game" (Rorty, 1982, p. 140), can be used to describe the language used in a purchasing context. Various alternative interpretations of textualism are available (Bochner, 1985; Granier, 1985; Harari, 1979; Mauss, 1985; Schank & Abelson, 1977). In the present study, textualism provides a foundation for the study of text as both the source and artifact of strategic social action. Theory suggests that we get our understanding of social reality from text; we express that understanding in the form of text; and we derive our individual and social identity "through the adoption and adaptation of [text]" (Cheney & Tompkins, 1988). The implications of this for the study of ethnic market segments is that the text produced in reference to a given situation constitutes a presentation of the world as perceived by the members of the market segment under investigation. The examination of such textual artifacts permits an interpretation of how buyers perceive the buying situation, and how their perspective motivates them to act as they do. This understanding offers strategic implications for the design of advertising and communication strategy.

Analysis of text can be divided into two basic approaches: a quantitative, systematic coding via content analysis mode or a qualitative, inferential, ethnographic summary mode. The principle difference is that the ethnographic approach relies more on direct quotation of the group discussion, whereas the content analysis typically produces numerical descriptions of the data (Morgan, 1988). This chapter relies on a blend of these approaches. The methodological foundation for our analysis of language use is based on the content analytic notion of indexing and the ethnographic notion of clustering.

Indexing

Indexing is a generic term referring to the creation of a coding (category) system pairing words with their location in the text for the purpose of retrieval (Miles & Huberman, 1984). The approach to indexing used in this chapter is based on Burke's (1964) theory of the index. Burke's work was selected to serve as the basis for our framework because the notion of cognition/symbolic action represented in our model derives most directly from his writings. Additionally, Burke's insistence that pragmatic communication (e.g., advertising) is symbolic action that induces behavior is consistent with our suggestion of a link between cognition/symbolic action, advertising strategy, and consumer behavior.

As a method, indexing begins with the development of an index and concordance—a listing of every word appearing in the text along with frequency and location. Each noun, verb, and modifier is then located in context and a decision is made to assign each word to a category according to a pentad of terms: *act*, *scene*, *agent*, *agency*, or *purpose* (see Table 12.1)

These five terms serve as a model for describing salient aspects of a generalized situation, the basis for action, or in Burke's terms, motives. In *A Grammar of Motives*, Burke stated:

> In a rounded statement about motives, you must have some word that names the act (names what took place, in thought or deed), and another that names the scene (the background of the act, the situation in which it occurred); also, you must indicate what person or kind of person (agent) performed the act,

TABLE 12.1
Coding Definitions for Content Categories

Content Categories	Coding Definitions
Act	1. Focus is on what took place in thought or deed during an event.
Scene	2. Focus is on the background of an act, or the situation in which it occurred (time and space).
Agent	3. Focus is on the person or kind of person (attributes of the agent) that performed an act.
Agency	4. Focus is on the means or instruments used to perform an act.
Purpose	5. Focus is on the ends, goals, or communal values certified or sought by performing an act.

what means or instruments he used (agency), and the purpose. (Burke, 1969, p. xv)

The pentad of terms is a model used to describe what buyers representative of various subcultures view as the controlling elements in a purchase situation. This understanding is revealed by an indexing and content analysis of text. What is important in this phase of analysis is the relative weight placed on each element of the pentad. We use the weighting placed on any one or combination of situational elements to make inferences about what is perceived as the basis for action and situational control. Relating the categories to basic philosophical perspectives, Burke suggested that the idealist, having faith in mind over matter, will place greatest emphasis on terms referencing agent. In contrast, the pragmatist, believing that the outcome of any situation is dependant on what one has to work with, will emphasize terms referencing agency. The realist will emphasize acts, and so on (Burke, 1969). That is, for the members of one subculture it may be acts that determine the outcome of a given situation; for another subculture the outcome may be perceived to depend on agents, or the people involved in the situation. These differences in perception are presented and maintained through the use of language. Because language induces behavior, language referencing a dominant pentadic category provides insight into what in "reality" will ultimately form the basis for strategic adaptive action.

Ling (1970) provided an example that may serve to illustrate this point more clearly:

an individual who describes the problem of slums as largely a matter of man's unwillingness to change his environment will propose self-help as the answer to the problem. The person who, looking at the same situation, describes man as a victim of his environment will propose that the slums be razed and its inhabitants be relocated into a more conducive environment. (p. 82)

In the first instance, analysis of the extended textual description, if it were recorded and available for analysis, would show that words for agent dominate the description. Change requires agent change; that is, the solution to the problem rests in changing the nature of the people involved. In the second instance, the individual views the scene as the determining factor in the situation. Action to alter the environment is called for if change is desired. An analysis of the second individual's extended textual description would show the dominance of terms referencing the time and place of interaction. Thus, in similar fashion, in the present investigation the indexing and context analysis of terms forms the basis for inferences about a market segment's perception of the controlling elements of the marketing exchange.

Clustering

Clustering is an interpretive tactic used to better understand the meaning of important terms identified through indexing and content analysis. The conceptual definition or interpretive meaning of an important term is developed by extracting from the text a list of words implicitly and explicitly related to the important term of interest. Whereas the categories used in the indexing of the text are theory based and thus preexisting, the clusters of terms used to make inferences about the meaning of key pentadic terms emerge from the text. The focus here is on the meaning of key or pivotal terms revealed by an index.

The selection of key terms is an interpretive task. The significance of terms in each of the dominant pentadic categories is determined on the basis of intensity or frequency. That is, terms that seem to the researcher to be naturally charged (e.g., rip-off, haggle, etc.), or that seem to offer conceptual content (e.g., justice, freedom, fairness, etc.) relevant to the purpose of the study, and/or terms used over and over again to reference elements of the buying situation, are identified and included in the initial clustering effort. Key terms are necessarily selective.

Following the selection of key terms, clusters (groups of terms) that define the situation under investigation are constructed on the basis of terms that cluster around the key terms in various ways. Cluster terms may appear in close proximity, relating terms may appear merely by their appearance in the same place and the same time. Cluster terms may be connected to the key terms by a conjunction such as "and," associating objects, concepts, ideas, actions, or attitudes. Or, cluster terms may appear to add meaningful definition or suggest a cause-and-effect relationship between the key term and another term.

A PILOT STUDY OF TEXT ELICITATION AND ANALYSIS

As suggested in the beginning this chapter, the exploratory technique illustrated herein is based on the notion that text, an artifact of cognition/symbolic action, can be used to gain insight into subcultural "reality." Our focus, in this pilot study, is more on illustrating how the technique can be applied in the analysis of text to develop more effective advertising strategy than on presenting definitive advertising recommendations. However, some suggestions and recommendations are offered based on the pilot study results.

In designing the pilot study, we needed to address two important considerations involving: (a) the consumer behavior situation and (b) the source of text. In addressing the first issue, we decided on an automobile purchasing behavior context to explore the use of language by African American and White consumers. We felt that this might be an appropriate context because auto industry analysts argue that, in today's economy, research aimed at understanding customers may be more important than price, design, or quality considerations (Treece, Zellner, & Konrad, 1989). Pressured to better understand why people buy, car makers and sellers are moving beyond their traditional reliance on simple demographics to address the "whys" and "hows" of exchange relationships (Wallace, 1984). Also, previous research on new car buyers and ethnic influences has suggested that there are some differences between White and minority car buyers, specifically in seeking out salespersons of the same ethnic background (Saegert, Hoover, & Hilger, 1987).

For the second issue, we decided to use transcriptions of text from focus groups conducted with African American and White consumers. Although there have been other studies using language as a means to better understand cognition (e.g., Angelmar & Stern's [1978] assessment of written communication and Graham's [1985] assessment of verbal communication in buyer–seller negotiations only one (Bush & Boller, 1991) applied Burke's (1964) rhetorical theory to advertising. That study assessed transcriptions from television advertising campaigns. However, for our purposes focus groups offered a much better source of the textual data produced by relevant market segments.

The focus group discussions in our pilot study revolved around characteristics of car dealers and attributes of cars that focus group members thought were positive or negative. The text was transcribed from audio recordings, and an index and concordance were produced with the aid of a microcomputer.

The focus group interview is probably used more often than any other form of marketing research to produce the qualitative data needed for textual analysis. The established effectiveness of this qualitative research approach in aiding researchers' understanding of the nature of business situations makes the focus group technique of special value in exploring socially constructed aspects of marketing. Although there are numerous articles and books available on collecting focus group data (i.e., setting up interviews, recruiting subjects, prescriptions about group moderators, group dynamics, etc.), less attention has been given to analyzing and interpreting the output of focus group interviews – qualitative data (Nelson & Frontczak, 1988). With this in mind, this chapter attempts to make explicit, and thus render replicable, a systematic method for drawing conclusions about how different segments of car buyers give expression to their perceptions of the objects, events, and persons in the context of automobile purchasing.

Sample

We conducted two focus group sessions, one consisting of White consumers and another consisting of African American consumers. This allowed for the interpretive analysis and comparison of the two market segments. All participants were in the 25-49 age group and represented consumers from central Pennsylvania communities.

Each group was homogeneous on demographic dimensions such as gender (all males) and socioeconomic status (professional as opposed to blue-collar occupations). We felt that it was particularly important during this exploratory investigation of the technique to maintain gender homogeneity (in this case using all males) because other research has suggested that there are some distinct cognitive and language differences between men and women: for example, differences in the performance of verbal, spatial, mathematical, and mechanical tasks, which generally is attributed to differences in brain development and brain functioning — that is, men and women think differently, not better or worse, just differently (Pearson, 1985).

Also, typical women's speech is viewed as unassertive, passive, more expressive, supportive, affiliative, compliant, and conforming, whereas men's speech is perceived as more aggressive, instrumental, and task oriented. These generalizations may be accounted for, at least in part, by the language patterns that appear to emerge from the two sexes. Elsewhere in this volume, Stern (chapter 4) points out how women can be viewed as a distinct cultural group in terms of how they use language and how language uses them. She discusses how three characteristics that mark women's language as special, namely its propriety, hesitancy, and verbal excess (Lakoff, 1975), can help advertisers more effectively position products to men's and women's markets. Therefore, by focusing only on males in this pilot study, it was possible to extract meaningful segment-related information and to make comparisons between groups based on ethnicity, without worrying about a possible confounding with gender.

Coding and Cluster Charting Procedures

Formalized coding definitions were developed to minimize subjectivity and permit the assessment of interjudge reliability in the initial content analytic phase of the analysis. The choice of coding categories was based on the notion of cognition/symbolic action discussed heretofore. Three judges, two seniors in marketing and one graduate student, were recruited to code each focus group index on the basis of category definitions. A text sample, unrelated to the car buying context, was used to train the judges in the coding task. Coder differences were resolved through discussion and consensus during the initial training period. Next, judges were given typed copies of the index of terms and their frequencies from each of the focus group transcripts. In addition, each coder was provided with a microcomputer and a machine readable copy of each focus group transcript. Coders were instructed to use an installed computer search function to locate each term in the index in context of the corresponding focus group transcript. Judgement as to the category assignment of each term was based on each term's use in context. Each judge independently coded each index by assigning a number code identifying the appropriate category for each of the terms in the index. A zero or "no code" designation was given to any term not assigned to a category. These terms were usually prepositions, conjunctions, or terms used in ways that resulted in conflicting categorization. This procedure was followed, in turn, for each of the focus group texts.

The independent index codings were examined for interjudge agreement. Interjudge agreement was assessed by a procedure developed by Holsti (1969), suggested by Smith and Houston (1985), and previously applied in a marketing context by Leigh and McGraw (1989). In the actual text coding phase, no attempt was made to resolve coder differences; thus, the procedure is considered very conservative. Composite interjudge reliability ranged from.84 to.86 for the two focus group texts.

To develop an objective foundation for the interpretive phase of the analysis, if two judges agreed on the code for an index term, the term and frequency count were considered present in the agreed upon pentadic category. An initial set of high frequency and high intensity terms appearing in each of the pentadic categories was then developed independently for each focus group by one of the authors and a trained coder. The independently developed lists of key terms were then combined judgmentally for each representative market segment. The resultant selective lists of key terms focus attention on salient aspects of the purchase situation as voiced by the members of each market segment (Table 12.4). Key terms serve as the basis for cluster analysis.

Next, an initial set of cluster terms related to each of the key terms on the basis of proximity, or other implicit or explicit interconnection in the text, was developed independently by one of the authors and a trained coder. Cluster terms were located in the context of each text with the aid of a microcomputer, listed independently, and then combined judgmentally to produce a key term and cluster formation for each market segment (Tables 12.5, 12.6, & 12.7). The procedure called for again locating each of the previously identified key terms in the context of the focus group text and examining its relationship to other terms in the text. This procedure was followed for each set of key terms and for each focus group text. The resultant judgmentally established clusters serve to define each of the key terms previously presented as important to participants in the car buying situation.

RESULTS

Our primary purpose is to explore the language characteristic of identified market segments and to provide an interpretive account of how different market segments of car buyers manage language to create meaning and present social reality as they view it. Two focus groups consisting of White men and African American men allowed for the interpretive analysis and comparison of two market segments. For each market segment we describe and compare the weighting of pentadic categories, key words, and cluster terms.

Pentadic Word Classification by Market Segment

Table 12.2 presents a summary of word usage classification by market segment. In an effort to verify the general assumption that each market segment tends to approach the car buying situation from a somewhat different perspective, we examined the percentage of words falling into each situational (pentadic) category — each category being theoretically representative of an alternative philosophical perspective, or world view. An overall chi-square statistic indicates that these percentages are significantly different from each other ($x^2 = 215$, $df = 4$, $p < .001$). The distribution of percentages of words in the categories corresponding to each situational perspective differs from market segment to market segment, demonstrating a dependent relationship; that is, the perspective with which focus group participants, as a unit, approach the car buying situation appears to differ by ethnic orientation as represented by group participants.

TABLE 12.2
Word Classification Data by Market Segment

	Classification				
Segment	Act	Scene	Agent	Agency	Purpose
White male					
Number of words	1766	594	1655	1608	70
Percentage	31.0%	10.4%	29.1%	28.2%	1.2%
African American male					
Number of words	1652	183	1100	1294	4
Percentage	39.0%	4.3%	26.0%	30.6%	0.1%

Note. Overall $x^2 = 215$. $df = 4$. $p < .001$.

TABLE 12.3
Two Sample Proportion Test Word Classification by Market Segment

Segment	Classification				
	Act	Scene	Agent	Agency	Purpose
White male	−7.53	11.49	4.02	−1.85	6.58
African American male	.0000*	.0000*	.0001*	.0641	.0000*

*p < .001.

To further develop the point from our theoretical perspective, Table 12.3 presents a two sample proportion test used to determine whether the proportion of words observed in each category are significantly different for the two market segments. The results of the test demonstrate that White males talk proportionately less about what is done in the buying situation (acts) than African American males ($Z = -7.53$, $p < .0001$). Furthermore, White males tend to be more concerned with the setting or location of the car buying transaction (scene) than African American males ($Z = 11.49$, $p < .0001$). The White male market segment also tends to express more concern over the nature of participants in the buying situation (agents) than African American males ($Z = 4.02$, $p < .0001$)). However, no statistical difference was found between groups in terms of the emphasis placed on the means or instruments associated with the situation (agency), whereas White males placed greater emphasis on situational goals (purpose) than African American males ($Z = 6.58$, $p < .0001$).

Keep in mind that not all of the categories are likely to play a major or even important role in determining the overall outcome of the buying situation from the perspective of the individual car buyer. A cursory, interpretive explanation of the categorical weighting presented in Table 12.1 suggests that representatives of the White male segment are influenced most by a combination of what is done (acts), who does it (agents), and how or with what it is done (agency), in that order. The interpretation is supported by the categorical weighting of 31.0%, 29.1%, and 28.2% for the three categories of act, agent, and agency, respectively, with the why (purpose) and where (scene) aspects of the situation playing relatively minor roles in the outcome. The group representative of African American males views acts (39.0%), or what is done, as the principle determinant of the outcome of the buying situation. How, or with what, the outcome is accomplished is secondary (30.6%), followed by consideration for agents (26.0%). Again, scene and purpose play limited roles.

Key Terms

Although statistically significant differences are demonstrated for most of the pentadic categories across market segment groups, we have limited the

TABLE 12.4
Key Words by Market Segment

Segment	Key Words		
	Act	Agent	Agency
White male	Buy	I, me	Car
	Want	Dealer	Price
		Salesperson	Problem
African American male	Buy	I	Car
	Want	Dealer	Price
	Look	Salesperson	

Note. No key words were identified for scene or purpose categories. Key terms are arranged in order of frequency from high to low.

interpretive portion of our analysis to those categories felt to be most likely to play a major or important role in the outcome of the buying situation for each subcultural market segment. Thus, the interpretive analysis that follows is limited to act, agent, and agency aspects of the generalized purchase situation.

Table 12.4 identifies key words for the three important pentadic categories by market segment. Although the words are simple, they represent, in terms of frequency of use, the central or pivotal concepts around which the text of each market segment's discussion of the buying situation appears to be organized. In the following paragraphs we examine the meaning of each key term for each market segment based on associational word clusters.

Key Acts and Cluster Terms

Key *acts* and the cluster terms used to define them are presented in Table 12.5 for each market segment. For White males, car buying is a challenging problem situation, a competitive game involving bargaining. The uncertainty of the game makes them reluctant to finalize their purchase decision. This uncertainty is reduced by interaction with a known entity, a salesman with whom they are familiar, and by the acquisition of factual information both from printed materials and physical inspection of the automobile in question. The following quote captures, in part, the salient action as experienced by a participant in this consumer group: " . . . he is going to dicker and you are going to dicker. One of you is going to loose out . . . it is a hard game to play."

The African American male consumer segment in our study views car buying as a business-like process in which relationships are established, agreements are reached, and contracts are signed. The process, however, involves inherent risk and the use of a certain amount of technique. African

TABLE 12.5
Key Acts and Cluster Terms by Market Segment

Segment	Key Acts		
	Buy	*Want*	*Look*
White male	Fun	No argument	Magazine
	Dealing		Consumer reports
	Horsetrade	Known entity	
	Hard game	(salesperson)	data
	Bargaining		
	Ball game		Appearance
			Physical condition
	Hesitate		
	Problem		
	Decision		
	Agreement		
African American male	Deal	Answers	Shop around
	Technique	Information	
	Risky		
		No hassle	
	Relationship		
	Agreement		
	Contract		
	Process		
	Business		

American males seek information through direct contact with sales organization representatives from various dealerships. That is, they tend to shop around, not necessarily for the right car, but for the right relationship. In part, their view is summarized in the following statement by one of the participants in our study: "I think the most important thing about purchasing in general is that you're making a contractual arrangement. I don't know whether it's a matter of so much trust . . . but I feel that if you rely on just a feeling of trust every time you make a business deal, I think you . . . [are] more vulnerable"

Key "Agents" and Cluster Terms

Table 12.6 presents a summary of key "agents" involved in the automobile purchasing context and cluster terms by market segment. White males present themselves as concerned and distrustful, having had both satisfying and disappointing purchasing experiences (i.e., wins and losses). They tend to be brand loyal ("Ford/Chevy man") and feel that they are knowledgeable in terms of the mechanical operation and condition of automobiles in general. They view the dealer as part of the local "hometown" community,

TABLE 12.6
Key Agents and Cluster Terms by Market Segment

Segment	Key Agents		
	I/Me/We	Dealer	Salesman
White male	Satisfied	Hometown	Reputation
	Disappointed	Local reputation	Personality
	Concerned	Honest	High turnover
	Distrustful		Key to Sale
	Ford/Chevy loyal	Reliable	Acquaintance
	Knowledgeable	Fair	Rapport
	Mechanical	Rip people off	
	Experienced		
African American male	(Not) satisfied	Relationship	High Pressure
	(No) allegiance	Acquaintance	Courteous
	Knowledgeable	Independent	Adaptive
	Experienced	Urban	Not technical
	Sophisticated	Small town	Bond
	Distrustful	(Not) important	Owner
	Visceral	Means to:	
	Objective	Purchase	
	Personable	Warranty	
	Resentful	Service	
	Emotional		
	Reserved		

with a known community reputation. In general, dealers are honest, reliable, and fair. But, caution is indicated because sometimes they rip people off. However, the key to the sale is the salesperson. Although salespeople often move from dealership to dealership, it is the salesperson's personality, reputation, and rapport with the buyer that is most important in closing the deal. White males prefer to buy cars from a salesperson with whom they have established an acquaintance relationship. Their general view of the agents involved in the purchase situation is summarized by this representative quotation: "we're not dealing with car dealers, we're dealing with salesmen. [The] car dealer, that poor guy might be in Florida for the next two years and he's not ever there and doesn't even know what his manager is doing. This is where it all comes down to the ball game, the general manager, the people under him and the salesman. Your talking to the salesman. That's the key.

The African American males participating in our focus group present themselves as objective, knowledgeable, experienced, "sophisticated" buyers. One participant said: . . . I think that many Blacks in America right now are in a cultural flux. And, we're changing now in our way of evaluating things. They have these terms for us called, 'we're getting to be more sophisticated buyers,' they say. What that translates into is we're asking more questions." Another individual stated: "You're being specifically marketed to. You better be a more sophisticated buyer."

African American males have had both positive and negative car buying experiences and hold "no allegiance" to any particular dealer. They are also distrustful, as well as "visceral," "personable," and "emotional," yet somewhat "reserved" in their expressed reactions. For the most part, they do not view the dealership as significant to the outcome of the purchase situation: "I feel no allegiance from the time I buy that particular car. If I don't want to buy the next one from him [the dealer] I don't. I don't feel like I have to go back."

Thus, for African American males, the dealer is more a means to an end (e.g., warranty, service) and probably more appropriately categorized as an "agency" from their perspective. It is possible, however, for them to overcome their initial reservations and establish a "relationship" or "bond" with a dealer or dealer representative. Salesmen are viewed as "high-pressure," "courteous," and adaptive, nontechnical individuals who facilitate the business process.

Key "Agencies" and Cluster Terms

Table 12.7 presents a summary of the "agencies" or instruments involved in the purchase situation. White males view the traditional "big [American] car" as serviceable, dependable, comfortable, affordable, and offering a level of performance suitable for both work and family use. However, they express displeasure with the fact that current automobile designs "all look the same," and "foreign." They view the price of the automobile as "jacked up" and "inflated by gimmicks," and just want to know the "best price," or "bottom line price."

Note that problems are included in the agency category because they represent the negative of solutions. Solutions are instruments, means, or answers that enable the act to be done (agency). For White males the problems associated with the buying situation involve mechanical accessibility and repair. Additional problems are associated with "throw-away" small cars, workmanship, and restrictions imposed by the Environmental Protection Agency. A representative quote from a study participant illustrating the White male perspective on agency follows: "How many people change their own oil and filters? I'd say that probably 70% of the people today. At least around here I'd say, probably change their own oil and their fuel filters. But what happens like, I was just talking. You had a fuel filter and you didn't have the clamp tightened up and it leaked. You aren't going to know enough to look behind that panel inside the door to reset the fuel switch. Things like that they could put out underneath the hood . . . They could have it available."

TABLE 12.7
Key Agencies and Cluster Terms by Segment

Segment	Key Agencies		
	Car	Price	Problem
White male	Serviceable	Bottom line	Brakes
	Dependable	Best price	Tie rods
	Comfortable		Engine
	Affordable	Haggle	Accessibility
	Performance	Inflated with gimmicks	
	Family type	Jacked up	EPA
	Big is good		Workmanship
	New/used		
	All look the same		Small car
	U.S./foreign		
African American male	Durability	Good price	Level of mechanic knowledge
	Value	Bottom line	
	Economy	Drive away price	
	Mileage		Transmission
	Depreciation	Jacked up	Small town service
	Performance		
	Safety		
	Comfort		
	Handling		
	Fascinating		
	Pleasure		
	Appearance		
	Body style		
	Make and model		
	Flashy		
	Image		

Finally, African American males present their view of the car as a blend of business and pleasure. Cars are, or should be, durable, economical, safe, and comfortable. Cars should offer value, good mileage, and limited depreciation.

On the other hand, they express interest in the subtle pleasures of car ownership associated with appearance (e.g. body style, make, and model), performance, handling, and image. This conflict is captured in the following quotation: "when I bought the last car, image was important. If I were to buy today, I would go for what the use would be. So, if I were to buy today, it would be a pretty hard decision to go with the function, or to go with a small car, partly for economy because it's small, but also I like the nice flashy-looking small cars."

Like the White males, African American males view the price as "jacked up," and are only interested in a "good price," the "bottom line," or "drive away price." Their principle concern or problem is the small town mechanic's low level of technical knowledge, which reflects on the car owner's ability to obtain adequate service.

CONCLUSION AND SUGGESTIONS
FOR FUTURE RESEARCH

Language can play a central role in marketing segmentation, although it has been largely ignored. Specifically, it is useful in understanding the symbolic nature of reality as presented by subcultural market segments. We believe language mirrors this cognitive "reality," and by analyzing market segment language, we can be more effective in developing advertising and marketing strategies to affect consumer response behavior.

In this exploratory study, we illustrated a technique for the analysis of textual data using both quantitative and qualitative procedures (i.e., a theory driven coding scheme for content analysis supplemented by theory consistent interpretive procedures). The approach displayed good reliability although the validity of the interpretation cannot easily be established. However, as Hirschman (1986), referencing Lincoln and Guba (1985), pointed out: "there is no concrete benchmark for validating one's interpretation, either in principle or by technical adjustment using the falsification principle" (p. 244). Thus, convincing alternative means of validation appropriate to humanistic inquiry must be explored.

The specific situation examined in this study involved automobile purchasing behavior as presented symbolically in the form of text by representatives of two market segments, i.e. African American and White males. Assuming a link between cognition and language, there is both statistical and interpretive evidence to support the conclusion that these subcultural market segments view the salient aspects of the purchase situation differently.

Findings suggest that White males are less concerned with the nature and type of action taken by themselves and others to influence the outcome of the purchase situation than African Americans, although both groups view action taken as the principal determinant force in the outcome of the purchase situation. Consistent with previous research findings, African American males appear to focus on actions to establish relationships and the use of interpersonal skills and trust-based exchange processes to reach agreement. White males view the situation as one involving competitive game-like actions and physical acts.

Furthermore, results suggest that the nature and role of agents or people involved in the automobile purchase situation differs across subcultural segments. White males view agents as secondary only to action taken in the determination of the outcome of the purchase situation. It seems clear that if one is to engage in competitive gamesmanship, an opponent (e.g., the salesman) is required. Black males, however, express limited faith in the agent's ability to influence situational outcomes. Note that the agent most often referred to is themselves. Thus, it can be argued that this perspective is consistent with a psychology and cultural script that values affiliation and group orientation over personal aggression.

Finally, our interpretation suggests that African American males rank the influence of agency as second only to action in the determination of situational outcomes, whereas White males view agency as the least important factor in the outcome of the automobile purchasing situation. Representatives of both subcultures view the automobile itself as the principle "instrument" involved in the purchase process. Both subcultural groups appear to consider functional value important in their evaluation of automobiles. However, White males emphasize physical components, whereas African American males place considerable emphasis on emotional and visual components. Again, this can be related to a greater need for affiliation and peer acceptance hypothesized in the literature.

Advancing the cognition/symbolic action, marketing strategy, and consumer behavior link, these findings suggest that advertisers might benefit from the development of separate advertising strategies for each of the subcultural groups analyzed. For example, White males appear more likely to respond to game-and-deal related promotions and physical activities such as test drives, whereas African American males are likely to respond more favorably to promotions aimed at building trust and bonding, that is dealer/personality advertisement and open house promotions.

The results of this study also could be used to assess the effectiveness of various spokespersons used in advertising cars to African American and White consumers. For example, Triandis et al. (1984) suggested that minorities might seek advice on medical and legal issues from friends, that is, those with referent social power, over someone more qualified to answer the questions, that is, those with referent social power, but not a peer. Therefore, African American males might identify more with an advertisement featuring two African American professional workers discussing the attributes of a car rather than two laboratory engineers discussing all the tests that they have performed on the car.

Finally, advertisements directed to African American males might emphasize fantasy themes, appearance, image, and group acceptance with proportionately less emphasis on comparisons of performance and service records. The latter might be more appropriately focused on influencing the purchase behavior of white males.

However, our findings must be placed in proper perspective. We are limited in generalizing these results because we have analyzed the language transcriptions from only two focus groups, both from one geographic area in central Pennsylvania. The degree to which the participants in each focus group are representative of all African American and White male car buyers is uncertain. Clearly, a study involving a greater number of focus groups, groups from a wider geographic area, and groups with more diversified demographic characteristics (e.g., women focus groups and groups from a greater range of occupational and socioeconomic categories) will be required before further generalizations can be made.

One of the major limitations of this method, as with most qualitative methods, is labor intensity and time. However, the results gained from additional studies should help advertisers assess the trade-offs of the value of the additional information gained in developing better advertising strategies for the segments analyzed versus the considerable time and effort required to implement this technique.

Based on our pilot study, we feel the exploratory findings provide sufficient evidence to support continued research with larger samples on the use of language as a mirror to the cognitive processes of different market segments. These expanded studies would allow a better understanding of the links between language, cognition, and effective advertising strategy. Although recognizing the limitations of this study and the technique, we feel that it offers a significant first step in gaining that understanding.

REFERENCES

Angelmar, R., & Stern, L. W. (1978, February). Development of a content analytic system for analysis of bargaining communication in marketing. *Journal of Marketing Research, 15*, 93–102.

Bochner, A. P. (1985). Perspectives on inquiry: Representation, conversation, and reflection. In M. L. Knapp & G. R. Miller (Eds.), *Handbook of interpersonal communication*, (pp. 27–57). Newbury Park, CA: Sage.

Boykin, W. A. (1983). The academic performance of Afro-American children. In J. T. Spence (Ed.), *Achievement and achievement motives: Psychological and sociological approaches* (pp. 321–371). San Francisco: W. H. Freeman.

Burke, K. (1964). Facts, inferences, and proof in the analysis of literary symbolism. In S. E. Hyman (Ed.), *Terms for order by Kenneth Burke* (pp. 145–172). Bloomington: Indiana University Press.

Burke, K. (1969). *A grammar of motives*. Berkely: University of California Press.

Bush, A. J., & Boller, G. W. (1991). Rethinking the role of television advertising during health crises: A rhetorical analysis of the Federal AIDS campaigns. *Journal of Advertising, 20*(1), 28–37.

Caudle, F. M. (1982). Advertising as a basis for cross-cultural comparison. In L. L. Adler (Ed.), *Cross-cultural research at issue* (pp. 209–231). NY: Academic Press.

Cheney, G., & Tompkins, P. K. (1988). On the facts of the text as the basis of human communication research. In J. A. Anderson (Ed.), *Communication yearbook 11* (pp. 455–481). Beverly Hills, CA: Sage.

Cosmas, S. C., & Sheth, J. N. (1980, Spring/Summer). Identification of opinion leaders across cultures: An assessment for use in the diffusion of innovations and ideas. *Journal of International Business Studies, 11,* 66-73.

Durgee, J. F. (1986, August/September). Richer findings from qualitative research. *Journal of Advertising Research, 26,* 36-43.

Friedmann, R. (1989). Word associations in consumer research. In D. W. Schumann (Ed.), *Proceedings of division of consumer psychology American Psychological Association 1988 Annual Convention* (pp. 25-29). Atlanta: American Psychological Association.

Giles, H., Taylor, D. M., & Bourhis, R. Y. (1973). Toward a theory of interpersonal accommodation through speech: Some Canadian data. *Language in Society, 2,* 177-192.

Giles, H., Taylor, D., Lambert, W. E., & Albert, G. (1976). Dimensions of ethnic identity: An example from northern Maine. *Journal of Social Psychology, 100,* 11-19.

Graham, J. L. (1985, Spring). The influence of culture on the process of business negotiations: An exploratory study. *Journal of International Business Studies, 16* 81-96.

Granier, J. (1985). Perspectivism and interpretation. In D. B. Allison (Ed.), *The new Nietzsche* (pp. 190-200). Cambridge, MA: Harvard University Press.

Gregg, R. B. (1984). *Symbolic inducement and knowing: A study in the foundations of rhetoric.* Columbia: University of South Carolina Press.

Harari, J. V. (1979). Critical factions/critical fictions. In J. V. Harari (Ed.), *Textual strategies: Perspectives in post-structural criticism* (pp. 17-72). Ithaca, NY: Cornell University Press.

Haskins, J., & Butts, H. F. (1973), *The psychology of Black language.* NY: Barnes and Noble.

Hecht, M. L., Ribeau, S., & Alberts, J. K. (1989). An Afro-American perspective on interethnic communication. *Communication Monographs, 56,* 385-410.

Hedegard, J., & Brown, D. (1969). Encounters of some Negro and White freshmen with a public multiversity. *Journal of Social Issues, 25,* 131-144.

Hirschman, E. C. (1986, August). Humanistic inquiry in marketing research: Philosophy, method and criteria. *Journal of Marketing Research, 23,* 237-249.

Hofstede, G. (1980). *Culture's consequences: International differences in work-related values.* Beverly Hills, CA: Sage.

Holsti, O. R. (1969). *Content analysis for the social sciences and humanities.* Reading, MA: Addison-Wesley.

Hudson, L. A., & Ozanne, J. L. (1988, March). Alternative ways of seeking knowledge in consumer research. *Journal of Consumer Research, 14,* 508-521.

Hume, S. (1983, November 7). Stars are lacking luster as ad presenters. *Advertising Age,* p. 3.

Kochman, T. (1982). *Black and White styles in conflict.* Chicago: University of Chicago: University of Chicago Press.

Lakeoff, R. (1975). *Language and women's place.* New York: Harper & Row.

Leclezio, M. K., Louw-Potgieter, J., & Souchon, M. B. S. (1986). The social identity of Mauritian immigrants in South Africa. *Journal of Social Psychology, 126,* 299-310.

Leigh, T. W., & McGraw, P. F. (1989, January). Mapping the procedural knowledge of industrial sales personnel: A script-theoretic investigation. *Journal of Marketing, 53* 16-34.

Lincoln, Y. S., & Guba, E. G. (1985). *Naturalistic inquiry.* Beverly Hills, CA: Sage.

Ling, D. A. (1970). A pentadic analysis of Senator Edward Kennedy's address to the people of Massachusetts, July 25, 1969. *The Central States Speech Journal, 21*(2), 82-90.

Mauss, M. (1985). A category of the human mind: The notion of person; the notion of self. In M. Carrithers, S. Collins, & S. Lukes (Eds.), *The category of the person* (pp. 1-25). Cambridge: Cambridge University Press.

Miles, M. B., & Huberman, A. M. (1984). *Qualitative data analysis: A sourcebook of new methods.* Beverly Hills, CA: Sage.

Miller, G. A. (1990, January). The place of language in a scientific psychology. *Psychological Science*, *1*, 7-14.

Morgan, D. L. (1988). *Focus groups as qualitative research* (Qualitative Research Methods Series No. 16). Newbury Park, CA: Sage.

Morland, J. K. (1958). *Millways of Kent*. Chapel Hill: University of North Carolina Press.

Nelson, J. E., & Frontczak, N. T. (1988). How acquaintanceship and analyst can influence focus group results. *Journal of Advertising*, *17*(1), 41-48.

Nobles, W. (1976, Winter). Black people In White insanity: An issue for community mental health. *Journal of Afro-American Issues*, *4* 21-7.

Nobles, W. W. (1980). Extended self: Rethinking the so-called Negro self-concept. In R. L. Jones (Ed.), *Black psychology* (2nd ed., pp. 99-105). New York: Harper & Row.

Pearson, J. C. (1985). *Gender and communication*. Dubuque, IA: William C. Brown.

Peter, J. P., & Olson, J. C. (1987). *Consumer behavior: Marketing strategy perspectives*. Homewood, IL: Irwin.

Peterson, R. A. (1979). Revitalizing the culture concept. In A. Inkeles, J. Coleman, & R. H. Turner (Eds.), *Annual review of sociology* (Vol. 5., pp. 137-66).

Prus, R. C. (1989). *Pursuing customers: An ethnography of marketing activities* (Sage Library of Social Research 171). Beverly Hills, CA: Sage.

Rorty, R. (1982). *Consequences of pragmatism*. Minneapolis: University of Minnesota Press.

Saegert, J., Hoover, R. J., & Hilger, M. T. (1987). A study of Hispanic new car buyers. In R. L. King (Ed.), *Minority marketing: Issues and prospects. Proceedings of the Academy of Marketing science conference* (pp. 65-68). Charleston, SC: Academy of Marketing Science.

Schank, R., & Abelson, R. (1977). *Scripts, plans, goals and understanding: An inquiry in human knowledge structure*. Hillsdale, NJ: Lawrence Erlbaum Associates.

Schiffman, L. G., & Kanuk, L. L. (1987). *Consumer behavior*. Englewood Cliffs, NJ: Prentice-Hall.

Slavin, R. E. (1983). *Cooperative learning*. NY: Longman.

Smith, R. A., & Houston, M. J. (1985). A psychometric assessment of measures of script in consumer memory. *Journal of Consumer Research*, *12*(2), 214-224.

Taylor, D. M., Bassilli, J. N., & Aboud, F. E. (1973). Dimensions of ethnic identity: An example from Quebec. *Journal of Social Psychology*, *89*, 185-192.

Treece, J. B., Zellner, W., & Konrad, W. (1989, June 12). Detroit tries to rev up: Can better marketing reverse a sales slump? *Business Week*, pp. 78-82.

Triandis, H. C., Marin, G., Lisansky, J., & Betancourt, H. (1984). Simpatia as a cultural script of Hispanics. *Journal of Personality and Social Psychology*, *47*, 1363-1375.

Vanden Bergh, B., Adler, K., & Oliver, L. (1987, August/September). Linguistic distinction among top brand names. *Journal of Advertising Research*, pp. 39-44.

Wallace, K. M. (1984). The use and value of qualitative research studies. *Industrial Marketing Management*, *13*, 181-185.

White, J. L. (1984). *The psychology of Blacks: An Afro-American perspective*. Englewood Cliffs, NJ: Prentice-Hall.

Whorf, B. L. (1941). The relation of habitual thought and behavior to language. In L. Spier, A. I. Hallowell, & S. S. Newman (Eds.), *Language, culture, and personality* (pp. 75-93). Menasha, W: Sapir Memorial Publication Fund.

Wilcox, R. (1971). *The psychological consequences of being a Black American: A source book of research by Black psychologists*. New York: Wiley.

Williams, J. D., & Qualls, W. J. (1989, Winter). Middle-class Black consumers and intensity of ethnic identification, *Psychology and Marketing*, *6*, 263-86.

13

Toward a Universal Paradigm for Examining Processing of Brand Information: An Application of Illusory Correlation Theory

Anita M. Bozzolo
Timothy C. Brock
Ohio State University

Marketers have long been concerned with decisions related to product branding. The situations under which a strong brand image would lead to greater acceptance of the product are of continuing interest (Nedungadi & Hutchinson, 1985; Sappington & Wernerfelt, 1985); related issues include management of a brand image over time (Park, Jaworski, & MacInnis, 1986) and brand franchising (Aaker & Keller, 1987). Do strong brand images always lead to greater acceptance of the product? What characteristics are important in order to adopt a brand extension with optimal success? Better understanding of how brand information is processed (strong vs. weak brands and brand information vs. category information) is needed to address these issues.

In addition, the manner in which consumers receive brand information may have an important effect on the processing of this information. Specifically, there may be qualitatively different processing involved when information is presented by electronic (television, radio) versus print advertising.

A paradigm common in the social psychology literature lends itself well to investigating the issues of product branding and form of presentation: the illusory correlation paradigm. This paradigm includes a set of variable manipulations that have universal cross-cultural applicability in investigating brand processing: category versus brand information, strong versus weak brands (categories), impression versus memory-based processing (a major distinction in type of processing in the social psychology literature [Hastie & Park, 1986]), and serial versus summary presentation (simulating presentation of electronic vs. print media).

ILLUSORY CORRELATION THEORY APPLIED
TO BRAND PROCESSING

In general, an illusory correlation is any misperception of the degree of association between two variables. However, it is the illusory correlation based on the overestimation of association between variables that is pertinent to the issues that we are addressing. This type of illusory correlation is defined as the perception of a stronger relationship between two variables than what actually exists. For example, the perception that "all politicians are dishonest" represents an association between the group *politicians* and the trait *dishonesty* that is stronger than what actually exists. This type of illusory correlation has been demonstrated to occur between two distinctive variables (Chapman & Chapman, 1967; Hamilton & Gifford, 1976). Because an individual is most likely to attend to distinctive information, a co-occurrence of two distinctive entities may lead to a perception that they are associated to a greater degree than they actually are. This illusory correlation effect has been widely applied to explaining the formation of social stereotypes in the social psychology literature (see Hamilton & Sherman, 1989 for a review), where the relationship between a distinctive social group and particular distinctive traits or characteristics of the group is overestimated. Note that this illusory correlation effect is applied only to the formation of a stereotype, not to the changing of an already formed impression (Hamilton & Sherman, 1989).

Hamilton and Gifford (1976) conducted an experiment that employed what is now regarded as the standard illusory correlation paradigm. These authors asserted that a distinctive group is one with which a person interacts infrequently. In addition, infrequently occurring (nonnormative) behavior is also distinctive. The main hypothesis of the study was that perceivers would overestimate the frequency with which the distinctive group had engaged in the distinctive behavior.

Subjects were presented with information about two groups, Groups A and Group B. Twenty six statements were presented about Group A (which included 18 statements describing positive behaviors and 8 statements describing negative behaviors); 13 statements were presented about Group B (9 statements describing positive behaviors and 4 statements describing negative behaviors). According to the definition of distinctiveness by infrequency, Group B was the distinctive group and negative behavior was the distinctive behavior. Because the ratio of positive to negative behaviors presented about each group was equal, accurate perceptions of the information would lead to evaluations of equal positivity toward each group. However, the negative behavior of Group B was overestimated. Dependent variables included frequency estimates of the number of desirable and undesirable behaviors performed by each group, and cued recall.

This distinctiveness-based illusory correlation effect has also been demonstrated when processing information about products. Using the standard illusory correlation paradigm, Sanbonmatsu, Shavitt, and Sherman (1991) presented subjects with information about two types of pens. The amount of distinctive (infrequent) information about the distinctive (less frequently described) pen was overestimated. In addition, choice behavior was influenced.

Research has supported the notion that this illusory correlation effect is due to memory-based processing of information (Pryor, 1986). Upon presentation, each piece of information is stored in memory; when an evaluation is asked for, the information is retrieved from memory and the evaluation is based upon what is remembered. Because distinctive information is most likely to be remembered, an overassociation between the distinctive group and distinctive information results. It has been proposed that this memory-based processing occurs under nonthoughtful conditions (Sanbonmatsu, Shavitt, & Sherman, 1991), and when information about the group/product category is not expected to be highly consistent (Hamilton & Sherman, 1989).

In contrast, information about an individual is expected to be consistent. When processing information about individuals, the distinctive individual is paid most attention to and judgments are made at the time of input (on-line or impression-based processing). Thus, infrequent behaviors of the distinctive individual are subject to discounting processes in order to make all information consistent. This type of processing can lead to a different type of illusory correlation: an overassociation between the distinctive individual and his or her nondistinctive behavior—how the person acts most frequently (Sanbonmatsu, Shavitt, Sherman, & Roskos-Ewoldsen, 1987; Sanbonmatsu, Sherman, & Hamilton, 1987).

This illusory correlation research leads to hypotheses about the formation of evaluations about unfamiliar products. First, if a newly introduced product is unimportant to the consumer and information about the product is not expected to be highly consistent, then this information may be processed in a memory-based fashion. In this case, a distinctiveness-based illusory correlation may result, where distinctive (infrequent) information is overly attributed to a distinctive product. In contrast, if information about a product is expected to be consistent, then this information may be processed in an impression-based manner. As a result, a distinctive product may be overassociated with nondistinctive (frequently occurring) information about it (inconsistent, infrequent information should be discounted). These notions may be extended to the processing of brand versus category information. If a product category consists of multiple products, where there is some variation between these products, then information about the category may naturally be processed in a memory-based fashion. However, information about a single brand-name product within the category would probably be expected to be more consistent, resulting in impression-based processing.

Second, processing set may be induced by the kind of information that surrounds or is included in the advertisement. For example, obvious inductions such as "Remember these specific points" versus "We want you to form a general impression of the product" may be used. Also, the manner in which the information is presented may induce one or the other type of processing. Discrete, independent pieces of information presented in a jumbled order may induce memory-based processing. Advertisements may be presented where each ad includes a separate piece of information about the product and presents them in no particular order. Presenting information in an ordered, continuous fashion, like a story, may induce impression-based processing.

Third, illusory correlation effects have been demonstrated when the information is presented serially, one at a time without the opportunity of reviewing them (e.g., Hamilton & Gifford, 1976); these effects are not likely to occur when information is presented simultaneously (Hamilton, Dugan, & Trolier, 1985). It is reasonable to hypothesize that if product information is presented by electronic media (radio, television), illusory correlations are most likely. If product information is presented in print (simultaneously on one page), then misperceptions of the information are less likely.

PROPOSED PARADIGM FOR EXAMINING PROCESSING OF BRAND INFORMATION

The illusory correlation paradigm is useful for investigating how product information is processed (the proposed paradigm is displayed in Table 13.1). This paradigm is not (and should not be) restricted to hypotheses about illusory correlation effects in the formation of evaluations about a new brand/category. The paradigm may be used to manipulate variables that are basic to information processing of category versus brand information for both new and established products.

The frequency variable of the paradigm is employed in order to compare judgement making of strong (26 statements) product images versus weak (13 statements) product images. Here, product image strength is manipulated by amount of information presented. As in Hamilton and Gifford (1976), 18 positive and 8 negative statements are presented about one product and 9 positive and 4 negative statements are presented about the other product.

This paradigm is also useful for investigating processing of brand versus category information. Information may be presented about two brands or

TABLE 13.1
Paradigm for Investigating Brand Processing

Presentation Type	Brands		Generic Categories		Branded Categories	
	Strong	Weak	Strong	Weak	Strong	Weak
	18+, 8−	9+, 4−	18+, 8−	9+, 4−	18+, 8−	9+, 4−
Serial						
Impression-based processing						
Memory-based processing						
No processing set induction						
Summary						
Impression-based processing						
Memory-based processing						
No processing set induction						

categories. There are two ways one may learn about a product category: one may acquire information about a category in general, or one may learn about a category by acquiring information about different brands within the category. Therefore, the paradigm includes both types of category information: generic categories (where no brand names are mentioned) and branded categories (where each statement refers to a different brand in the category). Figure 13.1 presents examples of brand, generic category, and branded category statements.

We proposed that the distinctive category would be the category with the infrequent information (13 statements, as in Hamilton & Gifford, 1976), and that the distinctive brand would be the one in which information is presented most (26 statements), because this information would be most salient to subjects expecting a consistent "personality." In addition, the infrequent information (negative information) is defined as distinctive, and the frequent information (positive information) is defined as nondistinctive.

Two other between-subjects factors are included in the paradigm. Subjects are instructed to form a general impression about the information (impression set), to try and remember each statement presented (memory set), or are not given any processing set instruction. This factor enables comparisons of brand versus category information processing under "natural" (no set) processing conditions, and the influence of instructed processing set upon the final judgments.

In addition, style of presentation is manipulated: serial presentation (each

Positive Brand Information
1. Phenacin contains only natural compounds for better interaction with body chemicals.
2. Brontussin consists of tablets that are small and easy to swallow.

Negative Brand Information
1. Taking high doses of Phenacin may cause dizziness and disorientation.
2. Because of its high potency, an overdose of Brontussin is more likely than with other medications.

Positive Generic Category Information
1. Pain Relievers contain only natural compounds for better interaction with body chemicals.
2. Cold Remedies consist of tablets which are small and easy to swallow.

Negative Generic Category Information
1. Taking high doses of Pain Relievers may cause dizziness and disorientation.
2. Because of its high potency, an overdose of Cold Remedies is more likely than with other medications.

Positive Branded Category Information
1. Sylvan, a pain reliever, contains only natural compounds for better interaction with body chemicals.
2. Durrax, a cold remedy, consists of tablets that are small and easy to swallow.

Negative Branded Category Information
1. Taking high doses of Cosprin, a pain reliever, may cause dizziness and disorientation.
2. Because of its high potency, an overdose of Rondec, a cold remedy, is more likely than with other medications.

FIG. 13.1.   Examples of brand, generic category, and branded category information.

statement presented one at a time) versus summary presentation (all statements presented simultaneously). The assumption that these illusory correlation effects occur only when information is presented serially can be directly applied to testing differences in the processing of information by electronic (where information is presented serially) versus print (where all information is presented simultaneously) media.

CROSS CULTURAL UTILITY OF THE PARADIGM

The proposed paradigm consists of variable manipulations that are basic for understanding brand versus category processing. A main advantage of this paradigm is that it is easily transferrable from culture to culture; the specified procedures for manipulating variables in the paradigm can be used across cultures. Only language translation of product statements is necessary.

Consumer psychology has been concerned with both process issues and cultural limitations of particular manners of responding (Cohen & Chakravarti, 1990). Both functions can be served by the proposed brand processing model. Cross-cultural research can be a useful tool in the development of brand processing theory for a greater understanding of the processes involved (see Triandis & Brislin, 1983). In general, cross-cultural research is useful in identifying conditions under which a theory holds and conditions under which it does not (Greenwald, Pratkanis, Leippe, & Baumgardner, 1986). By specifying these conditions, limitations of the theory are identified and processes underlying a phenomenon are elucidated.

The present paradigm may also be used to determine universal differences in the processing of brand versus category information. Once these universal processes are specified, this information has direct application to the creation of global marketing and advertising strategies. In addition, the elucidation of specific differences between cultures is useful for the formulation of effective within-culture marketing plans. For example, if individuals in a particular society have little choice of brands within a product category so that they expect little variation between products in the category, then they may process both brand and category information in an impression-based fashion. Therefore, branding products in such a society may not greatly influence the manner in which the information is processed. In contrast, product branding may be especially influential in countries that offer consumers many product choices (e.g., United States, Japan). The social perspective of the culture may also influence the processing of brand information. Individuals with a collectivist orientation may feel little control over product choice, resulting in less thoughtful consideration of product information and memory-based processing of such information. In contrast, individuals with an individualist orientation may thoughtfully consider product information, because they feel the power to choose among products.

The amount of advertising presented may also influence brand processing. In more complex societies, where there is much information about products (e.g., United States, Britain), less attention can be exerted in processing the information for a greater likelihood of memory-based processing. Greater attention to advertising can be more easily exerted in simple cultures (e.g., Peru, Taiwan), so that impression-based processing is more likely.

AN EXPERIMENTAL INVESTIGATION OF THE PARADIGM

An experimental investigation using the proposed paradigm was conducted. The study investigated the processing of known product categories and unknown brands within these categories. A second objective was to evaluate the industry preference for nonstudent subjects by exact replication of the experiment with both student and nonstudent subjects.

Overview of the Study

Information was presented about two brands, two generic categories, or two branded categories. Eighteen positive and eight negative statements were presented about one brand (category), and nine positive and four negative statements were presented about the other brand (category). One-third of the subjects were instructed to process the information in an impression-based fashion, one-third were instructed to process the information in a memory-based fashion, and one-third were given no processing set instructions. Subjects were presented the information serially (one at a time) or in summary format (all statements on one page). Lastly, both student and nonstudent subjects participated in the experiment in order to test for differences between these two populations.

Detailed Account of the Study

262 male and female undergraduate and 205 female nonstudent subjects participated in the experiment. Nonstudent subjects consisted of members of a women's charity group, ranging from 25 to 65 years of age. The design of the study was a 2 (Sample; student vs. nonstudent subjects) × 2 (Form; serial vs. summary) × 3 (Category; brands vs. generic categories vs. branded categories) × 3 (Processing Set; memory set vs. impression set vs. no set) × 2 (Product Strength; 26 vs. 13 statements) × 2 (Assignment of Product to strength condition) mixed factorial design. Product strength (number of statements about each product) was manipulated within subjects, whereas all other factors were manipulated between subjects.

Subjects were presented with an information packet and a questionnaire. The first page of the information packet informed subjects that they were going to read information consisting of statements about two products. Some subjects were told that they would read information about two brands, Phenacin (a pain reliever) and Brontussin (a cold remedy); other subjects were told that they would read information about two product categories, pain relievers and cold remedies. Also on this first page, subjects were instructed to either try to remember the statements presented about each product (memory set), to try and form a general impression about each product (impression set), or were given no processing set information (no set). Similar to Pryor (1986), the processing set instructions were as follows:

Memory Set Instructions. Later on you will be asked to try to recall as many statements as you can. So, concentrate on remembering as many of the statements as you can.

Impression Set Instructions. Try to form a general impression of what each product is like. Consider the extent to which you might find each product as a whole to be likeable to unlikeable. Afterwards, you will be asked a few questions about your overall impression of each product.

The remainder of the product information packet consisted of 39 product statements either about Phenacin (a fictitious brand-name pain reliever) and Brontussin (a fictitious brand-name cold remedy), or about pain relievers and cold remedies. In the brand condition, each statement was about Phenacin or Brontussin; in the generic category condition, each statement was about pain relievers or cold remedies with no brand names mentioned; in the branded category condition, each statement was about pain relievers or cold remedies, and each statement was associated with a different brand name in the category (see Fig. 13.1 for examples of these statements).

Each subject received 18 positive and 8 negative statements about one product and 9 positive and 4 negative statements about the other product. The statements were randomly ordered and this same random order was used for all subjects. The assignment of product to the strength condition was also varied; half of subjects received 26 statements about pain relievers (Phenacin) and 13 statements about cold remedies (Brontussin), and half received 26 statements about cold remedies (Brontussin) and 13 statements about pain relievers (Phenacin).

In addition, half of the subjects were presented the information in serial fashion and half were presented the information in summary fashion. Subjects in the serial condition were presented with each statement on a separate page and were given 10 seconds to read each statement. At the end of every 10 seconds a soft tone instructed the subjects to turn to the next page and read the next statement. Subjects in the summary condition were presented with all statements on the same page and were given $6\frac{1}{2}$ minutes to read the information.

Immediately after reading the product information, subjects completed the questionnaire. In the questionnaire, subjects indicated their attitude toward each product on four 7-point semantic differential scales (good-bad, beneficial–harmful, favorable–unfavorable, wise–foolish) and indicated their intention to purchase each product on a single 10-point scale for each product. The next item in the questionnaire instructed subjects to estimate the number of desirable and undesirable statements presented about each product. On the next page, subjects tried to recall each statement (free recall). Then subjects were presented with all statements without the product name and were asked to indicate the product that each statement was previously presented about (cued recall). Subsequently, subjects listed their thoughts about each product and rated each thought as positive, neutral, or negative. Lastly, subjects filled out questions used to check the manipulation of processing set. They were asked the extent to which they tried to remember each statement, the extent to which they tried to form an impression about the information, the importance of being able to remember the information presented, and the importance of being able to form a general impression of the products. Subjects were then fully debriefed by the experimenter and dismissed.

In the brand condition, subjects answered questions about Phenacin and Brontussin, and in the category conditions subjects answered questions about pain relievers and cold remedies. Therefore, all dependent variables were standardized separately for brand, generic category, and branded category conditions. All analyses were conducted on these standardized scores.

The semantic differential ratings (good-bad, beneficial-harmful, unfavorable-favorable, wise-foolish) were highly correlated with each other (all intercorrelations were greater than .70). Therefore, the attitude score for each product was computed as the mean of all four semantic differentials.

For the frequency estimates, the number of positive statements estimated, number of negative statements estimated, and a composite score reflecting the relative positivity of estimation were used in the statistical analyses. The composite was computed by taking the number of positive statements estimated minus the number of negative statements estimated divided by the total number of statements estimated.

For the cued recall and free recall measures, the number of positive and number of negative statements recalled were counted and used in the analyses. In addition, a composite was computed for each subject that consisted of the number of positive statements recalled minus the number of negative statements recalled divided by the total number of statements recalled. Accuracy of recall was not investigated.

In addition, the number of positive and number of negative thoughts were counted. A composite representing the relative positivity of thoughts was computed for each subject that consisted of the number of positive thoughts minus the number of negative thoughts divided by the total number of thoughts.

Differences Between Student and NonStudent Samples

A MANOVA was conducted on the attitude and behavioral intention variables to test for differences between student and nonstudent samples on these variables. This multivariate main effect of Sample was nonsignificant

$[F(4,388) = 1.08, p > .10]$. Univariate ANOVAs resulted in nonsignificant differences between student and nonstudent samples.

A MANOVA was conducted on the memory variables: frequency estimates, cued recall, and free recall. The main effect of Sample was marginally significant $[F(4,388) = 2.20, p = .052]$; however, univariate ANOVAs revealed nonsignificant differences between samples.

A Sample × Form × Processing Set × Category × Assignment of Product ANOVA was conducted on each processing set manipulation check. Again, significant differences were not found between student and nonstudent samples. From these results, we can conclude that student and nonstudent samples did not act differently on any of the dependent measures.

Processing Set Manipulation Checks

Questions were asked at the end of the questionnaire that attempted to assess perceived effort toward memorizing the information presented, perceived effort toward forming a general impression with the information, and perceived importance of remembering and forming an impression about the products. A Sample × Form × Processing Set × Category × Assignment of Product ANOVA was conducted on each manipulation check. The Sample × Set interactions were nonsignificant; therefore, student and nonstudent subjects were combined for the following analyses.

All means of these manipulation checks were in the correct direction (see Table 13.2). Memory set subjects exerted more effort in memorizing the information and thought it was more important to do so than impression set and no-set subjects; impression-set subjects exerted more effort in forming a general impression and thought it was more important to do so than memory-set and no-set subjects.

Orthogonal contrasts were used to determine significant differences between means. Memory set subjects perceived their effort toward remembering the information presented marginally significantly higher than

TABLE 13.2
Processing Set Manipulation Check Means[a]

Effort	Impression Set	Memory Set	No Set
Perceived memory effort[b]	5.77	6.25	5.96
Perceived importance of memory effort[c]	2.46	2.77	2.38
Perceived impression effort[b]	6.38	6.03	6.32
Perceived importance of impression effort[c]	2.69	2.44	2.46

[a]Higher numbers designate greater effort/importance.
[b]Perceived effort was measured on a 10-point scale.
[c]Perceived importance was measured on a 4-point scale.

impression set subjects [$F(1,343)$ = 2.89, p < .09], but not significantly higher than the no-set subjects [$F(1,343$ = 1.58, p > .10]. Memory set subjects rated remembering the information as significantly more important than impression-set subjects [$F(1,339)$ = 7.24, p < .008) and no-set subjects [$F(1,339)$ = 11.92, p < .0006]. Impression-set subjects rated perceived effort toward forming a general impression with the information as marginally significantly higher than no-set subjects [$F(1,343)$ = 2.66, p < .103], but not significantly higher than memory-set subjects [$F(1,343)$ < 1, p > .10). Impression-set subjects rated perceived importance of forming a general impression as significantly higher than both memory-set subjects [$F(1,341)$ = 6.83, p < .009] and no-set subjects [$F(1,341)$ = 6.11, p < .013].

According to these data, the processing set instructions clearly influenced perceived importance of remembering or forming a general impression of the information presented in the predicted directions. In addition, memory- and impression-set groups differed significantly in perceived effort toward memorizing or forming an impression with the information. The fact that the no-set group did not differ from the other groups on these manipulation checks indicates that unless specifically instructed to process in one or the other manner, subjects seemed to process in both memory and impression fashions simultaneously.

Moderate correlations were revealed between impression-and memory-set manipulation checks for each processing set condition (r > .34). According to these correlations, memory-based and impression-based processing are positively associated, in contrast to the inverse relation assumption in the social cognition literature (Hastie & Park, 1986).

Differential Processing of Brands Versus Categories

The processing-set manipulation checks were used to investigate the type of processing used when learning information about brands versus generic and branded categories. In the full ANOVA, the Sample × Category interaction was nonsignificant. Therefore, student and nonstudent subjects were combined for these analyses.

For both memory-set and impression-set manipulation checks, branded category subjects exhibited the lowest means, generic category subjects exhibited the next lowest means, and brand subjects exhibited the highest means (see Table 13.3). Orthogonal contrasts were used to test differences between means. Subjects in the brand condition rated perceived effort toward remembering the information significantly higher than both generic category subjects [$F(1,343)$ = 4.08, p < .04] and branded category subjects [$F(1,343)$ = 26.34, p < .0001]. In addition, subjects in the brand condition

TABLE 13.3
Processing of Brand Versus Category Information[a]

Effort	Brands	Generic Categories	Branded Categories
Perceived memory effort[b]	6.54	6.11	5.23
Perceived importance of memory effort[c]	2.75	2.53	2.28
Perceived impression effort[b]	6.95	6.21	5.46
Perceived importance of impression effort[c]	2.70	2.47	2.40

[a]Higher numbers designate greater effort/importance.
[b]Perceived effort was measured on a 10-point scale.
[c]Perceived importance was measured on a 4-point scale.

rated remembering the statements as more important than both generic category subjects [$F(1,339) = 7.53, p < .006$] and branded category subjects [$F(1,339) = 21.96, p < .0001$].

In addition, subjects in the brand condition rated perceived effort toward forming a general impression with the information significantly higher than both generic category subjects [$F(1,343) = 8.73, p < .003$] and branded category subjects [$F(1,343) = 36.95, p < .0001$], and rated forming a general impression as more important than both generic category subjects [$F(1,341) = 6.20, p < .013$] and branded category subjects [$F(1,341) = 10.45, p < .001$].

These results suggest that subjects in the brand condition processed the information in both a higher memory fashion and a higher impression fashion.

Attitudinal, Behavioral Intention, and Memory Effects

Sample × Form × Processing Set × Category × Strength × Assignment of Product ANOVAs resulted in a main effect of Form for the attitude scores [$F(1,393) = 6.43, p < .012$], behavioral intention scores [$F(1,392) = 3.77, p < .05$], frequency estimate scores, number of positive statements estimated [$F(1,354) = 9.58, p < .002$], number of negative statements estimated [$F(1,354) = 9.33, p < .003$], composite score [$F(1,354) = 9.27, p < .003$], and the free recall composite [$F(1,349) = 4.53, p < .034$]. Table 13.41 reveals that overall, serial presentation resulted in more positive ratings of the products than summary presentation. These results suggest that negative or infrequent statements may not be discounted as easily when presented in summary fashion.

Under serial conditions, significant Set × Category interactions emerged on the attitude [$F(4,198) = 3.16, p < .02$], thought composite [$F(4,198) = 4.03, p < .01$], and recall composite [$F(4,198) < 3.96, p < .01$], revealing

TABLE 13.4
Mean Product Ratings Under Serial and Summary Presentation Conditions[a]

Measures	Serial Presentation	Summary Presentation
Attitude[b]	.094	− .094
Purchase intention	.084	− .084
Frequency estimate composite[c]	.255	.170
Recall composite[d]	.173	.102

[a]Standardized scores.

[b]An index composed of the mean of four semantic differential scales

[c]An index composed of the number of desirable statements estimated minus the number of undesirable statements estimated, divided by the total number of statements.

[d]An index composed of the number of positive statements recalled minus the number of negative statements recalled, divided by the total number of statements recalled.

that ratings of branded categories were more negative under memory set conditions than under impression-set or no-set conditions. Generic category and brand ratings did not become more negative under memory-set conditions.

As displayed in Table 13.5, when subjects were told to process in a memory or impression set, the strong brand was consistently rated more favorably than the weak brand across dependent variables. This pattern of means did not occur under no-set conditions. Strong generic categories were also rated more favorably than weak categories under impression-set conditions on the attitude ratings, thought composite, recognition, and frequency-estimate scores. Strong branded categories were not consistently rated more favorably than weak branded categories.

For brands, the Strength main effect was significant for the free recall composite [$F(1,74) = 7.33, p < .01$], the frequency estimate composite [$F(1,71) = 4.01, p < .05$], and the cued recall composite [$F(1,77) = 4.81, p < .03$]. In addition, the Strength × Processing Set interaction was marginally significant for the cued recall composite [$F(2,77) = 2.57, p < .08$]. Therefore, overall the strong brand was rated as significantly more positive than the weak brand. Processing set approached a significant difference only on the cued recall composite.

Orthogonal contrasts conducted on difference scores (strong product rating minus weak product rating) revealed that the difference between strong and weak products was significantly greater under processing set conditions than the difference under no-set conditions on the attitude ratings [$F(1,393) = 6.48, p < .01$] and recognition ratings [$F(1,394) = 3.63, p < .06$]. This effect approached significance for brands on the thought composite [$F(1,365) = 2.21, p < .13$], recognition index [$F(1,394) = 6.66, p < .01$], and frequency estimate composite [$F(1,354) = 2.75, p < .10$].

Therefore, results revealed that when either type of processing effort was exerted (impression or memory effort) toward processing brand informa-

TABLE 13.5
Mean Product Ratings[a] of Brands and Categories under Serial Presentation:
Effects of Processing Set and Brand (Category) Strength

Measures	Impression Set		Memory Set		No Set	
	Strong[b]	Weak[c]	Strong	Weak	Strong	Weak
Attitude[d]						
Brands	.25	−.10	.22	−.04	.05	.11
Generic categories	.23	.11	.00	.16	.00	.29
Branded categories	.28	.12	.04	−.39	.02	.27
Purchase intention						
Brands	.07	−.17	.13	−.03	.17	.23
Generic categories	.13	.21	−.07	.15	.25	.05
Branded categories	.08	.01	.14	−.15	.20	.10
Thoughts[a]						
Brands	.39	.03	.25	−.39	−.12	.09
Generic categories	.25	−.07	−.08	.22	.08	.17
Branded categories	.28	.27	−.37	−.26	−.07	−.10
Frequency Estimates[4]						
Brands	.33	−.40	.23	−.13	.02	.04
Generic categories	.12	−.01	.08	.29	.14	.22
Branded categories	.14	.41	.21	−.10	.50	.13
Recall[e]						
Brands	.48	−.01	.33	−.34	.24	.05
Generic categories	.03	.11	.26	.21	.11	−.06
Branded categories	.33	.15	−.32	−.42	.26	−.25
Recognition[h]						
Brands	.23	−.27	.45	−.66	−.01	.12
Generic categories	.20	−.27	.01	.03	−.06	.11
Branded categories	−.07	.08	.17	−.15	−.03	−.13

[a]Standardized for brands and categories separately.
[b]Twenty-six statements were presented about the respective brand (category).
[c]Thirteen statements were presented about the respective brand (category).
[d]An index composed of the mean of four semantic differential scales.
[e]An index composed of the number of positive thoughts minus the number of negative thoughts, divided by the total number of thoughts.
[f]An index composed of the number of desirable statements estimated minus the number of undesirable statements estimated, divided by the total number of statements.
[g]An index composed of the number of positive statements recalled minus the number of negative statements recalled, divided by the total number of statements recalled.
[h]An index composed of the number of positive statements recognized minus the number of negative statements recognized, divided by the total number of statements recognized.

tion, strong brands were rated more favorably than weak brands. Processing effort toward category information did not consistently result in more positive ratings of the strong categories than the weak categories.

Conclusions

Some interesting and informative effects resulted from the present research. First, serial presentation of information resulted in more favorable product ratings overall than summary presentation. It may have been more difficult to discount negative information when all information was presented on the same page.

Differential processing of brand versus category information was also revealed. Ratings of branded categories became more negative when processed in a memory-type fashion. Ratings of generic categories and brands were not negatively influenced by memory-type processing. These results suggest that processing of branded category information is susceptible to negative influences of memory-type processing. Brand and generic category information were not susceptible to negative influences of memory-based processing.

In addition, the exertion of processing effort (memory or impression effort) in processing brand information resulted in more favorable ratings of strong brands than weak brands. Analysis of processing set manipulation checks revealed that subjects processed brand information in both a higher memory fashion and a higher impression fashion than category information.

Finally, significant differences were not found between student and nonstudent samples. Both samples were successfully instructed to process information in the fashion specified, and both samples exhibited nonsignificantly different ratings of brands versus categories. Therefore, evidence was not found supporting the industry preference for nonstudent subjects.

APPLICATIONS TO MARKETING AND ADVERTISING

Research using the proposed paradigm has many direct applications to marketing and advertising. The paradigm may be used to investigate the processing of information about both new and familiar products. Illusory correlation theory has applications to the formation of an evaluation toward a new or unfamiliar product category or brand. In addition, the present research is informative of evaluations of familiar product categories and unfamiliar brands within these categories.

First, serial versus summary presentation is akin to electronic versus print media presentation. Illusory correlation theory suggests that misperceptions of information are most likely when it is presented serially, without the possibility of reviewing the information. Therefore, misperceptions of information presented by electronic media (i.e., television, radio) are likely; however, print media enable the reviewing of information for more accurate perceptions of this information. The present research supports this hypothesis; greater discounting or forgetting of infrequent negative information occurred when information was presented serially. Therefore, when the presentation of infrequent undesirable information is necessary, it is best to present the information serially for greatest discounting of this information.

The paradigm accounts for both the processing of brand information and product category information. The target of most advertising is the brand-name product. However, advertising of category information has become more prevalent. For example, public service announcements concerning nutrition and health (i.e., milk advertisements), information about health risks (i.e., AIDS, drugs), and environmental conservation (i.e., rain forests, redwood trees, etc.) employ category information as the target. Consumers may acquire information about categories in two ways; consumers may be presented information that is general to the category (generic category information), and/or they may learn about product categories by acquiring information about specific subtypes or brands within the category (branded category information). The present paradigm encompasses both methods of processing category information.

Amount of information (26 vs. 13 statements) is useful for investigating the relative impact and survival of strong versus weak brands (categories). Here, a strong brand (category) is defined as one that consumers are most informed about. In addition, processing set may be induced by the kind of information that surrounds or is included in an advertisement. Results of the present experimental research suggest that inducing either type of processing effort leads to more positive evaluations of stronger brands over weaker brands; however, a memory-type processing induction should be avoided when presenting branded category information.

In sum, the present chapter proposes a paradigm for investigating brand processing that has direct applications to marketing and advertising. This paradigm may be employed to determine universal differences in the processing of brand information versus category information for enhanced global advertising strategies.

REFERENCES

Aaker, D. A., & Keller, K. L. (1987). Consumer response to brand extensions. Unpublished manuscript.

Chapman, L. J., & Chapman, J. P. (1967). Genesis of popular but erroneous psychodiagnostic observations. *Journal of Abnormal Psychology*, *72*, 193–204.

Cohen, J. B., & Chakravarti, D. (1990). Consumer psychology. *Annual Review of Psychology*, *41*, 243–288.

Greenwald, A. G., Pratkanis, A. R., Leippe, M. R., & Baumgardner, M. H. (1986). Under what conditions does theory obstruct research progress? *Psychological Review*, *91*, 216–229.

Hamilton, D. L., Dugan, P. M., & Trolier, T. K. (1985). The formation of stereotypic beliefs: Further evidence for distinctiveness-based illusory correlation. *Journal of Personality and Social Psychology*, *48*, 5–17.

Hamilton, D. L., & Gifford, R. K. (1976). Illusory correlation in interpersonal perception: A cognitive basis of stereotypic judgments. *Journal of Experimental Social Psychology, 12,* 392–407.

Hamilton, D. L., & Sherman, S. J. (1989). Illusory correlations: Implications for stereotype theory and research. In D. Bar-Tal, C. F. Graumann, A. W. Kruglanski, & W. Stroebe (Eds.), *Stereotypes and prejudice: Changing conceptions* (pp. 59–82). New York: Springer-Verlag.

Hastie, R., & Park, B. (1986). The relationship between memory and judgment depends on whether the judgment task is memory-based or on-line. *Psychological Review, 93,* 258–268.

Nedungadi, P., & Hutchinson, J. W. (1985). The prototypicality of brands: Relationships with brand awareness, preference, and usage. *Advances in Consumer Research, 12,* 498–503.

Park, C. W., Jaworski, B. J., & MacInnis, D. J. (1986). Strategic brand concept-image management. *Journal of Marketing, 50,* 135–145.

Pryor, J. B. (1986). The influence of different encoding sets upon the formation of illusory correlations and group impressions. *Personality and Social Psychology Bulletin, 12,* 216–226.

Sanbonmatsu, D. M., Shavitt, S., & Sherman, S. J. (1991). The role of personal relevance in the formation of distinctiveness-based illusory correlations. *Personality and Social Psychology Bulletin, 17,* 124–132.

Sanbonmatsu, D. M., Shavitt, S., Sherman, S. J., & Roskos-Ewoldsen, D. R. (1987). Illusory correlation in the perception of performance by self or a salient other. *Journal of Experimental Social Psychology, 23,* 518–543.

Sanbonmatsu, D. M., Sherman, S. J., & Hamilton, D. L. (1987). Illusory correlation in the perception of individuals and groups. *Social Cognition, 5,* 1–25.

Sappington, D., & Wernerfelt, B. (1985). To brand or not to brand? A theoretical and empirical question. *Journal of Business, 58,* 279–293.

Triandis, H. C., & Brislin, R. W. (1983). *Cross-cultural psychology.* Paper presented at the Annual Convention of the American Psychological Association Anaheim, CA.

Author Index

Subject Index